Student Resource Manual

for use with

Personal Finance

Sixth Edition

Jack R. Kapoor
College of DuPage

Les R. Dlabay
Lake Forest College

Robert J. Hughes
Dallas County Community College

Boston Burr Ridge, IL Dubuque, IA Madison, WI New York San Francisco St. Louis
Bangkok Bogotá Caracas Lisbon London Madrid
Mexico City Milan New Delhi Seoul Singapore Sydney Taipei Toronto

Student Resource Manual for use with
PERSONAL FINANCE, SIXTH EDITION
Jack R. Kapoor, Les R. Dlabay, Robert J. Hughes

Published by McGraw-Hill/Irwin, an imprint of the McGraw-Hill Companies, Inc., 1221 Avenue of the Americas, New York, NY 10020.

4 5 6 7 8 9 10 CRS 0 9 8 7 6 5 4 3 2 1

ISBN 0-07-241002-7

www.mhhe.com

STUDENT RESOURCE AND READINGS MANUAL

This publication is designed to help you learn and apply personal financial planning concepts. This *Student Resource Manual and Casebook* supplements *Personal Finance* (Kapoor, Dlabay and Hughes; McGraw-Hill, 2001) and will guide you through the content of the book. You will be given opportunities to learn, test, and apply personal financial topics.

Each chapter of the *Student Resource Manual and Casebook* has the following features:

Chapter Overview	This introductory paragraph provides an overview of the main topics and concepts developed in the chapter.
Objectives	These instructional goals from the introductory page of each chapter in the textbook offer a framework for desired behaviors related to chapter content.
Key Terms	This feature lists the vital words related to chapter content. The definitions of these terms are in the margins within each chapter for your review.
Pretest	This section allows you to assess your initial knowledge of the chapter material with a ten-item true-false quiz.
Self-Guided Study Questions	These open-ended questions are keyed to textbook headings and provide you with an opportunity to develop a knowledge of the content and concepts of a chapter.
Post Test	After reading and studying the material of a chapter, ten completion and ten multiple choice questions help you measure your mastery level.
Problems, Applications, and Cases	Several activities are provided to allow you to use personal financial planning concepts. These include computational exercises, financial planning activities, and situations requiring examples or further research.
Supplementary Cases	Real-world situations are presented for you to use your research and analytical skills related to personal financial decision making.
Supplementary Reading	To expand the content of *Personal Finance*, recent articles from *Business Week* are included in the Resource Manual. Each article is accompanied by study questions.

The answers to the pretests, post tests, problems, applications, and cases are presented at the end of this publication. These are provided so you can assess your knowledge based on the various tests and exercises in this Resource Manual.

CONTENTS

Chapter

1 PERSONAL FINANCIAL PLANNING: AN INTRODUCTION

Chapter Overview

This chapter provides the foundation for *Personal Finance* and the study of financial planning. The chapter starts with a discussion of decision making, including consequences of choices and the evaluation of associated risks. Next, the opportunity costs, or trade-offs, of decisions are considered in relation to personal and financial resources. This is followed by coverage of the personal, social, and economic factors that make up the financial planning environment. Next, the steps of the financial planning process are discussed, along with the main components of financial planning (obtaining, planning, saving, borrowing, spending, managing risk, investing, and retirement and estate planning). Finally, strategies for creating and using a financial plan are introduced.

Learning Objectives

After studying this chapter, you will be able to:

Obj. 1 Analyze the process of making personal financial decisions.

Obj. 2 Develop personal financial goals.

Obj. 3 Assess the personal and economic factors that influence personal financial planning.

Obj. 4 Determine the personal and financial opportunity costs associated with personal financial decisions.

Obj. 5 Identify strategies for achieving personal financial goals for different life situations.

Key Terms

adult life cycle
bankruptcy
economics
financial plan
future value
inflation
liquidity
opportunity cost
personal financial planning
present value
time value of money
values

Pretest

True-False

______ 1. (Obj. 1) Every person uses decision-making techniques every day.

______ 2. (Obj. 2) The risks associated with financial decisions are easy to measure.

______ 3. (Obj. 3) Ideas and principles that are considered correct, desirable or important are examples of opportunity costs.

______ 4. (Obj. 4) Financial opportunity costs can be measured using time value of money calculations.

______ 5. (Obj. 3) A career change can influence a person's financial decisions.

______ 6. (Obj. 3) Inflation results in increased buying power for consumers.

______ 7. (Obj. 1) Financial planning starts with setting personal economic goals.

______ 8. (Obj. 1) Financial planning requires an ongoing reevaluation and revision of financial goals.

______ 9. (Obj. 5) Liquidity is the ability to convert financial resources into useable cash without a loss of value.

______ 10. (Obj. 5) The primary purpose of a financial plan is to report a person's or household's current financial situation.

Self-Guided Study Questions

Obj. 1

The Financial Planning Process (p. 3)

1. What is personal financial planning?

2. What are some advantages of personal financial planning?

3. What are the steps of the financial planning process?

4. How do opportunity costs influence decision making?

5. What types of risks affect personal financial decisions? How can these risks be considered when making financial choices?

6. Why is information important for successful financial decisions? What are the main sources of financial planning information?

Obj. 2

Developing Personal Financial Goals (p. 8)

7. How does timing affect goals?

8. What are four qualities of effective financial goals?

Obj. 3

Influences on Personal Financial Planning (p. 12)

Life Situation and Personal Values (p. 12)

9. What factors affect a person's life situation?

10. How do values affect financial planning?

Economic Factors (p. 13)

11. What does the study of economics involve?

12. What function does supply and demand serve?

13. What are the main financial institutions that operate in our society?

14. How do global business activities affect individuals in our society?

15. How are people on fixed incomes, lenders of money, and borrowers of money affected by inflation?

16. What does the consumer price index (CPI) measure?

17. How do changing interest rates influence personal financial decisions?

Obj. 4

Opportunity Costs and the Time Value of Money (p. 17)

Personal Opportunity Costs (p. 17)

18. What are some examples of opportunity costs that cannot be measured in terms of money?

Financial Opportunity Costs (p. 17)

19. What are some examples of the time value of money affecting personal financial decisions?

20. How is interest computed?

21. How are future value calculations used in financial planning?

22. What information is provided by present value calculations?

Obj. 5

Achieving Financial Goals (p. 21)

Components of Personal Financial Planning (p. 21)

23. What are the eight areas of financial planning that require decisions by all people at some time in their lives?

24. Why is a savings and investment program a necessity for future financial security?

25. What problems can the overuse of credit cause?

26. What are some common types of investments?

Developing a Flexible Financial Plan (p. 23)

27. What is a financial plan?

Implementing Your Financial Plan (p. 23)

28. What are some examples of short-term and long-term financial strategies that can help a person achieve his or her financial goals?

Post Test

Completion

1. (Obj. 1) ____________ ____________ ____________ is the process of managing your money to achieve personal economic satisfaction.
2. (Obj. 3) The stages in the family situation and financial needs of an adult are referred to as the ____________ ____________ ____________.
3. (Obj. 1) The second stage of the financial planning process is to develop financial ____________.
4. (Obj. 1) If you decide to use your savings to pay for school instead of going on vacation, this is an example of ____________ ____________.

5. (Obj. 3) ____________ is the study of how wealth is created and distributed.
6. (Obj. 4) The ____________ ____________ ____________ ____________ refers to increases in the amount of money as a result of interest earned.
7. (Obj. 3) A rise in the general level of prices is referred to as ____________.
8. (Obj. 5) ____________ is the ability to readily convert financial resources into usable cash without loss in value.
9. (Obj. 3) ____________ are ideas and principles that a person considers correct, desirable and important.
10. (Obj. 5) A financial ____________ is a formalized report that summarizes your current financial situation, analyzes your financial needs, and recommends a direction for your financial activities.

Multiple Choice

_____ 1. (Obj. 1) The main purpose of personal financial planning is to
A. plan for retirement.
B. control your spending habits.
C. reach personal economic goals.
D. increase the amount in your savings.

_____ 2. (Obj. 1) The first step in financial planning is to
A. create a financial plan of action.
B. analyze your current situation.
C. develop financial goals.
D. implement your financial plan.

_____ 3. (Obj. 4) Which of the following time value of money computations would be used to determine the value of $100 three years from now?
A. Future value of a single amount
B. Future value of a series of deposits
C. Present value of a single amount
D. Present value of a series of deposits

_____ 4. (Obj. 3) An example of a personal factor that would affect financial planning is
A. inflation.
B. household size.
C. interest rates.
D. tax laws.

_____ 5. (Obj. 3) Prices in the American economy are most influenced by
A. government.
B. supply and demand.
C. taxes.
D. interest rates.

_____ 6. (Obj. 3) Increased consumer borrowing is likely to cause
A. an increase in interest rates.
B. a decrease in interest rates.
C. lower taxes.
D. reduced consumer prices.

_____ 7. (Obj. 1) The final step of the financial planning process is to
A. implement the financial plan.
B. create a financial plan of action.
C. develop financial goals.
D. re-evaluate your actions.

_____ 8. (Obj. 5) ________ is necessary to have funds available for long-term financial
security.
A. Borrowing
B. Spending
C. Saving
D. Liquidity

_____ 9. (Obj. 5) Making a will is involved in the __________ component of financial planning.
A. spending
B. obtaining
C. managing risk
D. estate planning

_____ 10. (Obj. 5) The main purpose of a financial plan is to
A. budget for current spending.
B. determine your insurance needs.
C. recommend financial activities.
D. plan risk management activities.

Problems, Applications, and Cases

1. Compute the future or present value for the following:
   a. What is the future value of $430 earning 8 percent for two years?
   b. What is the future value of $200 deposited each year for six years earning 6 percent?
   c. What is the present value of $700 earning 7 percent for 12 years?
   d. What is the present value of a withdrawal of $300 at the end of each year for 8 years with an interest rate of 8 percent?

2. For each of the following life situations, (a) suggest some short-term and long-term goals that would be unique to this group; and (b) recommend specific financial activities that could help these individuals achieve these goals.

Life situation	Short-term goals	Long-term goals	Financial activities
Single person, age 43, no dependents			
Married couple, both working, children ages 3 and 7			
Married couple, ages 56 and 51, no dependent children			
Divorced woman with a 10-year-old daughter			
Married couple, one income, child age 14 and dependent parent, age 73			

3. Using the Internet, *The Wall Street Journal*, the business section from the newspaper, or business periodicals such as *Business Week*, *Forbes*, and *Fortune*, obtain current information on various economic conditions. Indicate how this information might affect a person's financial decisions.

Economic indicator	Current trend	Source of information	Possible impact on financial planning
Inflation; Consumer prices			
Interest rates			
Employment			
Consumer spending; Retail sales			

4. Listed here are the main components of financial planning. For each situation below, indicate which area is being neglected. More than one may apply to a situation.

- obtaining
- planning
- saving
- borrowing
- spending
- managing risk
- investing
- retirement and estate planning

a. Alice Kendall does not have a will to make sure that her children will receive her financial resources should she die. ____________________

b. Janet and Brad Collins spend money as they need or want without a budget. ____________________

c. Ken and Barb Kolar rent an apartment but don't believe they need insurance for their furniture or other personal belongings. ____________________

d. John Brubeck charges frequent restaurant visits and clothing purchases to his credit cards and other charge accounts. ____________________

e. Mona Collins can't get a promotion at her place of employment because she lacks adequate education. ____________________

f. Joyce and Tom Hallar are not able to save more than a few dollars each month. ____________________

g. Bill Cartwright had to borrow money to pay taxes he owes for last year. ____________________

h. Jeanne Holland has $14,000 in a savings account that pays five and one-half percent interest. ____________________

5. With the use of a telephone directory, advertisements in local newspapers, the Internet, information from friends, and by contacting one or more financial advisors, develop a list of people available in your community who provide financial planning assistance. Obtain the following information:

   a. Name, address, telephone number, and e-mail

b. Area of expertise, training, and background

c. Type of fee charged

d. Comments from previous customers

(Note: Refer to Appendix A for additional questions to ask when selecting a financial planner.)

6. Based on the format in Exhibit 1-10, outline a financial plan for you or your household.

Supplementary Case 1-1: Winners Can Still Be Losers*

Topic: Financial Planning and Budgeting

Text Reference: pp. 3-24

Poor personal financial management is the most important cause of bankruptcy and the greatest cause of anxiety in American households. Consider the case of Erika Earnhart of Lexington Park, Maryland, who won $1 million in the Maryland lottery. Erika says she is in debt, lives in a trailer park, and is unable to work because of a knee injury.

"I thought I'd be on easy street the rest of my life," said Erika. "Now I live from April to April. I admit I've had some fun, but it's not everything it's cracked up to be."

Each April, Erika receives her annual $50,000 check, a prize guaranteed for 20 years. Erika spent the first $50,000 on a four-bedroom house, gifts of money to her parents and sister, a Volkswagen, and some travel. She did not pay taxes on this money, so when her second check came, she had to pay $18,000 in taxes on the first year's winnings plus advance taxes for the second year. Consequently, the second annual windfall immediately plunged from $50,000 to about $20,000.

Now—after two divorces, a still unresolved child custody case, two knee operations without any health insurance to defray the costs, and moves to Michigan, Colorado, California, and back to Maryland—Erika is broke. She sold her house and lives in a nearly new, extra-wide trailer. She visits her bank frequently. The bank vice president does not even ask Erika the purpose of her visit. He knows that Erika is borrowing against her next lottery check, and he just needs to know what amount she wants to withdraw. "When I got this year's check, I already owed the bank $10,000," she said.

There are still several checks to come, but Erika said that if she had known what would happen after she won the million dollars, "I'd have torn up the ticket or put it in someone else's name." Still she continues to play the Maryland lottery periodically in the hope of winning again, "to pay off my debts."

---

* Adapted from "'I'm Broke,' Says Winners of Lottery," *Chicago Tribune*, October 11, 1984, sec. 1A, p. 32.

Erika's financial woes demonstrate that using money effectively is one of the biggest problems in the lifetime of any individual or family. But personal financial planning and money management are skills that can be learned, developed and enjoyed.

The job of managing your money is lifelong. Some people do it well and live smoothly and pleasantly, free from monetary cares and worries. They enjoy the pleasures and satisfactions of a full life. Others ineptly stumble from one financial mess to the next. They never seem to solve their personal financial problems. Some families can live comfortably and save money on an annual income of $30,000. Others, with annual incomes of more than $100,000 can't make ends meet. Most of us work hard for our money. We should make an additional effort to see that it is managed and used wisely.

Case Questions

1. What financial planning mistakes did Erika Earnhart make?
2. How did the misuse of credit contribute to Erika's problems?
3. Did Erika's changing household situation affect her financial planning difficulties? Explain.
4. If you were in a situation similar to Erika's, how would your actions differ from her actions?

Supplementary Case 1-2: Emily's Personal Financial Plan

Topic: Developing a Financial Plan

Text Reference: pp. 3-24

Emily Burton, 23, completed college two years ago with a degree in physical therapy. The major cost of her education was covered by a scholarship. Through wise planning by her parents, Emily has $32,000 which they set aside for her education. This fund consists of savings certificates and stocks that increased in value over the years.

Emily works for a hospital in Lincoln, Nebraska, and earns $32,000 a year. In about three years, she would like to go to graduate school to get a master's degree. Then she would like to buy a house. Emily wants to live on her salary and invest the $32,000 for her education and future needs.

Case Questions

1. How did Emily benefit from her parents' financial planning?
2. What decisions does Emily need to make regarding her future?
3. How could various personal and economic factors influence Emily's financial planning?
4. What would be the value of Emily's $32,000 in three years if it earned an annual interest rate of 7 percent?

Supplementary Case 1-3: Maternity Leave for Margo

Topic: Financial Planning

Text Reference: pp. 8-24

Having children has always been important to Margo Sanchez; however, so has her career. Within the next few years, she would like to take a leave of absence from her employment to start a family. To obtain the necessary financial resources for this goal, Margo estimates that she will need to accumulate $16,000 over the next four years.

Currently Margo and her husband, Alex, rent an apartment and have a combined household income of $53,000. While they have very few debts, their savings consist of less than $2,000.

Case Questions

1. How does Margo's personal goal affect her financial planning activities?
2. What information sources might be helpful to Margo when making decisions related to her goal?
3. What amount would Margo need to deposit today for that amount to grow to $16,000 in four years at a 6 percent annual interest rate?
4. What actions would you suggest for Margo and Alex?

Supplementary Reading 1

Barbara Hetzer, "The Second Income: Is It Worth It?" *Business Week*, August 25, 1997, pp. 192-194.

The Second Income: Is it Worth it?

Edited by Amy Dunkin

For Nancy McCardel, the days start early. At 5:30 a.m., she gets up to feed her 3-month-old daughter before showering and dressing in a blouse and suit ($300, plus $12 a week for dry cleaning). She rouses her 8-year-old son, and during the summer, whisks him off to a day-care center ($112 per week). She then drops off her daughter at another center ($210 per week) across town. She drives downtown to her job ($4 roundtrip, plus $22.50 per week for parking) as managing supervisor for a public relations firm in Atlanta and picks up a gourmet cup of coffee ($3 a day). She eats lunch ($4) at her desk. At 4:30 she races from the office to get the kids. After a quick dinner, she bathes the children, reads to them, tucks them into their freshly made beds ($70 for bimonthly housecleaning), and does chores. By 10:30, she tumbles into bed. At week's end, this 35-year-old mother wonders: Is it worth it?

Financially, the answer isn't clear. Although more than half of all women with preschool children hold paid jobs, many of them soon discover that much of their earnings are eaten up by the costs of child care, a professional wardrobe, and other work-related expenses. Ultimately, some women (and many men) argue it doesn't pay for women to work when the kids are small.

The numbers certainly seem to support that assumption. For example, a hypothetical suburban couple working in New York City and whose combined income is $150,000 saves more than $15,000 in federal taxes, $5,070 in FICA taxes, and $5,184 in state and local taxes when they live on a single income of $80,000. The couple will save an additional $32,634 when they lop off the mother's costs of working: child care, commuting, and such. Instead of losing $70,000 in income, the actual loss is only $4,544 (table).

Each family's spending habits vary so widely, of course, that it's almost impossible to generalize about how lucrative a second income actually is. And having the option to choose between working or staying at home with your child is a luxury that millions of single mothers and less-affluent families don't have. Still, on paper, it often seems that a second salary for a higher-income family doesn't mean much improvement in their standard of living—especially in the child's early years.

That determination is shocking, but also somewhat misleading. While a good chunk of a working mother's salary does foot those work-related expenses, it's questionable how much would be saved if the woman stayed at home. Whether you work in an office or stay at home, you still have to eat, says Jane Bermont, a consultant with Boston-based WFD, a leading provider of corporate work-life programs.

Grabbing a tuna on rye from the fridge isn't as pricey as the lunch special downtown, but you may wind up eating out lunch frequently with other stay-at-home moms and their tots. Even a quick chat over a cup of coffee and Danish will set you back three bucks. What's more, you may find yourself doing more shopping now that you have the time. That's not altogether a bad thing, if you shop the sales. Your babysitter costs won't be eliminated entirely. You'll still need to get away from the kids—to run errands or enjoy time by yourself.

The real problem in this tally, however, is its short-term view. Even if your take-home pay covers little more than your expenses, argues Cindy Hounsell, executive director of the Women's Institute for a Secure Retirement in Washington, from a financial standpoint, it would still pay to work. "By remaining in the workforce, you're making a long-term investment in your career and future earnings," says Houndsell.

Child-care costs, the heftiest expense by far for most working mothers, don't last forever. Eventually, Junior will grow up and go to school. And by that time, most working moms will have gotten a raise, maybe even a promotion, and regularly siphoned some cash into a 401(k) or similar retirement fund. Our New York professional would stockpile $186,386 in her retirement plan over 10 years—if she keeps working.

Building up a 401(k) nest egg—if that's an option for you at your job—may be a hidden benefit of remaining in the workforce, both in the short and long term. The 401(k) contributions give you an immediate tax break by reducing your current adjusted gross income. "Every dollar that you put in will save you about 35¢ in federal taxes today," says Douglas Mollin, a certified financial planner with ProPlan in Elmhurst, N.Y. Over the long haul, the money you sock away into a 401(k) grows tax-deferred. Obviously, the more you put in over the years—and the earlier in your life that you do so—the larger your holdings will be upon retirement. And, if your employer matches all or part of your contribution, you're getting free money. "Think of it as an annual, tax-deferred bonus," says Mollin, "that you'd be forfeiting if you quit." Using that logic, our New York professional earns not $70,000 but $73,500 annually.

Meanwhile, women who step out of the paid workforce for an extended period may find that they're (sic) earning power has diminished. "It's especially troublesome for women reentering who are over age 40," says Bermont. Unless they update their skills, returnees may earn less now than they did 5, 10, even 15 years ago when they stopped working to raise their kids.

FINANCIAL JEOPARDY. Stay-at-home moms may even be putting themselves in financial jeopardy. It's risky to depend on a single wage-earner, given the constant threat of layoffs. And divorce and widowhood—two real possibilities—often put nonworking wives in a precarious position, says Hounsell, if they forgo all responsibility for their financial future.

The bottom line doesn't tell the whole story, of course. "For many women, the decision to work, or not, involves more than money," says Norman M. Berk, managing partner of Berk Patterson, a financial planning firm in Birmingham, Ala. Some parents don't believe in day care. "Do I really want someone else raising my child?" asks Denise Larkin. For this 33-year-old former international portfolio trader, the answer was no. Larkin quit shortly after the birth of her first child last year.

Other mothers feel they must take a more active parenting role—at some point in their child's life. Ellen Bartel, 42, recently quit her job as vice-president for institutional advancement at Alverno College in Milwaukee. While she has worked full-time since her children were born, Bartel feels that her two boys, aged 8 and 9, need her full-time now. "They're asking more complicated questions," she says. "And you only have a small window of opportunity when you can be influential in their lives."

Women who are committed to a career, on the other hand, often see their job—as many men do—as an integral part of their identity. And they may not be willing to give that up. Playing peek-a-boo and singing *Twinkle, Twinkle, Little Star* all day long can be tedious—even for the most nurturing of parents.

The spouse of working mothers are apparently happier, too. In *She Works/He Works: How Two-Income Families are Happier, Healthier, and Better Off* ($24, Harper San Francisco), clinical psychologist Rosalind Barnett explains the findings of her three-year study, funded by the National Institute of Mental Health, of 300 families in the Boston area. "When the husband and wife both work, it puts less stress on their marriage," says Barnett. "They have more security, and more flexibility."

If only real life were so simple. But add a sick child or a trusted nanny who has just quit, and even the best-laid plans go awry. "I have to go out of town next week," says McCardel. "That'll really upset everyone's schedule." But she wouldn't think of giving up her job. "My work is challenging, and I need that," she says. Besides, that second income is keeping the family on track financially. The McCardels recently bought a new car and are trying to beef up their savings for the kids' college educations. "We couldn't do that if I didn't work," says McCardel. "Two incomes give us more choices."

Barbara Hetzer

A FINANCIAL ANALYSIS FOR WORKING PARENTS

The numbers in these worksheets are based on a suburban married professional couple working in New York City with a child under age 3, a 30-year $200,000 mortgage at 7.5%, and separate 401(k) plans.

DATA: PRICE WATERHOUSE PERSONAL FINANCIAL SERVICES

He Works, She Stays Home

Gross Income (Husband)	$80,000
Minus 401(k) Contribution:	-8,000
Adjusted Gross Income (AGI)	72,000
Minus Taxes	
Federal	-5,883
State & Local	-2,891
FICA	-5,215
Total Taxes*	-13,989
What's Left	58,011
Plus Pretax Value of 401(k) Savings **	10,893
TOTAL	68,904

*The taxes are based on a taxable income of $39,222, which results after deductions of $14,937 for mortgage interest, $7,000 for real estate taxes, and $2,891 for state and local taxes, plus three exemptions worth $7,950.
**Assuming a 10% annual contribution, 8% annual return, and 50% employer match.

He Works, She Works

Gross Income (Husband)	$80,000
(Wife)	70,000
Total Gross Income	150,000
Minus 401(k) Contribution:	
His	-8,000
Hers	-7,000
Adjusted Gross Income (AGI)	135,000
Minus Taxes*	
Federal	-21,931
Dependent-Care Expense Credit	480
State & Local	-8,075
FICA	-10,285
Total Taxes*	-39,811

After-tax income	95,189
Minus Additional Expenses	
Child Care ($400/week)	-20,800
Payroll taxes for Nanny	-2,444
Commuting**	-2,160
Lunches Out ($7/day)**	-1,680
Dry cleaning ($50/month)**	-550
Take-Out Dinner ($50/week)**	-2,400
House cleaning ($50/week)	-2,600
Total Expenses	-32,634
What's Left	62,555
Plus Pretax value of 401(k) Savings***	23,343
TOTAL	85,898

*The taxes are based on a taxable income of $97,452, which results after deductions of $14,937 for mortgage interest, $7,000 for real estate taxes, and $8,075 for state and local taxes, plus three exemptions worth $7,950.

**Based on a 52-week year—minus 2 weeks of vacation and 10 holidays.
***Assuming a 10% annual contribution, 8% annual return, and 50% employer match.

What She Loses Long-Term

	Salary*	401(k) Balance**
Year 1	$70,000	$10,894
Year 5	83,476	69,454
Year 10	104,027	186,386
Year 15	129,636	360,596

*Assumes a 4.5% increase per year
**Balance at yearend, given a 10% contribution of her salary per year, a 50% match of that 10% by her employer, and an annual return of 8%.

DATA: Price Waterhouse Personal Financial Services

Study Questions

1. Other than financial factors, what might influence both parents to work?

2. What actions might be taken to reduce costs associated with a two-income household?

3. What recommendations would you offer to parents who both want to work?

2 FINANCIAL ASPECTS OF CAREER PLANNING

Chapter Overview

A person's career and work situation is frequently overlooked in financial planning. Your career will influence the financial resources you have available for spending, savings, and investing. In addition, a career interacts with a person's lifestyle, interests, and values, all of which influence financial decisions. This chapter provides a basic understanding of career planning, job selection, and obtaining an employment position. Included is practical information regarding career information sources, creating a resume and cover letter, and interviewing. Finally, material on evaluating a job offer and considering a career change is presented.

Learning Objectives

After studying this chapter, you will be able to:

Obj. 1 Describe the activities associated with career planning and advancement.

Obj. 2 Evaluate the factors that influence employment opportunities.

Obj. 3 Implement employment search strategies.

Obj. 4 Assess the financial and legal concerns related to obtaining employment.

Obj. 5 Analyze the techniques available for career growth and advancement.

Key Terms

cafeteria-style employee benefits
career
cover letter
informational interview
job
job creation
mentor
networking
résumé

Pretest

True-False

_______ 1. (Obj. 1) Increased education increases a person's potential earning power.

_______ 2. (Obj. 1) A person's career selection influences many aspects of his or her lifestyle.

_______ 3. (Obj. 1) Aptitude tests are designed to measure a person's interests.

_______ 4. (Obj. 2) Foreign competition has resulted in fewer manufacturing jobs in the United States.

_______ 5. (Obj. 3) An informational interview is designed to gather information about a career or an organization.

_______ 6. (Append) References are not usually included on a résumé.

_______ 7. (Append) A functional résumé is suggested for individuals with diverse skills who may be seeking employment in a new career area.

_______ 8. (Append) A screening interview is designed for in-depth discussion with the finalists for a job.

_______ 9. (Obj. 4) Salary is only one of the financial factors that should be considered when accepting an employment position.

_______ 10. (Obj. 5) Continuing career education can involve both formal and informal methods of training.

Self-Guided Study Questions

Obj. 1

Financial and Personal Aspects of Career Choice (p. 37)

1. Describe the differences between a job and a career.

Trade-Offs of Career Decisions (p. 37)

2. What are some trade-offs a person may face when making a career decision?

Career Training and Skill Development (p. 38)

3. What is the common relationship between education and income?

4. What traits are commonly associated with successful individuals?

Personal Factors (p. 39)

5. How can aptitude tests and interest inventories assist a person with career planning?

6. How does a person's personality affect career decisions?

Career Decision Making (p. 40)

7. How would the career activities of a person seeking an entry-level position differ from a person planning to change careers?

Obj. 2

Career Opportunities: Now and in the Future (p. 41)

Social Influences (p. 41)

8. How can demographic and geographic trends affect job opportunities?

Economic Conditions (p. 42)

9. What types of employment opportunities would be most affected by higher interest rates?

Trends in Industry and Technology (p. 42)

10. How have foreign businesses affected career opportunities?

11. What career areas are likely to have the most demand in the next few years?

Obj. 3

Employment Search Strategies (p. 44)

Obtaining Employment Experience (p. 44)

12. How can a person obtain work-related experience without having a job?

Using Career Information Sources (p. 45)

13. What are the main sources of career planning information and assistance?

14. In what ways could the *Occupational Outlook Handbook* and the World Wide Web assist a person with career planning decisions?

15. What is the value of personal and business contacts in the career planning process?

Identifying Job Opportunities (p. 48)

16. What are some methods for finding available employment positions?

Applying for Employment (p. 49)

17. How does a résumé differ from a cover letter?

Obj. 4

Financial and Legal Aspects of Employment (p. 49)

Accepting an Employment Position (p. 49)

18. What factors of the working environment of an organization should be considered when evaluating a job offer?

19. What factors affect a person's salary?

Evaluating Employee Benefits (p. 50)

20. What is the advantage of a cafeteria-style employee benefits program?

21. What analytical techniques could be used to assess the financial value of employee benefits?

22. How do tax-deferred employee benefits differ from tax-exempt benefits?

Your Employment Rights (p. 53)

23. What are some rights employees have that are protected by law?

Obj. 5

Long-Term Career Development (p. 54)

24. What daily work activities can contribute to long-term career success?

Training Opportunities (p. 54)

25. What are some common sources of continuing education experiences?

Career Paths and Advancement (p. 54)

26. How can a mentor contribute to your career development?

Changing Careers (p. 55)

27. What factors might a person consider when deciding whether or not to change employment situations?

Appendix: Résumés, Cover Letters, and Interviews (p. 61)

Developing a Résumé (p. 61)

28. What are the main components of information on a résumé?

29. Should a career objective be presented on a résumé?

30. What types of school and community experiences are relevant work experiences?

Types of Résumés (p. 62)

31. How does a chronological résumé differ from a functional résumé?

32. When should a targeted résumé be used?

Creating a Cover Letter (p. 65)

33. What is the purpose of a cover letter?

34. What are the main sections of a cover letter?

The Job Interview (p. 66)

35. What actions are suggested before going to an interview?

36. How does a screening interview differ from a selection interview?

37. What actions could be taken after an interview to add to a person's chances of successful job hunting in the future?

Post Test

Completion

1. (Append) A(n) ____________ interview is an initial meeting, usually brief, that reduces the pool of job candidates to a workable number.
2. (Append) A(n) ____________ résumé is used to apply for a specific job.
3. (Obj. 1) An employment position that is obtained mainly to earn money is commonly referred to as a(n) ____________.
4. (Obj. 5) A(n) ____________ is an experienced employee who serves as a teacher and counselor for a less experienced person in a career field.
5. (Obj. 3) A(n) ____________ ____________ is designed to express your interest in a job and obtain an interview.
6. (Append) The ____________ résumé presents your education, work experience, and other information in a reverse time sequence.
7. (Append) The purpose of a(n) ____________ interview is to gather information about a career or an organization.
8. (Obj. 1) A commitment to a profession that requires continued training and offers a clear path for occupational growth is a(n) ____________.
9. (Append) A(n) ____________ interview is limited to the finalists in a job search.
10. (Append) The ____________ résumé emphasizes a person's abilities and skills in categories such as communication, supervision, and training experiences.

Multiple Choice

_____ 1. (Obj. 2) Aptitudes refer to
   A. areas of interest.
   B. natural abilities.
   C. skills requiring technical training.
   D. supervisory skills possessed by managers.

_____ 2. (Obj. 3) The purpose of an informational interview is to
   A. obtain career information.
   B. select a job for which to interview.
   C. make a final selection of an employee.
   D. select the best candidates for a position.

_____ 3. (Append) The item least likely to be included on a résumé is
A. volunteer work.
B. school club activities.
C. employment experience.
D. references.

_____ 4. (Append) A ___________ résumé would be best for a person with many skills who is applying for employment in a new career area.
A. targeted
B. functional
C. chronological
D. placement

_____ 5. (Obj. 3) The purpose of a cover letter is to
A. obtain career planning information.
B. determine the jobs available in an organization.
C. apply for a specific position.
D. inquire about employee benefits with a prospective employer.

_____ 6. (Append) The final section of a cover letter should
A. express your interest in the job.
B. request the opportunity for an interview.
C. highlight portions of your background.
D. communicate your career goals.

_____ 7. (Append) The purpose of a screening interview is to
A. obtain information on a career area.
B. select the best candidate for an available position.
C. make an initial contact with an employer.
D. discuss the working environment with current employees.

_____ 8. (Append) The final step in the interview process involves a(n) ________ interview.
A. selection
B. transition
C. screening
D. informational

_____ 9. (Obj. 4) Which of the following is considered a long-term employee benefit?
A. Salary
B. Overtime pay
C. Profit sharing
D. Paid vacations

_____ 10. (Obj. 4) A cafeteria-style employee benefits program is designed to
A. minimize taxes for workers.
B. reduce benefit costs for the company.
C. meet the needs of individual employees.
D. provide food service for workers while on the job.

Problems, Applications, and Cases

1. With the use of the World Wide Web, *Business Week*, other business periodicals, and the daily newspaper, obtain information about increased or decreased career opportunities based on the following factors that influence the job market. (Refer to text pages 41-44 for additional information.)

Factor	Influence on the job market
Economic trends	
Industry trends	
Technology	
Social factors	
Geographic trends	

2. Investigate one or more careers in which you are interested. Be sure to use information from the library, mass media sources, the World Wide Web, your campus placement office, community organizations, professional associations, and personal and business contacts (see text pages 45-48).

3. Conduct a personal inventory of your background, and prepare a chronological résumé (refer to text pages 61-63). Your data should include information in the following areas:

   a. personal data

   b. career objective

   c. education

   d. experience

   e. related information

   f. references

   If a functional or targeted résumé (see text pages 61-63) is more appropriate for your personal situation, create one of these personal information sheets.

4. Select a specific job opportunity and develop a cover letter (see text page 66) that would be appropriate. This correspondence should have the three main sections:

   (1) the introductory paragraph

   (2) the development section (one or two paragraphs)

   (3) the concluding paragraph

5. Talk to several people who have recently interviewed for a job and obtain information on the questions they were commonly asked. (Or refer to Exhibit 2-E, text page 68, for sample questions.) Make notes as to how you would respond to these questions.

Interview question	Possible response

6. Contact one or more companies to obtain information about the types of employee benefits they offer, or talk to friends who work to gather this data (see text pages 50-53).

Company		
Paid holidays		
Vacation time		
Sick days		
Health insurance		
Life, other insurance		
Retirement program		
Profit sharing		
Other benefits:		

Supplementary Case 2-1: Wise Career Choices

Topic: Job Search Strategies

Text Reference: pp. 44-49; 61-69

Barb Collins was recently promoted from regional sales manager to vice president of marketing for a telecommunications company. Many people would say they could never achieve that kind of success. However, Barb also had that attitude when she graduated from college eight years ago. What changed her attitude and put her on a successful career path? She didn't always take the right actions, but after awhile Barb started to learn from every experience.

During college, Barb majored in history and also took several English, psychology, math, computer, and business classes. When she graduated, she wasn't sure how to get a job. Barb obtained help with her résumé from the career placement office on campus. Not sure about the type of work she wanted to do, Barb sent out letters and résumés to nearly 200 companies that advertised positions open. She received very few responses and was invited to interview for only three jobs. None of the three interviews went well.

To pay her living expenses, Barb took a job as a sales clerk. One day, Barb was talking to her supervisor, Joan Sanders, about the trouble she was having getting a job that used more of her skills. Joan suggested that Barb visit some companies for which she would like to work.

Joan also advised Barb to strengthen her career planning portfolio before the visits. First, she told Barb to make sure her résumé communicated the skills and experiences the company wanted. Barb had completed several class projects involving field research, human relations, and communication skills. Her campus activities demonstrated leadership and organizational planning. These qualifications were not clearly presented on her current résumé. Joan also stressed the importance of emphasizing in an interview how Barb's past accomplishments would benefit the employer in the *future*.

Next, Joan suggested that Barb prepare questions about the jobs available, the skills required, and the working environment of the company. These questions would show her personal initiative and desire to work for that company.

Finally, Joan encouraged Barb to talk to as many people as possible at different companies, both on and off the job, and to ask questions about everything related to their companies and their duties. This information would prepare Barb to better target her job search.

Things started to go a little better with Barb's career planning activities. She started to get more interviews, but still no job. Then, one day, while talking to someone while waiting for an interview, she heard about a company that was opening a new sales office in the neighboring city. It was at this company that Barb Collins became vice president of marketing.

Case Questions

1. How could Barb Collins have improved her chances of getting the job she wanted before meeting Joan Sanders?
2. What types of school and work experiences helped Barb obtain the job she wanted?
3. Which of Joan's suggestions do you believe will be most helpful to you when planning a career or changing jobs?

Supplementary Case 2-2: A Dead-End Career Path

Topic: Career Planning Activities

Text Reference: pp. 44-49

Joanne Nash has tried to get a sales job for three months. She has applied for a position with companies that sell everything from automobiles and electronic products to medical supplies and restaurant equipment. Joanne has always worked in an office. She completed two years of college and took several business courses. She sees sales as a chance to meet interesting people and earn a higher salary.

During interviews, Joanne displays a very pleasant and outgoing personality. The company representatives like talking with her, but they have not offered her a job due to her limited knowledge and her limited sales experience.

Case Questions

1. As a career counselor, what suggestions would you offer Joanne?
2. What experience might Joanne have that could be adapted to a sales career?
3. How could a specific career objective be valuable to Joanne?
4. What types of career information materials could Joanne use to improve her chances of obtaining a sales job?

Supplementary Case 2-3: A Midlife Career Search

Topic: Changing Careers

Text Reference: pp. 44-49

Bob Thomas faces a difficult situation—two children in college, a dependent parent, and a job eliminated in a corporate merger. After 20 years with the company, Bob, age 47, must seek employment elsewhere. Bob's wife still has her job. Her income, however, will not support all of the family's financial obligations. Bob has the options of taking out his pension funds, leaving them in the same pension plan, or transferring them to a different retirement account.

During the two decades Bob was with the company, he was promoted several times. He started as an accounting clerk, then became credit manager, and most recently served as manager of the company's southeastern regional office.

Bob's former employer will allow him to continue his health insurance coverage. Bob, of course, will be required to pay monthly premiums. The company is also providing a career consultant to assist former employees with their job search.

Case Questions

1. How can the family's spending be revised to cope with financial difficulties while Bob is between jobs? What sources of funds are available to Bob and his family?
2. What actions should Bob consider regarding his pension funds?
3. What employment skills is Bob likely to have that will make him an attractive prospect to other organizations?
4. What career planning advice would you recommend to someone in Bob's situation?

3 MONEY MANAGEMENT STRATEGY: FINANCIAL STATEMENTS AND BUDGETING

Chapter Overview

Successful money management is based on organized financial records, accurate personal financial statements, and effective budgeting. This chapter offers a discussion of the importance and type of financial documents. This is followed by an explanation of the components and procedures for preparing personal financial statements—the balance sheet and the cash flow statement. Next, the chapter covers the basics of developing, implementing, and evaluating a budget. Finally, savings techniques for achieving financial goals are discussed.

Learning Objectives

After studying the chapter, you will be able to:

Obj. 1 Recognize the relationships among financial documents and money management activities.

Obj. 2 Create a system for maintaining personal financial documents.

Obj. 3 Develop a personal balance sheet and cash flow statement.

Obj. 4 Create and implement a budget.

Obj. 5 Calculate savings needed for achieving financial goals.

Key Terms

assets
balance sheet
budget
budget variance
cash flow
cash flow statement
current liabilities
deficit
discretionary income
income
insolvency
liabilities
liquid assets
long-term liabilities
money management
net worth
safe-deposit box
surplus
take-home pay

Pretest

True-False

_______ 1. (Obj. 2) Most financial records and documents should be stored in a safe-deposit box.

_______ 2. (Obj. 3) A balance sheet reports the current financial position of an individual or family.

_______ 3. (Obj. 3) An individual retirement account (IRA) is an example of a liquid asset.

_______ 4. (Obj. 3) Your net worth is computed by adding total assets to total liabilities.

_______ 5. (Obj. 3) If your assets exceed your liabilities, this is referred to as insolvency.

_______ 6. (Obj. 3) Wages, salaries, and commissions are cash inflows.

_______ 7. (Obj. 3) If a person's payments are greater than income for a month, this will decrease net worth.

_______ 8. (Obj. 4) Food, clothing, and transportation expenses are commonly referred to as fixed expenses.

_______ 9. (Obj. 5) A budget deficit occurs when actual spending exceeds planned spending.

_______ 10. (Obj. 5) Future value computations are used to determine the amount in savings at some later date.

Self-Guided Study Questions

Obj. 1

Planning for Successful Money Management (p. 71)

Opportunity Cost and Money Management (p. 71)

1. What are examples of trade-offs associated with money management decisions?

Components of Money Management (p. 72)

2. What are the major money management activities encountered by most people?

Obj. 2

A System for Personal Financial Records (p. 72)

3. Why is an organized financial records file important?

4. What is the purpose of a safe-deposit box?

5. What suggestions could be offered to a person designing a system for organizing and storing financial records and documents?

Obj. 3

Personal Financial Statements for Measuring Financial Progress (p. 74)

6. What are the main purposes of personal financial statements?

The Personal Balance Sheet: Where Are You Now? (p. 74)

7. What is the purpose of a balance sheet?

8. What are the three categories of assets?

9. How do current liabilities differ from long-term liabilities?

10. How is a person's or household's net worth computed? What does this number represent?

11. What is insolvency?

Evaluating Your Financial Position (p. 77)

12. What information does a debt ratio, a current ratio, and other ratios provide?

The Cash Flow Statement: Where Did Your Money Go? (p. 77)

13. What purpose does a cash flow statement serve?

14. What are common sources of income?

15. What are commonly used categories for cash outflows?

16. What is the effect of a negative cash flow on a person's financial position?

Obj. 4

Budgeting for Skilled Money Management (p. 81)

17. What purposes does a budget serve?

Starting the Budgeting Process (p. 81)

18. What factors affect your daily financial choices?

19. What are some common financial goals?

20. What information sources are available to assist a person in developing a budget?

21. What is the difference between fixed and variable expenses?

22. What is a budget variance?

23. What factors should be considered when reviewing a budget for possible changes?

Characteristics of Successful Budgeting (p. 87)

24. What are the qualities of a successful budget?

25. What types of financial recordkeeping systems are available for maintaining budget information?

Obj. 5

Saving to Achieve Financial Goals (p. 89)

26. What are common reasons for saving?

Selecting a Savings Technique (p. 90)

27. What are methods that can be used to increase a person's savings?

Calculating Savings Amounts (p. 90)

28. How can the time value of money be used to reach savings goals?

Post Test

Completion

1. (Obj. 3) ____________ assets are cash and items of value that can easily be converted to cash.
2. (Obj. 4) A budget ____________ is the difference between the amount budgeted and the actual amount received or spent.
3. (Obj. 3) A(n) ____________ ____________ reports the assets, liabilities, and net worth of a family or individual.
4. (Obj. 3) A person's earnings after deductions is referred to as ____________ ____________.
5. (Obj. 3) Amounts owed to others are called ____________.
6. (Obj. 3) A summary of cash receipts and payments for a period of time is reported on a(n) ____________ ____________ ____________.
7. (Obj. 3) ____________ is the financial position in which your total liabilities are greater than the value of your assets.
8. (Obj. 4) Budget ____________ are amounts allocated for various spending categories.
9. (Obj. 3) The difference between total assets and total liabilities is referred to as ____________ ____________.
10. (Obj. 2) A(n) ____________ ____________ is a private storage area at a financial institution that offers maximum security for valuables.

Multiple Choice

______ 1. (Obj. 2) Which of the following items is most likely to be stored in a safe-deposit box?
   A. Paycheck stubs
   B. Savings` certificates
   C. Income tax returns
   D. Bank statements

______ 2. (Obj. 3) The purpose of a balance sheet is to
   A. report a person's or family's financial position.
   B. serve as a plan for spending.
   C. report current income and expenses.
   D. project a person's or a family's future financial position.

_____ 3. (Obj. 3) Which of the following would be an example of a liquid asset?
A. A savings account
B. Furniture
C. Stocks and bonds
D. An individual retirement account

_____ 4. (Obj. 3) The net worth of an individual or family is determined by
A. subtracting expenses from income.
B. adding income and expenses.
C. adding assets and liabilities.
D. subtracting liabilities from assets.

_____ 5. (Obj. 3) Which of the following would result in an increase in net worth?
A. Reduced income
B. Reduced spending
C. Increased amounts owed to others
D. Decreased value of personal belongings

_____ 6. (Obj. 3) A common example of a fixed expense is
A. food.
B. telephone.
C. rent.
D. clothing purchases.

_____ 7. (Obj. 3) The purpose of a cash flow statement is to
A. budget for future spending.
B. report current income and payments.
C. summarize assets and liabilities of an individual or family.
D. project the future value of investments.

_____ 8. (Obj. 4) The main purpose of a budget is to
A. determine the future value of investments.
B. plan spending.
C. determine a person's current financial situation.
D. report assets and liabilities.

_____ 9. (Obj. 4) A budget _____________ occurs when actual spending exceeds budgeted spending.
A. surplus
B. deficit
C. restriction
D. reduction

_____ 10. (Obj. 5) Which of the following time value of money computations would be used to determine the value of $100 three years from now?
A. Future value of a single amount
B. Future value of a series of deposits
C. Present value of a single amount
D. Present value of a series of deposits

Problems, Applications, and Cases

1. Develop a financial document and records filing system based on the categories and information presented on pages 72-74 of the text.

2. Create a balance sheet and income statement based on the following information for Gail Johnson; date the balance sheet September 30 of the current year and the income statement for the month ended September 30 of the current year.

Balance sheet data
Cash in checking account $460
Retirement account $7,690
Value of furniture $2,560
Credit card balances $563
Value of automobile $5,600
Jewelry $340
Auto loan balance $1,239
Savings certificate $3,000
Cash value of life insurance $2,298
Cameras $980
Savings accounts $1,256
Value of clothing $1,800
Credit union loan $315
Value of stereo $1,150
Amount owed to dentist $76
Antiques $2,100

Cash flow statement data
Food (home and away) $467
Gifts $45
Electricity $67
Rent $810
Clothing $108
Take-home pay $2,078
Auto loan payment $211
Water $22
Auto insurance $38
Telephone $43
Interest earned on savings $34
Heat $47
Cable television $26
Personal care/reading materials $63
Medical expenses $65

3. Through library research, the Internet, and discussion with others, determine the common budget category percentages for such expenses as food, housing, transportation, clothing, personal care, entertainment/recreation, and savings.

4. Conduct a survey of common financial goals of families and individuals. Categorize these goals using the following headlines:

Short-term goals less than two years)	Intermediate goals (2-5 years)	Long-term goals (over 5 years)

5. Create a budget for a month similar to Exhibit 3-7 (page 84 in text).

6. For each of the following living expenses, decide if the item is generally fixed or variable:

	Fixed or variable expense?
a. Personal care	
b. Transportation	
c. Mortgage payments	
d. Telephone	
e. Gifts	
f. Loan payments	
g. Food	
h. Savings	

Supplementary Case 3-1: A Money Management Mess

Topic: Financial Records and Savings Goals

Text Reference: pp. 72-74; 89-91

Jeff Conrad completed high school two years ago. Afterward, he continued to live with his parents while attending college across town. He had a part-time job as a sales and inventory clerk at a department store. With his income, he was able to pay his school expenses and save $1,000. Since his parents paid for housing and food, he was able to make car payments, buy clothes, and spend money on entertainment activities.

During the past two years, Jeff never kept track of his spending habits. His financial record-keeping consisted of depositing half of his income in a checking account and half in a savings account. Whenever he needed to pay a bill or make a purchase, he would write a check. If he didn't have enough money in checking, he would transfer funds from savings to checking. When he decided to get his own apartment, he didn't have a realistic picture of his finances and living expenses.

During the first few months in his apartment, Jeff was able to work full-time and could pay his bills on time. When school started in September, however, his income decreased since he worked fewer hours. Also, he had to use most of his savings to pay for tuition and books. These school costs were higher than those he had paid the previous year.

As time passed, Jeff had other expenses, such as automobile repairs, insurance for his car and other property, and medical bills. The cost of food, electricity, and telephone was higher than he had anticipated. Jeff's financial independence was not as pleasant as he had hoped it would be.

Budgeting and an understanding of living expenses are skills that many people learn only after difficult experiences. An ability to plan and document spending is the starting point of successful money management and effective financial planning.

Case Questions

1. What actions could Jeff Conrad have taken to prepare for his financial independence from his parents?
2. What common problems did Jeff encounter because he did not have an organized system of financial records and documents?
3. How effective would Jeff's financial record-keeping system be for developing personal financial statements and a budget? Explain.
4. What are common savings goals for persons in Jeff's situation? What money management activities would be most effective in achieving these goals?

Supplementary Case 3-2: Beth's Unbalanced Books

Topic: Personal Financial Statements

Text Reference: pp. 72-81

Beth Lyons is employed as a word processing supervisor for an investment company. She lives in a small house about 20 minutes from work, and she drives a two-year-old car. She is making payments on both the house and the car. Beth has a steady income and can afford to buy many other items. She recently redecorated several rooms in her house, and during each of the past five years she has taken a vacation.

Even though Beth handles business records and documents at work, she is frequently late in making payments to her creditors. Also, the insurance coverage for her home and car is not adequate to cover their value.

Beth has the following assets and liabilities:

Savings/investment account, $800
Market value of automobile, $11,000
Mortgage balance, $66,000
Household possessions, $18,500

Credit card balances, $8,600
Market value of home, $83,000
Checking account balance, $340
Personal loans, $1,700

Case Questions

1. Which financial documents does Beth need?
2. How could Beth become better organized in handling her personal finances?
3. Compute Beth's net worth based on the data provided.
4. How would a personal balance sheet and a personal cash flow statement assist Beth in her financial planning?

Supplementary Case 3-3: Mismanaged Money

Topic: Personal Financial Statement and Budgeting

Text Reference: pp. 74-80

Julie and Ralph Palmer have been married six years. They have a combined income of $50,000. With total assets of $110,000, they have only $500 in savings. Their liabilities total $80,600.

Each time the Palmers have a substantial amount of savings, they spend it for such things as vacations, furniture, or home entertainment equipment. Currently, their annual expenses include $11,325 listed as "unaccounted for." This amount is in addition to the amounts they spend for food, housing, utilities, transportation, loan payments, insurance, donations, gifts, and taxes. The Palmers live in a town house, but they would like to buy a detached house.

Case Questions

1. What is the net worth of the Palmers? What is your opinion of their current financial position?
2. How could the Palmers improve their financial position?
3. What changes would you suggest in the Palmers' budgeting techniques?
4. How could the Palmers be more effective in their financial planning?

Supplementary Reading 3

Jeffrey M. Laderman, "Stalking Those Elusive Financial Records," *Business Week*, September 1, 1997, pp. 94-95.

Stalking Those Elusive Financial Records

Edited by Amy Dunkin

The soaring stock market is running into turbulence. And the new tax bill slashes the capital gains rate to a maximum of 20% on assets held for more than 18 months. Perhaps you want to do some judicious selling, turning those fat paper profits into cold, hard cash.

But the elation you might enjoy over cashing in on a smart investment could turn into a major, and perhaps costly, headache at tax time if your financial records aren't in order. To know how much tax you would have to pay on your gains, you would need to know exactly how much you spent initially. Do you have that information—in tax terms, the "cost basis"—for all of your investments?

Old Suitcases. Knowing the amount of capital gains in your portfolio is essential for smart investment and tax planning. Mark Cohen, a CPA with the New York accounting firm of Newman & Cohen, recently sent a client to rummage through old suitcases and file folders for documentation that would establish a cost basis for a six-figure holding. "Depending on how much profit there is, my client may be better off donating the shares to charity than selling them and paying the taxes," says Cohen. "But I just can't advise her until I know."

If your financial records are spotty or if years of data seem to have evaporated, you're not alone. Even many well-to-do folks, the sort that use the services of a major trust company, often fail when it comes to financial fastidiousness. "A lot of people come to us with very poor records," says Edward Peller, a senior vice-president at U.S. Trust Co. of New York. We start by asking how the stock was obtained: purchase, inheritance, or gift. Depending on the answers, we can direct people to the sources."

It's easier to hunt for those missing numbers now than in those frantic first weeks of April. You'll need that info to complete the Schedule D (Capital Gains & Losses) on your federal income tax return, and most likely for your state form as well. Many mutual-fund companies provide average cost basis in yearly statements or when shares are sold. But if the fund has been held for more than a decade, that basis may not include older investments.

Not having those numbers could cost you. If you report a basis that's too high and thus show a lesser gain and tax liability, you'll risk the wrath of the Internal Revenue Service. You might have to pay not only the back taxes, but penalties and interest. Tax pros say the IRS rarely questions cost-basis reporting by itself, but auditors might ask for documentation if you're already undergoing the agency's scrutiny.

Without good records, you could also underreport your cost basis, and thus overpay your taxes. Accurate records are especially important if you reinvest dividends or the income and capital-gains distributions paid by a mutual fund. Each time you reinvest, you are actually buying new shares, and those purchases roll into your cost basis.

Even if you're not planning to sell right now, it's still a good idea to establish the cost basis for your holdings. In these days of merger mania, you might be forced to sell your stock if the company is bought out. If you receive cash, you'll likely have to report capital gains.

The first step in trying to determine cost basis on shares of stock or a mutual fund is to contact the firm that sold you the investment. Brokers and financial planners often keep their own records of clients' transactions in addition to those of their firms. That's handy if the broker has changed employers. Also, scores of brokerages have folded or merged, and old records don't always make it to their successors.

If you have stock certificates but can't find a brokerage record of the purchase, check the shares for the date they were registered to your name. That's usually done within four to six weeks of purchase, says Rosilyn Overton, a financial planner at Brown & Overton in Queens, N.Y. Once you establish a registration date, Overton suggests a trip to the library to check newspaper stock tables or Standard & Poor's *Daily Stock Price Record* for the prices four weeks and six weeks before the transfer date. Take one of them, or average them, and use that as a cost basis. "It's not exact, but close enough," says Overton. This method may be way off base, though, if there have been stock splits, spin-offs, or other corporate reorganizations over the years.

The business section of a large public library usually has some publications that may help you trace such events. They include *Capital Changes Reporter*, published by Commerce Clearing House, and two S&P publications: *Corporation Records* and *Dividend Record*. Try calling company shareholder-relations departments for assistance, but often they lose track of spin-offs once they are separated from the parent. Standard & Poor's Central Inquiry (212-208-1199) is a fee-based service that also can assist in searches. The cost depends on the amount of information you need, but there is a $35 minimum. Don't bother looking online. Daily quotes at Web sites commonly go back months, not decades.

Mutual-fund companies are used to getting requests for records, and you can order them by calling the funds' toll-free numbers. Even if you were making monthly purchases, you don't need a statement for every investment. Each year's final statement will include all the year's transactions, including reinvestment of dividends and capital gains. The same goes for the dividend reinvestment programs that many corporations run for shareholders.

Most fund companies will provide the current and previous year's statement gratis, but you may have to pay beyond that. T. Rowe Price Associates charges $10 per year for past statements, with a maximum of $75 for all searches. DST Systems, the transfer agent that handles the recordkeeping for more than 2,000 mutual funds and more than 2,400 companies, doesn't charge for the past five years of records. But going back six to 10 years costs $20; 11 to 16, $40; and 17 or more, $80. You can get computerized records in a few days, but older records on microfilm or ledger cards will take longer.

Suppose you have the cost of your original investment, but are missing reinvestment records. Old tax returns may help. Provided you reinvested all the dividends and distributions, you can assume the dividend and distribution income from each stock or fund reported on Schedule B of the tax return is the amount you invested.

If you're selling inherited stock, the cost basis is probably the stock's price on the benefactor's day of death. Executors have the option of using a valuation date six months after the day of death, so you should check with the executor or seek a copy of the estate tax return.

It gets tougher when you're dealing with gifts. Suppose you're in your 40s and you want to sell the stock your deceased Uncle Joe gave you when you were a tot. If he bought the stock in your name, the cost basis is the same as if you had purchased it yourself. But if he transferred shares from his ownership to yours, your cost basis is his. And who knows when he got those shares? The first place to check is with other family members who may have access to his records. Try the company, too. Exxon, for instance, has nearly 80 years of daily stock price information. If you can provide a purchase date or a stock certificate number, Exxon may be able to fill in the missing pieces.

But even after a long search, you may never solve this mystery. If you still want to sell and can't come up with the exact information, advisers suggest documenting your efforts to find the original cost basis, coming up with a reasonable estimate, and hoping the IRS understands.

Jeffrey M. Laderman

Strategies for Filling the Gaps

Brokers
Ask for cost-basis data at the firm where you made the investment. Firms usually archive even dormant account records.

Companies
The shareholder relations department can be of help, but the level of assistance will vary by company and how far back your request goes.

Mutual Funds
Call the shareholder service number. The last two years' records are usually free, but be prepared to pay after that.

Tax Returns
If you've reinvested dividends and distributions, you can fill in missing years' cost data by looking at how much income from those investments you've reported on past returns.

References
Check the business section of the public library for Commerce Clearing House's *Capital Changes Reporter*, or S&P's *Corporation Records, Dividend Record,* and *Daily Stock Price Record.*

DATA: Business Week

Study Questions

1. Why are financial records related to investments important?

2. What actions might be taken to obtain missing information related to investment records?

4 PLANNING YOUR TAX STRATEGY

Chapter Overview

The basics of taxes and their relationship to financial planning are presented in this chapter. The material starts with a brief discussion of types of taxes. Next, the fundamental aspects of federal income taxes are presented, including taxable income, deductions, exemptions, tax rates, and tax credits. The information on filing your federal income tax return covers filing status, types of tax forms, basic steps for completing Form 1040, tax assistance sources, and audit procedures. Finally, the chapter concludes with a discussion of tax planning strategies related to purchasing decisions, investment alternatives, and retirement plans.

Learning Objectives

After studying the chapter, you will be able to:

Obj. 1 Describe the importance of taxes for personal financial planning.

Obj. 2 Calculate taxable income and the amount owed for federal income tax.

Obj. 3 Prepare a federal income tax return.

Obj. 4 Identify tax assistance sources.

Obj. 5 Select appropriate tax strategies for different financial and personal situations.

Key Terms

adjusted gross income (AGI)
average tax rate
capital gains
earned income
estate tax
excise tax
exclusion
exemption
inheritance tax
investment income
itemized deductions
marginal tax rate
passive income
standard deduction
taxable income
tax audit
tax avoidance
tax credit
tax deduction
tax-deferred income
tax evasion
tax-exempt income
tax shelter

Pretest

True-False

_______ 1. (Obj. 1) Federal income tax is based on a person's earnings.

_______ 2. (Obj. 1) Inheritance taxes are also referred to as gift taxes.

_______ 3. (Obj. 1) An excise tax is a sales tax on specific goods and services.

_______ 4. (Obj. 2) Earned income refers to money received in the form of dividends or interest

_______ 5. (Obj. 2) Medical expenses, real estate property taxes, and home mortgage interest may qualify as itemized deductions for federal income tax purposes.

_______ 6. (Obj. 2) A tax credit is a deduction that reduces the amount of taxable income.

_______ 7. (Obj. 2) Most employees are required to make quarterly payments for estimated taxes owed.

_______ 8. (Obj. 3) The Form 1040A is used by a taxpayer who plans to itemize deductions.

_______ 9. (Obj. 4) A correspondence tax audit requires a person to report to a local IRS office.

_______ 10. (Obj. 5) An IRA is an example of a tax-exempt investment.

Self-Guided Study Questions

Obj. 1

Taxes and Financial Planning (p. 97)

1. What are common goals for tax planning efforts?

2. What is the main purpose of taxes?

3. What are the main types of taxes paid by individuals and households?

4. How does an excise tax differ from a general sales tax?

Obj. 2

Income Tax Fundamentals (p. 99)

Step 1: Determining Adjusted Gross Income (p. 99)

5. What is taxable income?

6. How does earned income differ from investment income?

7. What is the difference between tax-exempt income and tax-deferred income?

Step 2: Computing Taxable Income (p. 101)

8. How do deductions and exemptions affect taxes?

Step 3: Calculating Taxes Owed (p. 103)

9. What procedure is used to determine the amount of taxes due?

10. What is the difference between the marginal tax rate and the average tax rate?

11. What is a tax credit?

Making Tax Payments (p. 105)

12. What is the purpose of the tax withholding system?

13. Who must make estimated quarterly payments?

Deadlines and Penalties (p. 106)

14. What is the purpose of Form 4868?

Obj. 3

Filing Your Federal Income Tax Return (p. 107)

Who Must File? (p. 107)

15. Who is required to file a federal income tax return?

16. What are the main filing status categories?

Which Tax Form Should You Use? (p. 107)

17. What factors affect a person's decision to file the Form 1040EZ, Form 1040A, or Form 1040?

Completing the Federal Income Tax Return (p. 109)

18. What determines if a person receives a refund or owes an amount for taxes due?

Obj. 4

Tax Assistance and the Audit Process (p. 112)

Tax Information Sources (p. 113)

19. What services does the IRS provide to assist taxpayers in preparing their tax returns?

Tax Preparation Services (p. 116)

20. What individuals and organizations are available to help people with their tax returns?

What if Your Return is Audited? (p. 117)

21. What is a tax audit?

22. What are the main types of IRS audits?

23. What is the appeal process for an IRS audit?

Obj. 5

Tax Planning Strategies (p. 119)

24. What is the difference between tax avoidance and tax evasion?

Consumer Purchasing (p. 119)

25. What types of interest payments are tax deductible?

26. What are some job-related tax deductions?

Investment Decisions (p. 120)

27. What are the benefits of tax-deferred investments?

Retirement Plans (p. 122)

28. How do individual retirement accounts, Keogh plans, and 401(k) plans provide tax benefits for workers?

Post Test

Completion

1. (Obj. 2) A tax ____________ is an amount subtracted directly from the amount of taxes owed.
2. (Obj. 1) A tax imposed on specific goods and services is a(n) ____________ tax.
3. (Obj. 5) A(n) ____________ ____________ is a profit realized from the sale of a capital asset such as stocks, bonds, or real estate.
4. (Obj. 4) A detailed examination of your tax return by the IRS is called a(n) ____________ ____________.
5. (Obj. 2) ____________ income is money received by an individual for personal effort.
6. (Obj. 1) A(n) ____________ tax is levied on the value of property bequeathed by a deceased person.
7. (Obj. 2) ____________ ____________ are expenses that a taxpayer is allowed to deduct from adjusted gross income, such as real estate property tax and home mortgage interest.
8. (Obj. 2) A deduction from adjusted gross income for yourself, your spouse, or qualified dependents is a(n) ____________.
9. (Obj. 5) Tax ____________ income includes interest from municipal bonds.
10. (Obj. 2) An amount not included in gross income is a(n) ____________.

Multiple Choice

_____ 1. (Obj. 1) An estate tax is based on
A. income.
B. property value.
C. earnings.
D. retirement benefits.

_____ 2. (Obj. 1) A tax on specific goods and services is a(n)
A. social security tax.
B. general sales tax.
C. corporate income tax.
D. excise tax.

_____ 3. (Obj. 2) Money received in the form of dividends or interest is commonly referred to as ____________ income.
A. investment
B. earned
C. passive
D. excluded

_____ 4. (Obj. 2) Which of the following is an example of an itemized deduction?
A. Child care expenses
B. Expenses to travel to work
C. Real estate property taxes
D. Life insurance premiums

_____ 5. (Obj. 2) An exemption is a deduction from adjusted gross income for
A. yourself and your dependents.
B. money earned while living in a foreign country.
C. money donated to charity.
D. earnings from stocks and bonds.

_____ 6. (Obj. 2) Which of the following people is most likely to be required to make quarterly estimated tax payments?
A. A person who is employed by a non-profit organization
B. A person with excessive federal income tax withheld from his or her pay
C. An employee of a government agency
D. A person who earned large amounts of dividends and interest

_____ 7. (Obj. 3) Which of the following filing status categories would most likely be used by a person who is married with a dependent child, and is living apart from the spouse?
A. Single
B. Head of household
C. Married filing separate return
D. Married filing joint return

_____ 8. (Obj. 4) Government-approved tax experts who prepare tax returns are
   A. enrolled agents.
   B. IRS agents.
   C. auditors.
   D. accountants.

_____ 9. (Obj. 4) Which type of IRS audit requires a visit to your home or office?
   A. Research
   B. Office
   C. Correspondence
   D. Field

_____ 10. (Obj. 5) Interest paid on a(n) _____________ is fully deductible as an itemized deduction.
   A. credit card
   B. auto loan of less than $20,000
   C. home equity loan
   D. personal cash loan from a credit union

Problems, Applications, and Cases

1. Based on the following information, determine the amount of taxable income for Joanna Thompson. (Refer to text pages to review this material.)

   gross income $37,000

   exclusions $3,400

   exemption value $2,050

   standard deduction $3,000

   taxable income $ _____________.

2. Obtain current income tax forms and instructions. Use this material to prepare your own taxes. IRS Web site: www.irs.gov

3. Conduct a survey of people who prepare their own taxes and people who have someone else prepare their taxes. What are the main reasons given for the method of tax preparation selected by various individuals?

Supplementary Case 4-1: Taxes and Financial Planning

Topic: Tax Planning Activities

Text Reference: pp. 99-106; 119-123

Bob and Connie Martin have always considered themselves careful in their budgeting and savings activities. They never use credit cards; they pay all bills, including their monthly rent, on time; and they have several thousand dollars in savings certificates. However, tax planning is an area of weakness in what the Martins believe to be good financial planning and money management habits. Each year, they pay much more in taxes than they need to; quite often, they have had to take money out of savings to make their tax payment.

Case Questions

1. How might the Martins' housing situation be changed for better tax planning?
2. What savings and investment alternatives might reduce the Martins' tax liability?
3. What could the Martins do to prevent having to pay the government tax owed?
4. What additional suggestions with regard to effective tax planning could be offered to the Martins?

Supplementary Case 4-2: Taxes for a Home-Based Business

Topic: Tax Planning

Text Reference: pp. 99-112

In an effort to spend more time with their family and to have more flexible careers, Doris and Bob Hannon have decided to leave their current jobs and start a home-based business. They have years of experience in the areas of graphic arts, sales, marketing, and computers. As a result, the Hannons are operating a combination promotion and design company. Their main clients include local businesses and others who need brochures, newsletters, and promotional materials.

To get things started, the Hannons set up a portion of their home as an office and design studio. They purchased appropriate office equipment, computers, and software. The Hannons also had to purchase a variety of supplies and encountered more start-up costs than they estimated.

Next, they had to promote their business. They distributed fliers, put ads in local newspapers, and visited many businesses. One weekend, Doris and Bob attended a trade show of companies from around the state. This gave them names of potential clients for their services.

To keep up with personal living expenses, the Hannons received monthly interest payments from federal government securities and municipal bonds. In addition, Bob maintains a part-time job at a local retail store.

During their first year of business, the Hannons were able to generate $43,000 in revenue for the company. The expenses for the business were either $28,500 or $47,800 depending on what they included!

Doris asked, "Well Bob, did we make money or did we lose money?" "I'm not sure," Bob responded. "I'm not sure."

Case Questions

1. What are the main tax benefits of owning your own business?
2. What types of taxable income must the Hannons report for federal income tax purposes?
3. What factors could have accounted for the differences in total expenses for the Hannon's business?

Supplementary Reading 4

Susan Scherreik, "The Tax Man Still Biteth, The Audit Rate is Down—But Some Deductions Invite Scrutiny" *Business Week*, February 28, 2000, pp. 162, 164.

The Tax Man Still Biteth, The Audit Rate is Down—But Some Deductions Invite Scrutiny

Under pressure from Congress, the Internal Revenue Service is trying to shake its tough-guy image. Indeed, look no further than today's tax audit rate. The average person today has a less than 0.5% chance of an in-person audit. Five years ago, the odds of being audited were 0.7%, and in 1981, they were 1.6%. Budget and staff cuts are partly behind the fall-off. But audit rates are also down because the IRS has turned its attention to beefing up customer service.

Don't be lulled into complacency, though. The IRS recently asked Congress for money to conduct more audits, starting in 2001, and indications are it will get more funding for this purpose. More important for now, the IRS continues to target certain categories of taxpayers for audits. If you take a deduction for a home office, own a cash-based business such as a restaurant, or even pull down a six-figure salary in Los Angeles, your odds of being audited rise well above the norm. "There is no assurance that the kinder gentler IRS will be a pussycat with you," warns David Rhine, national director of family wealth planning at BDO Seidman in New York.

What triggers a tax audit? The most common way the IRS pulls returns for a closer look is by using a computer program called DIF, which stands for discriminate function. DIF scans every tax return and assigns it a score indicating the likelihood of questionable items. The IRS doesn't disclose what DIF might flag, but tax experts figure it searches for seemingly out-of-whack relationships, such as itemized deductions that are large compared with earnings.

There's evidence the DIF criteria, which were last updated in 1992 with data culled from 1988 returns, are not as relevant as they once were. Indeed, the IRS used DIF to select 29% of returns audited in 1998, down from 46% in 1992.

What also catches the IRS' eye are deductions most people don't qualify for—such as casualty losses or employee business expenses. Say a hurricane leaves your finished basement a soggy mess. Insurance should cover the damage, but if it doesn't, the IRS only lets you deduct unreimbursed casualty losses that exceed 10% of adjusted gross income, plus $100. If you claim this deduction, BDO Seidman's Rhine suggests trying to head off an audit by attaching supporting documents to your return such as newspaper clips on hurricane damage in your area.

SMALL-BIZ TARGET. Small-business owners remain targets for audits as well. The IRS zeros in on entrepreneurs because of concerns about lumping personal expenses with business deductions. Home-office deductions are scrutinized for the same reason. In 1998, 2.85% of returns with a Schedule C (the IRS tax form used by many small-business owners) showing income of $100,000 or more were audited. That audit rate is six times higher than the national average. The IRS especially reviews cash-based businesses such as restaurants and dry cleaners, to unearth unreported income. The agency has developed detailed manuals for 57 businesses to help its auditors. Many of these industry-specific *Audit Techniques Guides* are available for free on the Net at www.irs.gov and can help small-business owners and their accountants determine what is likely to catch the IRS' attention.

For instance, in the guide on bed and breakfasts, the IRS lists several sources of cash income, such as referral fees from local businesses that the B&B recommends to its guests. B&B owners "should substantiate and verify that they either have or don't have these sources of income," says Mark Ely, national partner in charge of tax controversies at KPMG in Washington. The guides, he adds, can help business owners track income they might have overlooked.

Taking a deduction for donating a car to charity is another red flag. Marcus Owens, director of the IRS division that watches charitable contributions, says anecdotal evidence suggests a growing number of people are overstating the value of vehicles given to charity. Owens says some used car or scrap-metal dealers also buy the use of a charity's name to fool people into thinking they are dealing with a charity. But "you don't get a deduction for giving your car to a for-profit organization," he says. In November, Owens sent a memo to the IRS' 33 districts directing them to look out for this abuse.

ADDRESS ALERT. Having your return pulled for an audit also depends on where you live. In 1998, individuals in Los Angeles reporting $100,000 or more in adjusted gross income were audited at a 2.56% rate, nearly six times greater than in Houston, which boasted a 0.45% audit rate, the lowest anywhere for the wealthy among the 33 IRS districts. Other areas with steep audit rates in 1998 were Brooklyn (1.78% rate and northern California (1.61%). Meanwhile, New Jersey (0.66%), Michigan (0.81%), and Illinois (0.89%) enjoyed among the lowest audit rates. Why the discrepancy? "We tend to do more audits where our research shows higher instances of noncompliance," says IRS spokeswoman Jodi Patterson.

The IRS is taking other measures to ensure compliance. For instance, the agency compares income reported on returns to W2 forms from employers and 1099s from banks and brokerage firms. It is also installing state-of-the art data-mining technology that will make it easier to identify patterns of cheating and fraud. When it is up and running in four to five years, "we will be better able to look at pieces of information to understand the entire profile of a taxpayer and changes from year to year," says Paul Cosgrave, chief information officer at the IRS.

When you're doing your 1999 return this spring, you may be tempted to avoid taking certain deductions out of fear of triggering an audit. Such behavior is silly if the deductions are legit, tax experts say, because you shouldn't ever pay more in taxes than you owe. Just be sure to deep detailed records—whether Uncle Sam comes calling or not.

Susan Scherreik

Study Questions

1. What factors might cause an IRS audit of a person's tax return?

2. What actions can taxpayers take to reduce the chances of an audit?

5 THE BANKING SERVICES OF FINANCIAL INSTITUTIONS

Chapter Overview

Using savings plans, checking accounts, and other financial services is a primary personal financial planning activity. This chapter starts with an overview of these services, followed by a discussion of electronic banking services. Next, discussion of the different types of financial institutions is offered, along with the factors to consider when selecting one. Coverage of choosing and using savings plans includes material on the types of accounts that are available. Finally, selection and use of checking accounts is presented.

Learning Objectives

After studying this chapter, you will be able to:

Obj. 1 Identify factors that affect selection and use of financial services.

Obj. 2 Compare the different types of financial institutions.

Obj. 3 Compare the costs and benefits of various savings plans.

Obj. 4 Identify the factors used to evaluate different savings plans.

Obj. 5 Compare the costs and benefits of different types of checking accounts.

Key Terms

annual percentage yield
asset management account
automatic teller machine
certificate of deposit
commercial bank
compounding
credit union
debit card
demand deposit
money market account
money market fund
mutual savings bank
NOW account
overdraft protection
rate of return
savings and loan association
share account
share draft account
time deposits
trust

Pretest

True-False

_______ 1. (Obj. 1) Increased borrowing is a quick source of cash, however your net worth is reduced.

_______ 2. (Obj. 1) Savings accounts are called time deposits.

_______ 3. (Obj. 1) A debit card allows a financial institution customer to charge purchases that can be paid for later.

_______ 4. (Obj. 1) Demand deposits refer to money in checking accounts.

_______ 5. (Obj. 2) A mutual savings bank is the financial institution that offers the widest range of services.

_______ 6. (Obj. 4) The more frequent the compounding on savings, the lower the rate of return that is earned.

_______ 7. (Obj. 3) Savings certificates usually have a higher liquidity than a regular savings account.

_______ 8. (Obj. 5) A NOW account is a type of interest-earning checking account.

_______ 9. (Obj. 5) An activity checking account is designed for people who write many checks each month.

_______ 10. (Append.) A blank endorsement requires the words "for deposit only."

Self-Guided Study Questions

Obj. 1

A Strategy for Managing Cash (p. 131)

Meeting Daily Money Needs (p. 131)

1. What are common sources of quick cash?

Types of Financial Services (p. 131)

2. What are the main financial services used by most consumers?

3. How do demand deposits differ from time deposits?

4. What are the benefits of an asset management account?

Electronic Banking Services (p. 133)

5. How does a debit card differ from a credit card?

6. What services are available with an electronic banking system?

Opportunity Costs of Financial Services (p. 136)

7. What common trade-offs are present when selecting financial services?

Financial Services and Economic Conditions (p. 136)

8. How can changing interest rates affect use of financial services?

Obj. 2

Types of Financial Institutions (p. 137)

9. What are nonbanks?

10. What types of organizations are considered to be "financial supermarkets"?

Deposit-Type Institutions (p. 138)

11. How are commercial banks organized and chartered?

12. What are the main services of a savings and loan association?

13. How does a mutual savings bank differ from other financial institutions?

14. What are the main advantages of using a credit union?

Nondeposit Institutions (p. 139)

15. How does a money market fund operate?

16. What costs are associated with using a pawnshop or check-cashing outlet?

Comparing Financial Institutions (p. 141)

17. What factors are commonly considered by consumers when selecting a financial institution?

Obj. 3

Types of Savings Plans (p. 142)

18. What are the main types of savings instruments available to consumers?

19. What are the main types of certificates of deposit?

20. How does a money market account differ from a money market fund?

21. What are the benefits of U.S. savings bonds?

Obj. 4

Evaluating Savings Plans (p. 146)

22. How does frequency of compounding affect the yield in a savings plan?

23. What is the purpose of the Truth-in-Savings law?

24. What is liquidity?

25. What is the purpose of the Federal Deposit Insurance Corporation?

26. What restrictions and fees may be associated with a savings account?

Obj. 5

Selecting Payment Methods (p. 150)

27. What are the common types of checking accounts available to consumers?

Evaluating Checking Accounts (p. 150)

28. What factors should be considered when comparing different types of checking accounts?

Other Payment Methods (p. 153)

29. What types of payment forms are available other than personal checks?

Appendix: Using a Checking Account (p. 159)

30. What are the benefits of a joint checking account?

31. What are the different types of endorsement? When is each appropriate?

32. What is the purpose of a bank reconciliation? What steps are involved in the process?

Post Test

Completion

1. (Obj. 2) A(n) ____________ ____________ ____________ ____________ specializes in savings accounts and loans for mortgages.
2. (Obj. 4) The percentage of increase in the value of savings due to earned interest is referred to as the ____________ ____________ ____________.
3. (Obj. 1) ____________ deposits are money held in checking accounts.
4. (Obj. 5) A(n) ____________ ____________ ____________ is an interest-bearing checking account at a credit union.
5. (Obj. 1) A(n) ____________ ____________ ____________ is a computer terminal for banking transactions.
6. (Obj. 3) A savings plan that requires you to leave a certain amount on deposit for a set time period in order to receive a certain interest rate is a(n) ____________ ____________ ____________.
7. (Obj. 1) A complete financial services program for a single fee is referred to as a(n) ____________ ____________ ____________.
8. (Obj. 2) A(n) ____________ ____________ is a non-profit financial institution.
9. (Obj. 4) Interest that is earned on previously earned interest is called ____________.

10. (Obj. 1) Savings accounts and savings certificates are referred to as ____________ deposits.

Multiple Choice

______ 1. (Obj. 2) Financial services would usually be most expensive at a
   A. credit union.
   B. check cashing outlet.
   C. commercial bank.
   D. financial supermarket.

______ 2. (Obj. 1) Which of the following would be an example of a demand deposit?
   A. A savings account
   B. A savings certificate
   C. A checking account
   D. A money market account

______ 3. (Obj. 2) Traditionally, the widest range of financial services has been offered by
   A. credit unions.
   B. investment companies.
   C. mutual savings banks.
   D. commercial banks.

______ 4. (Obj. 1) The purpose of a trust is to
   A. combine all financial services into one account.
   B. earn high rates of return on savings.
   C. manage funds for another person.
   D. obtain highly liquid investments.

______ 5. (Obj. 4) ____________ refers to the earnings received on savings.
   A. Yield
   B. Compounding
   C. Liquidity
   D. Insolvency

______ 6. (Obj. 4) Which of the following savings plans has the highest liquidity?
   A. An interest-earning checking
   B. A savings certificate
   C. A U.S. savings bond
   D. An individual retirement account

______ 7. (Obj. 4) A return of 6 percent on a savings account for a person with a 30 percent tax rate would mean an after-tax rate of return of ______ percent.
   A. 30
   B. 6
   C. 1.8
   D. 4.2

_____ 8. (Obj. 5) Which of the following is an interest-bearing checking account?
   A. EFT account
   B. Share-draft account
   C. Activity account
   D. Share account

_____ 9. (Obj. 6) A __________ endorsement includes the words "for deposit only."
   A. blank
   B. complete
   C. restrictive
   D. special

_____ 10. (Obj. 6) Which of the following items would be subtracted from your checkbook balance when preparing a bank reconciliation?
   A. Interest earned
   B. Outstanding checks
   C. Deposits in transit
   D. Service charges

Problems, Applications, and Cases

1. For each of the following influences on financial institutions and services, list an observed change that has occurred in recent years in your community.

Factor affecting financial services	Recent changes in financial institutions or services in your community
Legislative actions	
Economic conditions	
Technology	

2. Survey people in your community to determine which financial institution is strongest with regard to each of the following factors
   a. variety of services offered
   b. personal service
   c. convenience (location, hours, electronic banking services)
   d. return on savings
   e. low-cost checking

3. Survey several local financial institutions to compare the features of their savings plans (refer to text pages 134-141).

4. What would be the ending balance of the following savings accounts?

   a. $560 earning 7% (compounded annually) after one year

   b. $700 earning 8% (compounded quarterly) after three years

   c. $235 earning 5% (compounded annually) after two years

   d. $1,290 earning 12% (compounded monthly) after one year

5. With the use of the Internet (www.federalreserve.gov), *The Wall Street Journal*, *Business Week*, and other sources of current business news, update the interest rates presented on page 137.

6. Conduct a survey of checking services at financial institutions in your community. Also refer to text pages 141-145 for information on evaluating various types of checking accounts.

7. Prepare a bank reconciliation based on the information given below; also refer to text pages 146-148.

   Bank statement balance $436

   Unadjusted checkbook balance $234

   Total of outstanding checks $293

   Monthly service charge $4

   Deposit in transit $87

   Corrected (adjusted) checkbook balance $ __________

Supplementary Case 5-1: Evaluating Financial Institutions

Topic: Comparing Financial Institutions

Text Reference: pp. 137-142

Barb Kenton is a member of the credit union at her place of work. This financial institution offers regular savings accounts, share draft checking, and a variety of loans. It does not offer electronic banking, mortgages, or investment advice.

Barb's husband, Lance, is a manager at a department store in a local shopping center. Recently, an investment company opened a store in the mall. It offers free checking, low-cost loans, investment assistance, insurance, and real estate service. Lance believes that Barb and he should do business with this nationally known company.

Case Questions

1. What are the benefits of doing business with the credit union instead of the investment company?
2. What factors should Barb and Lance consider when they compare financial institutions?
3. What recommendations would you make to Barb and Lance about their use of financial services?

Supplementary Case 5-2: Selecting Financial Services

Topic: Comparing Financial Services

Text Reference: pp. 137-142; 150-154

Fran Hubbard lives with her two children and her father, Jerry. Although Jerry is retired, he is still very active in part-time consulting work and with various community volunteer programs. While Fran pays most of the household bills through her checking account, her father also wants to maintain his own checking account. Currently, Jerry's account requires a minimum balance of $1,500, pays a low interest rate, and has a $12 monthly charge if the balance falls below the minimum.

In recent weeks, unexpected expenses have resulted in Jerry's checking account balance dropping below the minimum balance. Jerry's pension checks are automatically deposited to his account, and he really likes the convenience of that service. In addition, Jerry is able to access various cash machines with the debit card from his bank.

Case Questions

1. What stated and implied factors probably encouraged Jerry to select his current checking account?
2. What alternatives may be available to Jerry for his checking services?
3. How might Fran and her father coordinate their financial services to minimize costs and maximize the services they receive?

Supplementary Case 5-3: Rate of Return versus Liquidity

Topic: Comparing Savings Plans

Text Reference: pp. 142-149

Martin Hoy recently obtained a bonus for a special project at work. His friends think that he should take a trip or buy a new car. However, Martin has decided to save these funds for the future.

Martin might like to buy a house in the next couple of years. Or he might want to go back to college for an advanced degree. In addition, his mother may need some financial assistance in her later years.

In viewing his alternatives, Martin has narrowed his choices to the following:

- Deposit the funds in a money-market account that earns 5.78 percent.
- Buy U.S. savings bonds, currently paying 5.67 percent.
- Purchase two-year certificates of deposit earning 6.83 percent.

Case Questions

1. What factors should Martin consider when deciding among the various savings plans?
2. Which of Martin's options has the greatest liquidity? When might liquidity be preferred over higher rate of return?
3. What action would you recommend for Martin?

Supplementary Reading 5

Geoffrey Smith, "Whisking Your Money Across the Web Will Soon Be a Snap," *Business Week Online: Business Week e.biz*, January 3, 2000

Whisking Your Money Across the Web Will Soon Be a Snap

Spurred by online auctions, dozens of startups are rushing to offer entirely electronic person-to-person payments over the Net—and for free.

Online commerce is not always an easy matter. For evidence, look no further than the Web site of one of the Internet's brightest e-commerce star, eBay (www.ebay.com). Bidding for items at an online auction is fun and entertaining, but for most eBay auction winners there is no online payment option. Some can pay by credit card, but more than 90% pay by check or money order and send the money via snail mail. Even if someone uses an online bill payment service, the money is still turned into a paper check that is sent through the mail.

It's a slow process. And there's a huge opportunity awaiting financial-services firms that can speed it up by offering person-to-person payments on the Internet. Dozens of startups are racing to fill the void, and already several companies let you zap payments to people over the Net. The rapid proliferation of this technology is going to add a convenient new dimension to our financial lives on the Web. While online auction-goers will be the prime beneficiaries, these services will also allow payments through handheld devices such as cell phones to virtually anyone with an e-mail account.

It's too early to tell precisely how this will work. But I'll make this prediction: Sending money online will be easy, and free. To be sure, visions of efficient new electronic payment schemes have been around for 30 years, and have been consistently overrated. In the early 1970s, the Federal Reserve Board predicted that the use of paper checks would plateau at about 22 billion checks a year and that checks would be replaced by technology for transferring electronic funds. In fact, both have steadily increased. Even with the emergence of online banking, check writing will increase 2.2% this year, to 68.8 billion checks, according to *The Green Sheet* (www.greensheet.com), an industry newsletter.

But the Web has spawned a whole new marketplace for individuals, mainly through auctions. And there's a huge need for simpler payment systems than those now commonly used. There have been widespread concerns about the security of e-mail. But it appears that e-mail security can now be made tight enough that financial transactions through this medium are now feasible.

One early entrant to the field, Billpoint (www.billpoint.com), is owned by eBay. And eBay has been testing an e-mail-based approach that is likely to resemble the standard person-to-person payment system of the future. eBay plans to begin offering the system early this year to its customers, which may make it the instant leader in a potentially huge new market. With its 8 million registered users, eBay's customer base is about the same size as the entire online banking industry in the U.S.

Here's how eBay's payment service will work. Sellers set up a Billpoint account through eBay that includes their bank account number. They use the service to send the winning bidder an e-mail invoice with the total amount due. The buyer enters their credit-card number in the e-mail, and sends it back to the seller. All payment information is encrypted, so the seller doesn't see the credit-card number. Once the buyer sends the payment information, the money is automatically deposited in the seller's bank account.

VERY PRICEY. There's one big problem with the Billpoint service. It's very expensive. eBay charges sellers 75 cents plus 4.5% of the total value of the transaction. That's a $3 fee on a $50 sale, and it's stiff enough that it will surely limit its appeal. But it's better than another person-to-person payment system offered by eBay: i-Escrow (www.i-escrow.com). This service allows buyers to receive and inspect merchandise before their funds are released. But the charge to sellers is 6% of sales up to $500, and $30 plus 5% of sales between $500 and $2,500. i-Escrow offers security above and beyond simple payments, which may make it worth the price for some high-priced transactions. But for simple financial transfers, there's a good chance eBay won't be able to sustain the fees on its Billpoint service because competitors will do it for less.

One such rival is Silicon Valley startup Confinity Inc., which operates a Web site called PayPal.com (www.paypal.com). Despite the goofy name, Confinity recently launched a no-fee, person-to-person e-mail payment service. Confinity's e-mail approach is similar to Billpoint's. But its no-fee business model is great for consumers. However, it's not an obvious moneymaker. It plans to earn its profits on the "float"—money held in Confinity's account between the time a payment is made and the time it is deposited into a recipient's account. Float is a major profit center for banks—but so are fees.

Will it work? The editor of the *Online Banking Report* (www.onlinebankingreport.com), Jim Bruene, gives the PayPal site rave reviews for ease of use. But Bruene says the key issue around PayPal is trust: "Will users turn over their bank account numbers to a new, unregulated, unlicensed company with 'pal.com' in its name? We think the answer is no."

Even so, there's promising technology behind both Confinity and Billpoint. If these new companies can convince consumers that their e-mail payments are safe, their services could become either successful stand-alone Web sites or a service offered by major Web sites, including auctioneers, portals, and financial-services firms.

There will be enormous competition for person-to-person financial transactions, and there is potential for high-stakes marketing battles. Microsoft, American Express, and other major players have developed digital wallets that simplify online transactions and can be easily adopted for person-to-person transfers, says Robert Sterling, an online finance analyst at Jupiter Research. What's more, most banks already have direct person-to-person transfer technology in place. They can move money from account to account with someone's bank account number and the standard nine-digit routing code (ABA number) of the recipient's bank. The lack of just two key ingredients prevents banks from offering person-to-person, electronic payment as a retail service online: bank account masking and integration into e-mail or online banking software.

Bruene thinks that two years from now, person-to-person transfers will be a standard offering of Net bank services. Thankfully it won't take that long before the early adopters make it easier to shop at eBay. If you've had any experiences with person-to-person financial transaction over the Internet, or if you have comments or questions, send an e-mail using the link below.

Smith covers a wide variety of topics, including personal finance issues, from Business Week's Boston bureau.

Have a question or a comment? Let him know at geoffsmith@ebiz.businessweek.com

Geoffrey Smith

Study Questions

1. What limitations are associated with online business?

2. How will online payment systems serve the needs of consumers?

3. What problems might consumers face as online payment systems develop?

6 INTRODUCTION TO CONSUMER CREDIT

Chapter Overview

This chapter defines consumer credit and analyzes its advantages and disadvantages. The importance of consumer credit in our economy is explained and uses and misuses of credit are discussed. Financial and personal opportunity costs of using credit are emphasized. Next, two types of consumer credit—closed-end and open-end credit—are differentiated. Then, general rules of measuring credit capacity such as debt payments-to-income ratio and debt-to-equity are explained. This is followed by coverage of building and maintaining credit rating. Next, the information that creditors look for in granting or refusing credit is identified, and the Equal Credit Opportunity Act is explained. Then, the steps in avoiding and correcting credit mistakes are outlined, and the provisions of the Fair Credit Billing Act are described. Finally, strategies for complaining about consumer credit are introduced, and the major consumer credit laws are summarized.

Learning Objectives

After studying this chapter, you will be able to:

Obj. 1 Define consumer credit and analyze its advantages and disadvantages.

Obj. 2 Differentiate among various types of credit.

Obj. 3 Assess your credit capacity and build your credit rating.

Obj. 4 Describe the information creditors look for when you apply for credit.

Obj. 5 Identify the steps you can take to avoid and correct credit mistakes.

Obj. 6 Describe the laws that protect you if you complain about consumer credit.

Key Terms

capacity
capital
character
closed-end credit
collateral
conditions
consumer credit
Consumer Credit Reporting Reform Act
credit
credit bureau
debit card
Equal Credit Opportunity Act (ECOA)
Fair Credit Billing Act (FCBA)
Fair Credit Reporting Act (FCRA)
home equity loan
interest
line of credit
open-end credit
revolving check credit

Pretest

True-False

_______ 1. (Obj. 1) Credit is an arrangement to receive cash, goods, or services now and pay for them in the future.

_______ 2. (Obj. 1) There are not many valid reasons for using credit.

_______ 3. (Obj. 2) With open-end credit, you pay back one-time loans in a specified period of time and payments are of equal amount.

_______ 4. (Obj. 2) Incidental credit is a credit arrangement that has no extra costs and no specific payment plan.

_______ 5. (Obj. 3) The debt payments-to-income ratio is calculated by dividing monthly debt payments (not including house payments) by net monthly income.

_______ 6. (Obj. 3) The debt-to-equity ratio is calculated by dividing total liabilities by net worth.

_______ 7. (Obj. 4) The Equal Credit Opportunity Act is not very specific about how a person's age may be used in credit decisions.

_______ 8. (Obj. 5) In case of a billing error, notify the creditor within 60 days after the bill was mailed.

_______ 9. (Obj. 5) If you think that your credit bill is wrong, you must notify the creditor in writing within 10 days after the bill was mailed.

_______ 10. (Obj. 6) The Fair Credit Reporting Act gives you the right to know what your credit file contains.

Self-Guided Study Questions

Obj. 1

What Is Consumer Credit? (p. 165)

1. What is the meaning of consumer credit?

The Importance of Consumer Credit in Our Economy (p. 165)

2. Why is consumer credit a major force in our economy?

Uses and Misuses of Credit (p. 166)

3. What are the uses and misuses of credit?

Advantages of Credit (p. 167)

4. How can credit be used to your advantage?

Disadvantages of Credit (p. 168)

5. What are the disadvantages of using credit?

Obj. 2

Types of Credit (p. 169)

6. What are the two types of consumer credit?

Closed-End Credit (p. 169)

7. Give examples of closed-end credit

8. What are the most common types of closed-end credit?

Open-End Credit (p. 169)

9. How does open-end credit differ from closed-end credit?

10. Give examples of open-end credit.

11. What is incidental credit?

12. What is a line of credit?

13. What is revolving check credit?

14. What is cobranding?

15. How do debit cards differ from credit cards?

16. How do you protect yourself against debit/credit card fraud?

17. What is a home equity loan?

18. What is a revolving line of credit?

Obj. 3

Measuring Your Credit Capacity (p. 176)

19. What is the importance of a family budget in measuring your credit capacity?

Can You Afford a Loan? (p. 176)

20. How can you determine whether you can afford a loan?

General Rules of Credit Capacity (p. 176)

21. What are the general rules of measuring credit capacity?

22. How can debt payments-to-income ratio and debt-to-equity ratio be used to measure credit capacity?

Cosigning a Loan (p. 177)

23. What would you do if a friend or relative asked you to cosign a loan?

24. Why do cosigners often pay?

25. What are a few caveats to consider if you do cosign a loan?

Building and Maintaining Your Credit Rating (p. 178)

26. What steps would you take in building and maintaining your credit rating?

Credit Bureaus (p. 178)

27. What is a credit bureau?

Who Provides Data to Credit Bureaus? (p. 178)

28. Who provides data to credit bureaus?

What's in Your Credit Files? (p. 179)

29. What information is contained in your credit files?

Fair Credit Reporting (p. 180)

30. What is the purpose of the Fair Credit Reporting Act?

Who May Obtain a Credit Report? (p. 180)

31. Can anyone obtain your credit report?

Time Limits on Adverse Data (p. 180)

32. How long can a credit bureau keep adverse information in your credit file?

Incorrect Information in Your Credit File (p. 180)

33. What can you do if there is incorrect information in your credit file?

What Are the Legal Remedies? (p. 181)

34. Do you have any legal rights and remedies if a credit bureau refuses to correct mistakes in your credit file? Explain your answer.

Obj. 4

Applying for Credit (p. 183)

A Scenario From the Past (p. 183)

35. Which federal consumer credit law starts all credit applicants off on the same footing?

36. What does the Equal Credit Opportunity Act (ECOA) state?

What Creditors Look For (p. 183)

37. What do creditors look for when they extend credit to their customers?

38. Describe the five Cs of credit.

39. Does public assistance affect your creditworthiness? Explain.

What if Your Application Is Denied? (p. 186)

40. What steps can you take if your application for credit is denied?

Obj. 5

Avoiding and Correcting Credit Mistakes (p. 187)

41. What are the major provisions of the Fair Credit Billing Act?

42. How does the Fair Credit Billing Act (FCBA) define a billing error?

In Case of Billing Error (p. 187)

43. What steps can you take if you think your bill is wrong or you want more information about it?

Your Credit Rating During the Dispute (p. 188)

44. What happens to your credit rating during the dispute?

Defective Goods or Services (p. 189)

45. Can you withhold payment on damaged or shoddy goods or poor services that you have purchased with a credit card?

Obj. 6

Complaining About Consumer Credit (p. 190)

46. What should be your first step if you have a problem with your creditor?

Complaints About Banks (p. 190)

47. What can you do if you have complaints about banks?

Protection Under Consumer Credit Laws (p. 190)

48. What protections are available to you under consumer credit laws?

49. What are the Truth in Lending and Consumer Leasing Acts?

50. What is the Equal Credit Opportunity Act?

51. What is the Fair Credit Billing Act?

52. What is the Fair Credit Reporting Act?

53. What are the provisions of the Consumer Credit Reporting Reform Act?

Your Rights Under Consumer Credit Laws (p. 193)

54. What are your rights under consumer credit laws?

Post Test

Completion

1. (Obj. 1) ____________ is an arrangement to receive cash, goods or services now and pay for them in the future.
2. (Obj. 2) With ____________ ____________ ____________, you pay back a one-time loan in a specified period of time and the payments are of equal amounts.
3. (Obj. 2) With ____________ ____________ ____________, loans are made on a continuous basis and you are billed periodically to make at least a partial payment.
4. (Obj. 2) ____________ ____________ ____________ is the maximum amount of credit you can use.
5. (Obj. 4) By ____________, we mean the borrower's attitude toward his or her credit obligations.
6. (Obj. 4) By ____________, we mean the borrower's financial ability to meet credit obligations.
7. (Obj. 4) ____________ is a valuable asset pledged to assure loan payments and is subject to seizure upon default.

8. (Obj. 3) Experts suggest that you spend no more than ____________ ____________ of your net income on credit purchases.
9. (Obj. 3) Most of the information in your credit file may be reported for only ____________.
10. (Obj. 5) ____________ ____________ ____________ ____________ ____________ sets the procedure for promptly correcting billing mistakes, for refusing to make credit card payments on defective goods, and for promptly crediting your payments.

Multiple Choice

______ 1. (Obj. 1) In which period did the use of installment credit explode on the American scene?
A. During the colonial times
B. Before WWI
C. In the early 1900s
D. In the 1980s

______ 2. (Obj. 1) Perhaps the greatest disadvantage of using credit is
A. the temptation to overspend.
B. to use it as leverage.
C. that you fail to carry cash.
D. that it results in bankruptcies.

______ 3. (Obj. 2) Which is a good example of an open-end credit?
A. A mortgage loan
B. An automobile loan
C. An installment loan
D. A VISA and MasterCard loan

______ 4. (Obj. 2) A credit arrangement in which loans are made on a continuous basis and you are billed periodically is called a(n)
A. closed-end credit.
B. installment sales credit.
C. single lump-sum credit.
D. open-end credit.

______ 5. (Obj. 4) The borrower's attitude toward his or her credit obligation is known as
A. capacity.
B. character.
C. capital.
D. collateral.

______ 6. (Obj. 4) The borrower's financial ability to meet credit obligations is called
A. conditions.
B. character.
C. collateral.
D. capacity.

______ 7. (Obj. 3) Spend no more than __ percent of your net income on credit payments.
A. 5
B. 10
C. 20
D. 35

______ 8. (Obj. 3) Which law regulates the use of credit reports, requires the deletion of obsolete information, and gives you access to your credit file?
A. The Fair Credit Reporting Act
B. The Fair Credit Billing Act
C. The Truth in Lending Act
D. The Equal Credit Opportunity Act

______ 9. (Obj. 5) Which law sets the procedure for promptly correcting billing mistakes and for promptly crediting your payments?
A. The Fair Credit Reporting Act
B. The Fair Credit Billing Act
C. The Truth in Lending Act
D. The Equal Credit Opportunity Act

______ 10. (Obj. 6) If you have a complaint against a bank regarding the violation of federal credit laws, the best place to complain is the
A. U.S. Department of Commerce.
B. U.S. Department of Labor.
C. Consumer Protection Agency.
D. Federal Reserve System.

Problems, Applications, and Cases

1. Do you wish to learn what is in your credit file? Check the Yellow Pages under Credit Bureaus or Credit Reporting Agencies. If several are listed, call to find the one that keeps your file. Credit bureaus may charge to give you file information. Their fees usually range from $10 to $20. (If your credit was denied, there is no charge if you examine your file within 60 days.)

2. Directions: Identify the type of credit described in each of the following examples and circle your answer.

   a. A consumer makes purchases at All Goods Department Store using an All Goods credit card.

      incidental closed-end open-end

   b. A consumer pays a bill for long-distance telephone calls made last month.

      incidental closed-end open-end

c. A doctor's office allows patients to pay their bills in installments, but does not charge interest on the unpaid balance.

incidental closed-end open-end

d. A loan from a credit union is paid back in 24 bimonthly payments.

incidental closed-end open-end

e. A contract is signed that states the terms and conditions of paying an orthodontist's fee.

incidental closed-end open-end

f. A local hospital sends a patient a bill for $50 for emergency room treatment.

incidental closed-end open-end

g. A consumer pays for dinner using a credit card issued by the restaurant.

incidental closed-end open-end

h. A bank credit card is used to make purchases at several retail stores.

incidental closed-end open-end

i. Furniture, Inc., requires customers to sign a contract each time they purchase a new item.

incidental closed-end open-end

j. An "overdraft protection" agreement allows a consumer to write a $150 check when his account balance is only $100.

incidental closed-end open-end

(Reprinted courtesy of Office of Public Information, Federal Reserve Bank of Minneapolis.)

Credit Use Surveys

3. **Would You Use Credit?**

Directions: Decide if you would use credit to make the following purchases. In the appropriate box, give the reasons for your decisions.

	Yes	No	Maybe
a. Would you use credit to buy a home or pay for a college education?			
b. Would you use credit to purchase appliances, furniture, etc. for a home?			
c. Would you use credit to pay for overdue bills?			
d. Would you use credit to purchase gasoline or food?			
e. Would you use credit instead of cash or checks to make several purchases in one store?			
f. Would you use credit to purchase an item that costs $8.50?			
g. Would you use credit to purchase an item on sale?			
h. Would you use credit to pay for a vacation?			
i. Would you use credit if you couldn't save enough money to buy something you wanted?			
j. Would you use credit to make a purchase even if you would pay cash?			

4. Directions: List examples of the four types of credit you or your family use (Column I). Under Columns II, III, and IV (optional), describe how you use and repay credit.

I Credit Sources	II How often is credit used?	III How is credit repaid?	IV How much is spent on monthly credit payments?
Public utility Ex: city water 1. 2.	Every day	Paid quarterly	Approx. $30
Incidental 1. 2.			
Open-end 1. 2.			
Closed-end 1. 2.			

(Reprinted courtesy of Office of Public Information, Federal Reserve Bank of Minneapolis.)

5. Alyssa purchased a dress from Amy's Boutique, a store in her home town, for $85 with her Discover Card. Before she paid her bill, she noticed that a seam was ripped and tried unsuccessfully to return the dress. Can Alyssa withhold payment?

6. Mark gets his television repaired by a local Ace TV Repair Shoppe. He uses a bank credit card to pay the $150 repair charge. A week later the TV breaks down again. Mark is fed up with Ace TV, so he calls a different repair shop. Can he withhold the payment of $150?

7. Amy purchases a $55 pair of shoes at DeKalb Shoemart, about 25 miles away from her home. She charged the shoes with her MasterCard. The heel falls off the shoe the next week. Can Amy withhold payment?

Supplementary Case 6-1

Topic: Applying for Credit and Getting It

Text Reference: pp. 183-186

Allison Allmart, a recent divorcee, applied for credit at Friendly Finance Company. She was denied credit and received a form letter stating that information had been obtained from a consumer reporting agency. The letter included the name, address, and phone number of Anytown Credit Bureau.

Allison called Anytown Credit Bureau to find out what information it had given the finance company. She was told that it generally did not give out such information on the phone but that she could come to the office to learn the contents of her credit file. Allison said that she would be able to come at 1 p.m. on Monday.

When Allison arrived at the credit bureau, she was asked to show her driver's license and one other piece of identification. A trained interviewer talked with her and revealed that the inquiry from Friendly Finance Company was the only inquiry about her that the credit bureau had received during the past six months. The only other information in her file was that an account held five years earlier with AAA Department store had been paid. Allison was surprised at the lack of credit information in her file, but she explained that until recently she had lived in a different state. The interviewer asked whether she could provide the names of her creditors there. The credit bureau would then check with those firms and add any new credit information. Allison did so and then applied for credit again at Friendly Finance Company. This time, she was granted credit.

Case Questions

1. Why did you think Ms. Allmart was denied credit?
2. Was it legal for the Friendly Finance Company to deny her credit request?
3. How could Ms. Allmart have avoided being denied credit the first time?

Supplementary Case 6-2

Topic: Measuring Credit Capacity

Text Reference: pp. 176-177

Hank Hansen, a recent college graduate, is 24 years old, single, and employed as a computer operator at a local manufacturing company. He recently purchased a two-bedroom condominium, and he plans to marry his high school sweetheart when she graduates from college in two years.

Hank's net monthly income is $2,000. He spends the following amounts each month for essential items:

Mortgage loan	$600
Utilities	130
Food	260
Transportation	130
Clothing	40
Medical expenses	40
Total	$1,200

Hank wants to buy a $10,000 car, and he has a down payment of $2,000. He figures that automobile insurance will be about $900 a year but that if he buys this new, fuel-efficient car, he will save about $30 a month on transportation.

Case Questions

1. How much can Hank spend on credit payments each month?
2. What percentage of his net monthly income can Hank spend safely on credit (not including housing) payments?
3. Will Hank get a loan from a bank if he applies for it?

Supplementary Reading 6-1

Gene Koretz, "Plastic Puts the Poor at Risk; Pocketbooks Suffer as Debts Grow" *Business Week*, June 10, 2000, p. 36.

Plastic Puts the Poor at Risk; Pocketbooks Suffer as Debt Grows

With consumer debt service payments claiming a lower share of disposable income than they did during most of the 1980s, household debt loads still seem quite manageable. If the economy were to slip into recession, however, the outlook would change significantly. And according to a recent study by Edward J. Bird of the University of Rochester and Paul A. Hagstrom and Robert Wild of Hamilton College, poor households would be especially vulnerable.

The study's focus is on the dramatic increase in credit-card usage by the poor. In 1989, it reports, only 17% of poor families had credit cards. Yet six years later, in 1995, 36% had at least one card, as did 57% of near-poor households (incomes from 100% to 150% of the poverty level). Meanwhile, the average monthly balance of the poor with cards soared from $343 to $1,380, as the average charge paid by those carrying balances (two-thirds of the group) jumped to $236 a month—and $317 for near-poor families.

That's not all. In the expansion of the 1980s, as more-affluent families boosted their credit-card balances, poor families actually reduced theirs. In the 1990-91 recession, however, as nonpoor families temporarily moderated their use of credit-card debt, poor families greatly increased their debt loads. More important, they have continued to do so in the subsequent recovery. This pattern raises some interesting questions. On the supply side, why have banks welcomed such presumably high-risk borrowers as poor households? Has the continuing economic boom led lenders to conclude that the poor are more credit-worthy than in the past? Or, has the sharp decline in banks' cost of funds, combined with their continued ability to charge 15% to 22% interest on card balances, made high-risk lending more profitable?

On the demand side, initial research has found that many former welfare recipients have trouble maintaining previous income levels, and it may be that greater use of credit-card debt has played a part in the relatively smooth introduction of welfare reform. In the short run, in other words, credit cards may be functioning as a safety net, easing the transition to the world of work.

Eventually, however, servicing such debt becomes a growing burden, lessening the cash available for consumption. And when a recession finally occurs, the government may find itself confronted not only with a rising number of poor families whose incomes have declined sharply, but with many who are saddled with large amounts of debt.

Gene Koretz

Study Questions

1. Who would be especially vulnerable if the economy were to slip into recession? Why?

2. What might be the reasons for the dramatic increase in credit-card usage by the poor?

3. Are the poor getting more credit-worthy now than in the past? Explain.

Supplementary Reading 6-2

Dennis Berman, "Card Sharps" *Business Week*, April 3, 2000, p. EB68.

Card Sharps

In April, 1998, Daniel Vasiliu zipped onto the Net from a PC in Bucharest, Romania. He ordered a $75.90 seasonal bouquet from FTD's Web site in Downers Grove, Ill., to be sent to Ruxanda Vasiliu, in the Romanian capital. "That's what parents are for," the accompanying card read. The gesture was anything but lovely for David V. Stien, CEO of Crane Federal Credit Union in Crane, Ind., 5,300 miles away. The credit-card number Vasiliu allegedly used belonged to one of Stien's customers—and the bill was just part of a flood of $21,000 in false charges his tiny credit union would sort through over the next six months.

Romanian police say there's no doubt that Vasiliu, who they claim is a mere two years out of high school, is the culprit. "He clearly is guilty," charges Colonel Mircea Alecsa, who says Vasiliu fessed up to the crime when police visited his apartment. And the flower purchase wasn't an isolated prank: Romanian police confirm that Vasiliu used 92 card numbers from Crane, and suspect he hit HSBC's U.K.-based Midland Bank for 120 more card numbers—which likely helped finance the computer equipment, Cuban cigars, and exotic billiard cues they found in his apartment.

Yet Vasiliu has never been charged with a crime, according to Romanian police, who admit they have neither the time nor the legal means to deal with online crimes. Reached by phone in Bucharest, Vasiliu would not comment. His lawyer, Varujan Udrea, also declined to comment except to say that Vasiliu has since returned all the goods to the Romanian police and that the case is closed. So far, U.S. merchants say they haven't received their products. "We haven't gotten anything back," says Debbie Ulrich, a sales manager for True Data Technology in Carlsbad, Calif., which shipped Vasiliu a Sony digital camera and Intel microprocessor worth a total of $1,700.

Amazon, Too. Vasiliu's story is a reminder that as electronic commerce booms, so does online credit-card fraud. Consider online retail giant Amazon.com. In December, the company referred a case to the FBI in which a Russian citizen was suspected of using 63 pilfered card numbers to buy electronics gear worth $70,000. Online fraud numbers are tough to come by, but research company TowerGroup, in Needham, Mass., estimates that .11% of all consumer Internet card transactions are bogus—which would put total Net fraud at about $43 million this year. By comparison, Visa's overall fraud rate (including online and the physical world) was .05% over the past two years—worth a total $911 million. "People who wouldn't have committed white-collar crime face-to-face or over the telephone are doing it over the Internet," says Lynne A. Hunt, section chief of the FBI's financial crimes division. "It's a wonderful means to commit crime."

The lure is especially great for foreign scammers, particularly those in Eastern Europe and Asia, where legal systems are less equipped to handle the dark side of e-commerce. There's also less motivation to prosecute there, because fraud victims are often faceless foreign corporations. "There are certain ex-iron-curtain countries where you might as well not ship," says Ben Narasin, CEO of fashionmall.com, a retail clothing site. In the strange, urgent logic of Internet retail, knowing the danger isn't always a deterrent, he says: "Companies take hits because they're rushing to book revenues. They decide to ship it and sort it out later."

That may be tough to do. One of the rarely mentioned pitfalls for e-tailers is that they are particularly vulnerable to credit-card fraud. Here's why: Conventional merchants are not liable for credit-card fraud if a criminal shows up in a store and charges something—in that case, the bank that issued the card eats the loss. But on the Net, it's different. Merchants assume full responsibility for what are called "card not present" transactions, which makes foreign transactions particularly risky.

Stien's travails illustrate the danger. Romanian police suspect that in early 1998 Vasiliu got credit-card numbers by using the Internet to download software called a card-number generator. These are widely distributed computer programs with names such as Credit Wizard that use algorithms to reconstruct valid card numbers. Such algorithm generators are "the biggest thing that has benefited the fraudster," says Malcolm MacDonald, a fraud prevention officer at HSBC in London. And Stien alleges Vasiliu took full advantage: Besides flowers, he used the fraudulent cards to buy $800 in Pentium II computer chips, an $8,000 Swiss watch, and to get on to porno sites in California.

Vasiliu's methods expose another hole in the way U.S. merchants handle foreign credit-card orders on the Net. Inside the U.S., merchants use an Address Verification Service to confirm any U.S. cardholder's name and billing address—an important safeguard against mail fraud. There's no similar system for cards issued by foreign banks, which means U.S. merchants accepting foreign Net orders are authorizing them based solely on a card number and expiration date—all easily duplicated with a number generator and some persistent guessing. "You get 16 digits flying over the wire, you have no idea where they came from," says Steve Herz, Visa's former senior vice-President for electronic commerce.

It was just such a scenario that blindsided Stien. His credit union serves 14,500 members at the tight-knit Crane Naval Surface Warfare Center. When word of the fraud spread, the rumors got nasty. "What's really destroyed is the confidence of your members," he says.

In an effort to win it back, the 53-year-old former bill collector set off to solve the case himself.

His first call was to CyberNet Ventures Inc., an Encino (Calif.) porn site that had accepted one of the Crane charges. Stein got an IP address (an Internet Protocol number unique to each computer) from CyberNet and easily traced it back to an Internet service provider in Romania. But then he slammed into a roadblock: Officials at the Net service provider wouldn't hand over any information about their users. Stien flooded Romanian bureaucrats with faxes—but he got no help. According to Stien, the FBI was only slightly more cooperative. Although it agreed to help Stien deal with foreign authorities, its agents would not run the investigation. That was his job.

Stien caught a break in the spring of 1998. After much cajoling, FTD agreed to share records showing that Vasiliu had used both his personal e-mail address and an anonymous Hotmail e-mail account to order the flowers for Ruxanda Vasiliu. According to Stien's complaint with the Romanian police, Vasiliu had used the free Hotmail to test numbers at CyberNet and other sex sites. After they proved valid, he would then log on with a personal account to order goods sent to Romanian addresses (many e-commerce sites won't process orders from customers with "freebie" e-mail). Stien said he eventually was able to link Vasiliu to 70 of Crane's 92 compromised numbers that used the same Hotmail address.

Even though Stien had pieced this evidence together by October of 1998, his quest was far from over. He still had to convince domestic and foreign authorities his case was worth taking abroad. That meant months of affidavits, translations, and certifications with the FBI, which eventually cooperated and forwarded his 470-page file to the U.S. Embassy in Romania. Finally, his plight caught the attention of the Romanian Ministry of Interior, which in November, 1998, agreed to investigate. But according to court officials, the ministry never prosecuted Vasiliu. "It's a rather empty feeling," says a dejected Stien. "It was all a waste of time."

With the credit-card heist wiped clean from his members' accounts, Stien has returned to the relatively intrigue-free duties of running a credit union. Still, he can't forget what he has been through. "Maybe people in Romania don't care," he says. "But this guy may live to find out he was wrong." If and when he does, Stien is poised to celebrate. Just don't send fresh flowers to congratulate him.

Dennis Berman

Study Questions

1. How was Daniel Vasiliu financing Cuban cigars, exotic billiard cues, a digital camera, and an Intel microprocessor?

2. Why is online credit-card fraud increasing?

3. How did Vasiliu get all those credit card numbers?

7 CHOOSING A SOURCE OF CREDIT: THE COSTS OF CREDIT ALTERNATIVES

Chapter Overview

All of us get into credit difficulties if we do not understand how and when to use credit. This chapter identifies major sources of consumer credit—commercial banks, savings and loan associations, credit unions, finance companies, life insurance companies, retailers, parents, and relatives. Next, in determining the cost of credit, we emphasize the finance charge and the Annual Percentage Rate (APR). Then we show how the cost of credit can be determined by calculating interest with various interest formulas. In dealing with your debts, we discuss the Fair Debt Collection Practices Act, consumer credit counseling, and the serious effects of debt. We describe various private and governmental sources that assist consumers with debt problems. Finally, we explain and distinguish between Chapter 7 and Chapter 13 bankruptcy laws to assess the choices in declaring personal bankruptcy.

Learning Objectives

After studying this chapter, you will be able to:

Obj. 1 Analyze the major sources of consumer credit.

Obj. 2 Determine the cost of credit by calculating interest with various interest formulas.

Obj. 3 Develop a plan to manage debt.

Obj. 4 Evaluate various private and governmental sources that assist consumers with debt problems.

Obj. 5 Assess the choices in declaring personal bankruptcy.

Key Terms

add-on interest method
adjusted balance method
annual percentage rate (APR)
average daily balance method
Chapter 7 bankruptcy
Chapter 13 bankruptcy
Consumer Credit Counseling Services (CCCS)
credit insurance
declining balance method
Fair Debt Collection Practices Act (FDCPA)
finance charge
previous balance method
rule of 78's
simple interest
Truth in Lending Law

Pretest

True-False

_______ 1. (Obj. 1) By evaluating your credit options, you can reduce your finance charges.

_______ 2. (Obj. 1) The least expensive loans are available from finance companies and retailers.

_______ 3. (Obj. 2) The finance charge is the total amount you pay to use credit.

_______ 4. (Obj. 2) The annual percentage rate (APR) is the percentage cost of credit.

_______ 5. (Obj. 3) If you are having trouble paying your bills, immediately turn to a debt consolidation company.

_______ 6. (Obj. 3) Paying only the minimum balance each month on credit card bills is one of the danger signals of potential debt problems.

_______ 7. (Obj. 4) A Consumer Credit Counseling Service provides debt counseling service for families and individuals with serious financial problems.

_______ 8. (Obj. 4) Most services provided by a Consumer Credit Counseling Service are not free.

_______ 9. (Obj. 5) The Bankruptcy Recovery Act of 1978 made personal bankruptcy easier.

_______ 10. (Obj. 5) A person filing for relief under the bankruptcy code is called a bankrupt.

Self-Guided Study Questions

Obj. 1

Sources of Consumer Credit (p. 199)

1. What three questions must you ask yourself before deciding whether to borrow money?

2. In what two situations should you avoid the use of credit?

3. When you need money, what kind of loan should you seek? Closed-end or open-end credit?

4. What are the sources of inexpensive loans?

5. What are the sources of medium-priced loans?

6. What are some advantages of borrowing from a credit union?

7. What are the sources of expensive loans?

8. What types of loans are made by commercial banks?

9. What types of loans are made by consumer finance companies?

10. Why do life insurance companies charge lower interest rates than some other lenders?

11. What types of loans are made by savings and loan associations?

12. What online computer services may be used to compare interest?

13. How will the smart cards facilitate banking and bill paying?

Obj. 2

Cost of Credit (p. 204)

14. What is the Truth in Lending Law of 1969?

15. What two key concepts should you consider when determining the cost of credit?

16. What is a finance charge?

17. What is the annual percentage rate (APR)?

18. How do finance charge and APR differ?

Tackling the Trade-Offs (p. 206)

19. When you choose your financing, what are the trade-offs between the features you prefer and the costs of your loan?

Calculating the Cost of Credit (p. 207)

20. How do you calculate the cost of credit?

21. What are the two most common methods of computing interest?

22. What is the simple interest formula?

23. When is the declining balance method used in calculating the cost of credit?

24. How is interest calculated with the add-on interest method?

25. What are the three methods creditors use to calculate the finance charge on open-end credit?

26. How do adjusted balance, previous balance, and average daily balance methods differ from one another?

27. How do lenders consider the effects of expected inflation in determining the cost of credit?

28. How does the new tax law affect the cost of consumer credit?

29. Why should you avoid the minimum monthly payment trap?

When the Repayment is Early: The Rule of 78's (p. 211)

30. Why do creditors use the Rule of 78's?

Credit Insurance (p. 211)

31. What is credit insurance?

32. What is the most commonly purchased type of credit insurance?

33. Distinguish among three types of credit insurance.

34. What is a better alternative to credit life insurance?

Obj. 3

Managing Your Debts (p. 213)

35. What should you do if you find it impossible to pay your bills on time?

36. What special problems are caused if you fail to pay an automobile loan?

Debt Collection Practices (p. 213)

37. What is the Fair Debt Collection Practices Act?

38. Who enforces the Fair Debt Collection Practices Act?

39. What steps should you take if a debt collector calls on you?

40. What are the major reasons for consumers not paying their debts?

Warning Signs of Debt Problems (p. 213)

41. What are the serious effects of heavy indebtedness?

Obj. 4

Consumer Credit Counseling Service (p. 216)

42. What is a Consumer Credit Counseling Service (CCCS)?

What the CCCS Does (p. 217)

43. What are the two-part activities of the CCCS?

44. Are all CCCS counseling services free for the asking?

Alternative Counseling Services (p. 218)

45. What other alternative counseling services are available to consumers?

Obj. 5

Declaring Personal Bankruptcy (p. 219)

46. What are indicators of personal bankruptcy?

47. Why has the personal bankruptcy rate increased in recent years?

The U.S. Bankruptcy Act of 1978: The Last Resort (p. 219)

48. What are the major provisions of the Chapter 7 bankruptcy?

49. What is the Chapter 13 bankruptcy?

50. What are the differences between Chapter 7 and Chapter 13 bankruptcies?

51. What is the Chapter 11 bankruptcy?

Effect of Bankruptcy on Your Job and Your Future Credit (p. 220)

52. How does a personal bankruptcy affect your job and your future credit?

Should a Lawyer Represent You in a Bankruptcy Case? (p. 221)

53. Why is an attorney needed for the Chapter 13 bankruptcy?

54. What are the monetary costs of declaring a Chapter 13 bankruptcy?

55. What are a few intangible costs to bankruptcy?

Post Test

Completion

1. (Obj. 1) Paying cash is almost always ____________ than using credit.
2. (Obj. 1) The number of credit union members has been ____________ steadily.
3. (Obj. 1) The ____________ ____________ ____________ specializes in personal installment loans and second mortgages.
4. (Obj. 1) The ____________ ____________ seek customers with an established credit history.
5. (Obj. 2) The ____________ ____________ is the total amount you pay to use credit.
6. (Obj. 2) The ____________ ____________ ____________ is the percentage cost of credit on a yearly basis.
7. (Obj. 3) The Federal Trade Commission enforces the ____________ ____________ ____________ ____________ ____________.
8. (Obj. 4) A ____________ ____________ ____________ ____________ is a local non-profit organization affiliated with the National Foundation for Consumer Credit.
9. (Obj. 5) In a ____________ ____________ ____________, a debtor is required to draw up a petition of all assets and liabilities, and the term bankrupt is not used.
10. (Obj. 5) In a ____________ ____________ ____________, a debtor normally keeps all or most of his or her property.

Multiple Choice

______ 1. (Obj. 1) Which of the following lenders specializes in mortgages and other housing-related loans?
   A. Commercial banks
   B. Federal savings banks (savings and loans)
   C. Credit unions
   D. Finance companies

______ 2. (Obj. 1) Which of the following lenders specializes in personal installment loans and second mortgages?
   A. Consumer finance companies
   B. Credit unions
   C. Savings and loans
   D. Commercial banks

_______ 3. (Obj. 2) When creditors add finance charges after subtracting payments made during the billing period, this is called the
A. adjusted balance method.
B. previous balance method.
C. average daily balance method.
D. annual percentage rate method.

_______ 4. (Obj. 2) The Truth in Lending Law
A. sets the interest rates that creditors can charge.
B. tells creditors how to make interest calculations.
C. requires creditors to tell the interest calculation method to be used.
D. was repealed by Congress in 1986.

_______ 5. (Obj. 2) To determine how much interest you have paid at any point in a loan, creditors use a mathematical formula called the
A. formula of large numbers.
B. mathematical law of averages.
C. Rule of 72's.
D. Rule of 78's.

_______ 6. (Obj. 3) Who enforces the Fair Debt Collection Practices Act?
A. The Federal Trade Commission
B. The U.S. Justice Department
C. The U.S. Department of Labor
D. The Better Business Bureau

_______ 7. (Obj. 3) If you cannot make your loan payments on time, first contact your
A. friends or relatives for a quick loan from them.
B. employers and ask for a raise in your salary.
C. creditors at once and try to work out a modified payment plan with them.
D. local office of a consumer finance company.

_______ 8. (Obj. 4) Which one of the following organizations is a local, non-profit organization affiliated with the National Foundation of Consumer Credit?
A. Consumer Complaints Advisory Service
B. Consumer Credit Counseling Service
C. The Better Business Bureau
D. The Federal Trade Commission

_______ 9. (Obj. 5) Usually, the largest single item of cost for a person filing a Chapter 13 bankruptcy is
A. court cost.
B. attorney's fee.
C. trustee's fee.
D. transportation cost.

_______ 10. (Obj. 5) In which type of bankruptcy are many, but not all, debts forgiven?
A. Chapter 2
B. Chapter 5
C. Chapter 7
D. Chapter 13

Problems, Applications, and Cases

1. Suppose you borrow $2,000 at 10% simple interest and repay it in one lump sum at the end of one year. How much will you owe at the end of one year?

2. Now suppose the loan is for two years and you are required to repay the loan (principal and interest) at the end of two years. What will the interest charge be?

3. What is the interest cost and the total amount due on a six-month loan of $1,500 at 13.2 percent simple annual interest?

4. Decide whether the consumer, debt collector, or creditor bears the costs described below of the Fair Debt Collection Practices Act. Circle your answers.

   a. A debt collector raises his collection fees when it takes longer to collect debts.

      consumer debt collector creditor

   b. A creditor decides to impose stricter standards for granting credit in response to the higher cost of debt collection.

      consumer debt collector creditor

   c. A creditor raises the interest rate charged on new loans to cover the higher price of debt collection.

      consumer debt collector creditor

   d. A consumer pays for legal advice to find out whether or not an action threatened by a debt collector can legally be taken.

      consumer debt collector creditor

   e. Due to the increased costs of using debt collection services, a creditor decides to collect her own debts.

      consumer debt collector creditor

   f. A consumer spends 30 minutes writing a letter to a debt collector requesting communications to cease regarding an unpaid bill.

      consumer debt collector creditor

g. A debt collector sends a debt validation notice to a consumer who has been notified about the debt.

consumer debt collector creditor

h. Because the costs of debt collection have increased, a creditor provides less credit to his customers.

consumer debt collector creditor

(Reprinted courtesy of the Office of Public Information, Federal Reserve Bank of Minneapolis)

5. Decide whether the debt collection activities described below are legal or illegal, or whether the legality cannot be determined on the basis of the information give. Circle your answers.

a. A debt collector uses a post card to notify a consumer about a debt.

legal illegal cannot be determined

b. A creditor telephones a customer at work and tells the person who answers the phone the name of his company.

legal illegal cannot be determined

c. An employee of Northland Bank calls one of the bank's customers at 11 p.m. about late payments.

legal illegal cannot be determined

d. A debt collection agency telephones a consumer about a debt at 11 p.m.

legal illegal cannot be determined

e. ABC Stores, using the name ABC Collections, Inc., telephones a delinquent customer at 6 a.m.

legal illegal cannot be determined

f. A department store's collection division calls a customer repeatedly during a 12-hour period.

legal illegal cannot be determined

g. A credit union calls a member at his place of employment about a late payment.

legal illegal cannot be determined

h. A debt collection agency telephones a consumer at work even though that person's employer does not allow personal calls.

legal illegal cannot be determined

i. A person who collects debts for others threatens to "throw in jail" a consumer who refuses to pay.

legal illegal cannot be determined

j. A debt collector hired by a furniture store tells a customer that furniture purchased on credit will be repossessed if payment is not received.

legal illegal cannot be determined

(Reprinted courtesy of Office of Public Information, Federal Reserve Bank of Minneapolis)

6. What is the cost of credit (finance charge) and the annual percentage rate for the following loans?

	Amount financed	Payments per year	Length of loan (in months)	Monthly payment	Cost of credit	APR
A	$2,000	12	24	$93.00	$________	________%
B	$900	12	12	$84.50	$________	________%
C	$3,400	12	30	$130.00	$________	________%

7. Steve borrows $100 from a friend and repays the $100 a year later in one lump sum. What is the nominal rate of interest on the loan?

8. If prices increased 7 percent during the year Steve had the loan, what would be the real rate of interest on the loan?

Supplementary Case 7-1

Topic: Calculating the Cost of Credit

Text Reference: pp. 207-210

After visiting several automobile dealerships, Richard Welch selects the car he wants. He likes its $10,000 price, but financing through the dealer is no bargain. He has $2,000 cash for a down payment, so he needs an $8,000 loan. In shopping at several banks for an installment loan, he learns that interest on most automobile loans is quoted at add-on rates. That is, during the life of the loan, interest is paid on the full amount borrowed even though a portion of the principle has been paid back. Richard borrows $8,000 for a period of four years at an add-on rate of 11 percent.

Case Questions

1. What is the total interest on Richard's loan?
2. What is the total cost of the car?
3. What is the monthly payment?
4. What is the annual percentage rate (APR)?

Supplementary Case 7-2

Topic: Buying Now vs. Later

Text Reference: pp. 199, 204-207

Shirley Watson wishes to buy a freezer that now costs $600. Since the current inflation rate is 5 percent, she expects the freezer to cost $630 if she postpones the purchase for a year. If she buys it now, she estimates that it would save her $150 in food costs during the next year. It would enable her to purchase food at special sales and in larger quantities and to preserve vegetables from her garden. However, operating the freezer would increase her electricity bill. Shirley can use one of the following options in purchasing the freezer:

Option 1 Buy the freezer now, using $600 she has in a savings account that earns interest at an annual rate of 6 percent.

Option 2 Buy the freezer now, using credit at an annual rate of 10 percent. She would make 12 monthly payments of $52.50 each.

Option 3 Postpone the purchase until she saves an additional $600. Her savings earn interest at an annual rate of 6 percent.

Case Questions

1. What trade-offs should Shirley consider in deciding whether to buy the freezer now or later?
2. If Shirley wants to buy the freezer now, what trade-offs should she consider in deciding whether to use credit or pay cash from her savings?

Supplementary Reading 7

Joseph Weber, "The Perils of Plastic," *Business Week*, February 14, 2000, p 127.

The Perils of Plastic

After getting a couple of low-rate credit-card offers each week for months, Saundra Williams decided last fall to see if she could do better than the 18.5% annual interest rate on her cards. When she called to bargain, she thought she was doing well when Citibank promptly offered her a menu of fixed or variable rates, including a nifty 10.9%. But Bank of America did even better, slashing her rate to 9.9% and hiking her credit line to boot. "I was astounded at all of the options they offered me," says Williams, an assistant professor at North Carolina State University in Raleigh. "I never heard of negotiating a rate."

Negotiate with a credit-card company? It would have been unthinkable a few years ago. But it's happening. For many of the players in the industry, times are tough. Now that they've saturated the American public with plastic, they're finding it hard to expand. As more and more customers pay off balances each month—"freeloading" in industry parlance—card companies are working harder than ever before to squeeze out a buck.

But even though overall profits are recovering a bit as bank efforts to regain customers make headway, card issuers still have a hard row to hoe. Credit-card and revolving debt totals $589 billion but has grown little over the past few years. And Visa International and MasterCard International are fighting an $8.1 billion antitrust suit by Wal-Mart Stores Inc. and other retailers, accusing them of forcing stores to accept their high-cost debit cards. "The game is tougher now than it was 5 years ago, 10 years ago," says David R. Alvarez, president of the credit-card business for eighth-ranked Providian Financial Corp.

For some customers, the industry's woes are just fine, thank you. They mean easier credit, high loan limits, and bargain rates that fly in the face of the Fed's tightfistedness. With so many lenders tripping over themselves to help Americans go into hock, it's no wonder that, as of 1998, some 68% of American families were packing credit cards, according to the latest Federal Reserve figures.

Still, plenty of cardholders are paying through the nose. Miss a payment by a few days? You could be slapped with a $29 late charge, up from an average of $13 just three years ago. And, to drive home the point, your interest rate could be jacked up as an added penalty, perhaps to as high as 30%. Don't use the card much? You might see an inactivity fee and then get tagged with a closing fee if you cut the card up. "We call it a 'fee frenzy,'" says Robert B. McKinley, chief executive of CardWeb.com Inc., an industry tracking service. But such soak-the-customer tactics can backfire. First USA, which now boasts some 50 million customers, has lost millions of them in the last two years, cutting its total outstanding card loans by 1%, to $69.4 billion last year. Bank officials blame consumer anger over such practices as ratcheting up loan rates above 19%, from introductory 3.9% rates, if the borrower paid late just twice in six months. "We lost many of our best customers," William P. Boardman, vice-chairman of First USA parent Bank One Corp, told analysts on Jan. 11.

While First USA officials vow to treat customers better, the fallout of its actions could be far-reaching. Bank One's stock has plunged from above $63 a share last spring to under $30 now. Its CEO quit, and the bank is a subject of takeover speculation. "It's a real challenge to turn this organization around," says David Hochstim, an analyst with Bear, Stearns & Co.

First USA's woes will give a boost to its rivals. Weakened, it won't flood mailboxes with low-rate offers at anywhere near last year's pace. It even expects to keep its total of card loans in the market flat or let them shrink as much as 5%, so the competition could carve up an additional $3 billion or so in business. "They'll be much more inwardly focused," says Moshe A. Orenbuch, an analyst with Donaldson, Lufkin & Jenrette Inc. "The intensity of the competition in the industry will decline."

But card companies must still scramble for growth. For some, gains will come from customers that rivals shun, so-called subprime or nonprime clientele. These folks have blemishes on their records—missed payments, even bankruptcies—or lack long credit histories.

Providian, a hard-charging San Francisco card issuer, finds gold in the nonprime market. It has signed up so many cardholders in the last year that it posted a stunning 66.4% rise in loans outstanding, to $18.71 billion—the biggest gain among the top 10 issuers tracked by The Nilson Report.

It levies a steep 23.9% rate on its lower-end customers. Providian pays too—for betting on borrowers others won't touch. Its loss rates are a bit higher than industry norms of about 5.51%, though the rate dropped from 7.58% at the end of 1998 to 6.78% in last year's closing quarter. Its delinquency rate, which tracks borrowers who are at least two payments behind, is nearer industry norms, of just under 5%, at about 5.66% as of yearend 1999.

Many players are pursuing wealthy customers just as feverishly. American Express is offering the Centurion charge card—which must be paid off monthly to holders of its high-end Platinum card. The jet-black Centurion, offered by invitation only, carries a whopping $1,000 annual fee. That gets you upgrades on the Concorde and a personal counselor for travel needs. And you get special privileges at Neiman Marcus and Saks Fifth Avenue, with such amenities as private shopping hours. AmEx officials won't say how many of these cards—which they call a "niche product"—they expect to sell.

AmEx is seeking a broader audience with its four-month-old Blue credit card. It has an introductory 0% rate for six months, a regular rate of just 9.99%, and no annual fee. AmEx equips Blue with computer chips aimed at helping do business online. Alfred F. Kelly Jr., president of AmEx's consumer card service group, says its core market is younger people who want to "feel secure in shopping both the physical world and the interactive world."

Winning younger folks may be crucial, since baby boomers are getting to be a headache for card issuers. Boomers pay off their credit-card balances monthly and jump fast to lower-rate cards. The share of cardholders who pay off their balances in full each month has risen from 29% in 1991 to 44% in 1999, says CardWeb.com. "They are getting less dependent on revolving credit," adds The Nilson Report President David Robertson. "The demographics are completely against the industry."

For all the players, the newest frontier is the Internet. Already, some operators offer low card rates not available by mail. Still others are pioneering credit lines available exclusively for Internet shopping, such as Citigroup's ClickCredit service. In just three months, Citi has signed up 80,000 customers. "We are very busy exploring the medium," says A. Sami Siddiqui, chief of the North America cards unit of Citigroup.

As the growth game toughens, card companies will tap every potential vein. Some are even looking abroad, building operations in Canada, Ireland, and Britain. But wherever they go, they'll have to avoid carrying some of the baggage they've picked up lately. Unhappy customers would rather switch than fight.

Joseph Weber

Study Questions

1. Is it possible to negotiate interest rate with a credit-card company? Explain.

2. What are some "soak-the-customer" tactics that credit-card companies use?

3. "The demographics are completely against the credit-card industry." Explain.

8 CONSUMER PURCHASING STRATEGIES AND LEGAL PROTECTION

Chapter Overview

While most consumer purchases may not be considered in financial plans, these choices affect financial resources available for other purposes. This chapter starts with a discussion of the factors that influence buying habits. Next, a systematic approach to making purchase decisions is presented, along with a discussion of various consumer information sources. Selected purchasing strategies are then covered, including types of retail stores and comparison shopping methods. This chapter concludes with a discussion of consumer protection actions and legal alternatives available to individuals. A chapter appendix provides information on buying, leasing, and operating motor vehicles.

Learning Objectives

After studying this chapter, you will be able to:

Obj. 1 Assess the financial implications of consumer purchasing decisions.

Obj. 2 Evaluate the alternatives in consumer purchasing decisions.

Obj. 3 Implement strategies for effective purchasing.

Obj. 4 Identify the steps people can take to resolve consumer problems.

Obj. 5 Evaluate the legal alternatives available to consumers.

Key Terms

arbitration
class action suit
cooperative
generic item
impulse buying
legal aid society
mediation
open dating
rebate
service contract
small claims court
unit pricing
warranty

Pretest

True-False

_______ 1. (Obj. 2) Consumer information from business organizations is considered the most reliable source available when making buying decisions.

_______ 2. (Obj. 2) Consumer Reports publishes a listing of recommended companies in an area from which to purchase goods and services.

_______ 3. (Obj. 3) A cooperative is organized to benefit its members by saving them money on various products.

_______ 4. (Obj. 3) Brand name products usually offer the least consistency of quality.

_______ 5. (Obj. 3) Even without a written warranty, consumers will have some guarantee that a product will perform in an expected manner.

_______ 6. (Obj. 3) Service contracts are designed to cover expensive repair costs on appliances or automobiles.

_______ 7. (Obj. 4) Most consumer complaints are solved with assistance from state and local government agencies.

_______ 8. (Obj. 4) Arbitration provides a legally binding solution to a dispute without your having to appear in court.

_______ 9. (Obj. 5) Small claims courts allow individuals to present a case without the use of a lawyer.

_______ 10. (Obj. 5) Class action suits usually involve complaints of less than $1,000.

Self-Guided Study Questions

Obj. 1

Financial Implications of Consumer Decisions (p. 237)

1. What factors influence daily buying decisions?

2. What trade-offs are associated with daily buying decisions?

Obj. 2

Consumer Purchasing: A Research-Based Approach (p. 239)

Phase 1: Preshopping Activities (p. 239)

3. Why is problem identification a vital component of consumer purchasing decisions?

4. What are some of the different approaches to using consumer information?

5. What are the main sources of consumer information?

6. How do independent testing organizations assist consumers?

Phase 2: Evaluation of Alternatives (p. 242)

7. What attributes are commonly considered when assessing consumer goods and services?

8. To what extent is price an indication of product quality?

9. In what types of situation is comparison shopping most beneficial?

Phase 3: Selection and Purchase (p. 244)

10. How can a person be better prepared to negotiate in a consumer buying situation?

Phase 4: Postpurchase Activities (p. 245)

11. What common efforts are necessary after a purchase is made?

12. What is a "cooling-off" law?

Obj. 3

Practical Purchasing Strategies (p. 246)

Timing Your Purchases (p. 246)

13. How can the time at which you buy certain items be an effective buying strategy?

Store Selection (p. 247)

14. What factors influence a person's decision to shop at a certain store?

15. What is a consumer cooperative?

Brand Comparison (p. 247)

16. How do brand name, store brand, and generic items differ?

Label Information (p. 247)

17. What is open dating?

Price Comparison (p. 248)

18. What guidelines are helpful when comparing prices?

Warranty Evaluation (p. 250)

19. What are examples of implied warranties?

20. What is the purpose of a service contract?

Obj. 4

Resolving Consumer Complaints (p. 251)

21. What are the common causes of consumer complaints?

22. What are the steps suggested when attempting to resolve a consumer complaint?

23. How are most consumer complaints resolved?

24. How does mediation differ from arbitration?

Obj. 5

Legal Options for Consumers (p. 255)

Small Claims Court (p. 255)

25. What is the purpose of small claims court?

Class-Action Suits (p. 256)

26. When can a class-action suit be of benefit to consumers?

Using a Lawyer (p. 256)

27. What factors should be considered when selecting a lawyer?

Other Legal Alternatives (p. 256)

28. What is a legal aid society?

Appendix: Buying and Operating a Motor Vehicle (p. 262)

Buying a Used Vehicle (p. 262)

Sources of Used Vehicles (p. 262)

29. What are the sources from which people buy used cars?

Consumer Protection for Used Car Buyers (p. 262)

30. What actions has the FTC taken to regulate used car sales?

The Inspection Process (p. 263)

31. What factors should a person consider when conducting an inspection of a used car?

Used-Car Price Negotiation (p. 264)

32. How can a person determine if a fair price is being charged for a used car?

33. What factors affect the price of a used car?

Purchasing a New Vehicle (p. 265)

Gathering Information (p. 265)

34. Where can a consumer find information on the invoice price of a motor vehicle?

Selecting Options (p. 266)

35. What are the common types of optional equipment offered on new cars?

36. What are the common advantages and disadvantages of a service contract?

Determining a Purchase Price (p. 266)

37. What actions should be taken to negotiate a fair price for a new car?

38. What is the purpose of a car buying service?

Financing an Automobile Purchase (p. 268)

39. What financial institutions offer financing for buying an automobile?

40. What information is most helpful when comparing various financing alternatives?

Leasing a Motor Vehicle (p. 269)

41. What are the main benefits of leasing an automobile or other motor vehicle?

42. How does a closed-end lease differ from an open-end lease?

Financial Aspects of Automobile Ownership (p. 271)

Automobile Operating Costs (p. 271)

43. Which automobile costs are considered fixed costs? Which ones are usually variable costs?

Proper Maintenance (p. 273)

44. What are common maintenance activities that can extend the life of a vehicle?

Automobile Servicing Sources (p. 273)

45. What factors should a person consider when selecting a source of automobile servicing?

Selling Your Automobile (p. 275)

46. What actions are recommended to a person who is considering the sale of an automobile?

Post Test

Completion

1. (Obj. 3) ____________ ____________ uses a standard unit of measurement to compare the prices of packages of different sizes.
2. (Obj. 5) ____________ ____________ ____________ is used to settle minor legal differences.
3. (Obj. 4) Suggested solutions by a third party to settle differences is ____________.
4. (Obj. 3) ____________ ____________ is unplanned purchasing.
5. (Obj. 5) Publicly supported community law offices that provide legal assistance to consumers who cannot afford their own attorney are a(n) ____________ ____________ ____________.
6. (Obj. 4) ____________ is the settlement of a disagreement with a legally binding decision by a third party.
7. (Obj. 3) An agreement between a business and a consumer to cover the repair costs of a product is a(n) ____________ ____________.
8. (Obj. 5) A(n) ____________ ____________ ____________ is legal action taken by a few individuals on behalf of many who have suffered the same alleged injustice.
9. (Obj. 3) A nonprofit organization created so that its members can save money on certain products and services is a(n) ____________.
10. (Obj. 3) A(n) ____________ is a written guarantee from the manufacturer or distributor of a product that specifies the conditions under which a product can be returned, replaced, or repaired.

Multiple Choice

_____ 1. (Obj. 1) An example of a social buying influence would be
   A. taxes.
   B. interest rates.
   C. advertising.
   D. government regulations.

_____ 2. (Obj. 2) The least reliable source of consumer information is likely to be from
   A. a consumer testing organization.
   B. a store salesperson.
   C. a newspaper advertisement.
   D. the label on a package of food.

_____ 3. (Obj. 3) Prices of food and personal care products are likely to be highest at a
A. cooperative store.
B. hypermarket.
C. convenience store.
D. supermarket.

_____ 4. (Obj. 3) Which of the following information is required to be on a food package?
A. Brand name
B. Freshness date
C. Unit pricing information
D. The address of the manufacturer or distributor

_____ 5. (Obj. 3) An unwritten guarantee that a product will perform its intended purpose
is called a(n)
A. express warranty.
B. service contract.
C. implied warranty.
D. limited warranty.

_____ 6. (Obj. 2) A "cooling-off" law is designed to help consumers
A. reduce unit prices.
B. cancel a contract.
C. hire a lawyer.
D. improve product safety.

_____ 7. (Obj. 4) Most common complaints are resolved by
A. returning to the place of purchase.
B. contacting a government agency.
C. taking legal action.
D. contacting the company's main office.

_____ 8. (Obj. 4) Arbitration differs from mediation in that arbitration
A. involves a third party.
B. is legally binding.
C. requires the use of a lawyer.
D. includes involvement of federal government consumer agencies.

_____ 9. (Obj. 5) The purpose of small claims court is to
A. settle difference between state and local government agencies.
B. handle legal problems involving severe injuries.
C. resolve minor legal differences.
D. assist lawyers with settling common legal problems.

_____ 10. (Obj. 5) Which of the following could qualify as a class-action suit?
A. A disagreement between a tenant and landlord
B. Injuries to several people caused by a defective product
C. An incorrect amount billed to your monthly charge account
D. Your attempt to obtain a refund of $37 for a product that was never delivered

Problems, Applications, and Cases

1. Conduct a study of an item you are planning to purchase or may consider purchasing in the future. Refer to text pages to review material on sources of consumer information.

2. John Blanchard is planning to purchase a compact disc player and is considering three brands. In his buying matrix (refer to Exhibit 8-4), he has assigned performance a weight of 0.4, warranty a weight of 0.3, store service a weight of 0.2, and product design a weight of 0.1. The following is a list of prices and ratings for the attributes:

	Price	Performance	Warranty	Store service	Product design
Brand A	$650	5	6	4	7
Brand B	$525	7	6	5	6
Brand C	$610	6	5	7	6

Based on this analysis, which brand would John buy? What other factors need to be considered in this buying decision?

3. Conduct a survey to determine the types of products (food, health care, clothing, and others) that are most likely to be purchased on brand name form, store brand form, and generic form. What factors influence people's decisions to select a specific brand?

4. For each of the following consumer problems, indicate the federal government agency (see Appendix B) that is most likely to provide assistance for the situation presented:

Situation	Government Agency
a. You desire information on whether certain used cars you are considering for purchase have had recalls.	
b. You have received some offers in the mail that appear to be deceptive and perhaps illegal.	
c. You have an allergic reaction to a soap that is supposed to medically cleanse your skin.	
d. A local company is offering an opportunity to invest in a stock that promises an unusually high rate of return.	

Supplementary Case 8-1: Buyer Beware

Topic: Buying Decisions

Text Reference: pp. 239-257

Each month, John and Tina Harper had difficulty making ends meet. They had three children, and their housing, food, and other living expenses were constantly increasing. One day at work, a friend told John about a food-buying plan that would help the Harpers save money. For a monthly payment of $165, all the food they needed would be delivered, and they would also qualify for a new refrigerator. Since the Harpers viewed this plan as a way to save money and since they also needed a new refrigerator, they signed up for the plan.

After making two payments, the Harpers were notified by the company with which they had signed up that delivery of their refrigerator had been delayed due to production problems. Meanwhile, they had received less food than they needed, so they still had to spend money for groceries.

Two months later, the refrigerator still hadn't arrived, and the Harpers were paying more for food than they had paid before they joined the plan. Two weeks later, the Harpers stopped receiving goods from the company. "Well, I guess we won't have to make any more payments," commented John, "since we aren't receiving any of the services we were paying for." He attempted to notify the company of his intention to stop making payments, but its phone had been disconnected, and its office was empty. He sighed, saying, "Now our food expenses can return to the amount they were before we got involved in this deal."

But the Harpers' problems weren't over. A few months later, a collection agency notified them that they still owed $495 for several months of service. The contract they had signed obligated them to pay for a minimum of eight months.

Such consumer problems occur frequently. People get involved in expensive situations that they could have avoided if they had known all the facts when they were making their purchasing choices.

Case Questions

1. What actions should the Harpers have taken before joining the food-buying plan?
2. How can the Harpers avoid paying the additional $495?
3. In what ways could effective financial planning help the Harpers cope with their situations?

Supplementary Case 8-2: Double Deception

Topic: Consumer Fraud

Text Reference: pp. 251-257

Melvin Hooper recently invested $8,000 in a land partnership that advertised an expected annual rate of return of 17 percent. He had read that the real estate company was responsible for some of the most successful housing developments and shopping centers in the southeastern United States. However, after four months, Melvin was no longer receiving the monthly statements that reported the value of his investment.

A couple of weeks later, Melvin saw a newspaper article stating that the company was being sued for deceptive sales practices. This was followed a few days later by a phone call from an organization who said they could help him get his money back. The organization would require a $250 fee, in advance, to help Melvin get his money back. However, this time Melvin was cautious since he had heard about "fraud recovery" services. Instead, he reported the organization to the state consumer protection office.

Case Questions

1. What actions might have helped Melvin avoid the land fraud?
2. Why are fraud recovery services able to take advantage of consumers who are recent victims of scams?
3. What legal action may be appropriate in this situation?

Supplementary Case 8-3: Used Trouble

Topic: Buying a Used Vehicle

Text Reference: pp. 262-264

Blake and Ellen Kenton recently purchased a used car for their daughter and for use by Blake's mother when she works in community programs for children and elderly citizens. The vehicle was purchased from a car rental company for $6,700. Most other sources were charging $8,200 for comparable vehicles.

After buying the car, the Kentons discovered the car need some minor repairs costing $600. They decided to have the work done at an auto repair shop a few miles away. The business, recently changed owners, but had been operating in the community for 15 years.

After the repair work was complete, the car ran well for two months. Then real trouble started; new problems arose. An oil leak was followed by a need for new brakes, which happened at the time the transmission needed major work. So ended the Kentons' used car bargain!

Case Questions

1. What actions should the Kentons have taken before buying the car?
2. How could the Kentons have made sure they were getting capable and cost-efficient repair service?
3. What additional actions might be recommended to the Kentons?

Supplementary Reading 8

Larry Armstrong, "Kicking Tires on the Web, By the Time You see Car Dealers, You Should Know as Much as They Do," *Business Week*, April 26, 1999, p. 120E1.

Kicking Tires on the Web

By the Time You See Car Dealers, You Should Know as Much as They Do

Psst. Wanna buy a car cheap? These days, you can get a better deal for almost anything via the Internet—and cars are no exception. You can't actually buy a car on the Net—franchise laws in most states prohibit it. But you can do everything right up to the point of signing on the dotted line.

The Internet puts you in control of the buying experience. The wealth of information available for free on thousands of Web sites has pretty much leveled the playing field for car buyers and sellers. Some would even say the buyer now has the advantage. "People now can walk into a dealership knowing more than what the dealer's salespeople often know," says Peter Steinlauf, president of Edmund Publications in Beverly Hills, Calif.

If you want to purchase a vehicle without dealing with a salesperson or dickering over price, submit a request for your dream car through a buying service such as Autobytel.com or Microsoft's CarPoint. You'll have a firm bid by E-mail or phone from a nearby dealer in a couple of hours, and can close the deal in a day. If you think you can save more, and like the negotiating process, you can shop the bid around to other dealers, inviting them to beat it. But have your guard up when you get to the showroom: The dealer may try to make up the difference by low-balling your trade-in or selling you a high-margin extended warranty or alarm system.

FIVE FOOLS. When you're beginning your online car search, Edmund's is a good place to start. It and CarPoint are the two most comprehensive auto sites on the Web. They give you all the tools you need to figure out what a car cost the dealer and how much you can expect for your trade-in. But Edmund's has the edge. It displays a keen sense of humor and pulls no punches when it comes to telling it like it is. Take April's "Top Five" column, "The Top Five Cars Fools Drive." The winners: The Mazda B-Series pickup, AM General Hummer, Cadillac Catera, Ford Excursion, and the entire Daewoo car line. The Korean-build Daweoos are "the most foolish cars in existence," Edmund's concludes.

If you don't know what car you want, the Internet offers lots of places to look. Every manufacturer has its own site with specifications and pictures. They're good for sorting out confusing option packages—whether, say, you can get the top-of-the-line audio package with CD changer without having to ante up an additional grand for leather seats. General Motors' new BuyPower service even lets you search dealers' lots to see where your car is in stock. But manufacturer sites omit the most important fact: what the dealer pays for the cars and trucks.

To unearth those details, go to such specialists as Edmund's, Kelley Blue Book, or AutoSite (www.autosite.com). Of the car-buying sites, only CarPoint has resources as complete. CarPoint also has three separate reviews for most cars, including one written from a woman's perspective.

What these sites provide is a way to calculate the dealer's invoice price on a car and its options, meaning what the dealer paid for the exact car you want. Just as important, they explain the hidden sources of dealer profit, such as "holdbacks"—a 2% or 3% kickback from manufacturers to dealers to help them finance their inventory. You can also use the Web to ferret out advertising fees some dealers try to add, and to keep track of customer rebates, which salespeople sometimes don't know about or forget to mention. And you can find dealer-incentive payments from carmakers. Retailers don't have to give them to you, but you can use them to exact a better price.

Links from these sites can also get you quotes on everything from financing to insurance to extended warranties. You may want to have these in hand when you show up at the dealer to buy your car. But be sure to shop around. Mostly, the links point to paying partners who may or may not offer the best deal. All that free information from Edmund's, for example, is paid for by fees or commissions Edmund's gets for referring you to Autobytel.com or NationsBank's CarFinance.com site. At a minimum, however, such sites can help you figure out how much car you can afford, whether you should buy a new or used car, and whether you should lease or buy. And www.financenter.com features a nice collection of online calculators. They'll walk you through such issues as whether it's better to use a home equity or auto loan or to take a carmaker's $2,000 rebate or its 1.9% financing deal.

About the only thing that's difficult to find on the Internet is an easy way to compare auto lease costs. Edmund's has a good primer with an example you can use as a template for your own deal, and there's a lease calculator at LeaseXpert.com. Consumer Reports has a leasing worksheet you can print out and fill in, though you'll feel like you're doing your income taxes when you use it.

A word about Consumer Reports. Long the standard print reference for car buyers, it comes up short online. While its site offers some free advice in its Bumper to Bumper section, to get ratings and reviews you'll need to subscribe, for $2.95 a month or $24 a year. Details such as invoice pricing, widely available elsewhere for free, cost $12 for the first vehicle, and $10 each for other reports ordered at the same time.

Before you make your final choice, you might want to check what the experts have to say. The car-enthusiast magazines' Web sites, such as www.caranddriver.com or www.roadandtrack.com, maintain archives of car reviews. As much as they claim otherwise, magazine reviewers pretty much find something to like about every car, and you have to read between the lines to figure out what they really think. More valuable are their drive-offs, where they review a series of like vehicles, such as four or five family sedans, and rank them.

WHEN TO WALK. Once you're ready to make a deal, log on to one of the car-buying sites. The largest is Autobytel.com, which sells as many cars as its two closest competitors—CarPoint and Autoweb.com—combined, according to market researcher J.D. Power & Associates. If you're having trouble finding a used car, try AutoConnect, which lists the largest inventory. All of them give you a firm quote in hours. If the quote turns out to be not so firm and the dealer wants to charge for extras, or the car's the wrong color, take a walk. Then go back to the buying service and report the dealer.

Chances are, though, you'll get what you want at the price you want. Take Bill Townsend, who bought his red 1995 Mazda Miata from a Sunnyvale (Calif.) dealer referred by Autobytel.com. "It was a huge savings of time and effort," the 33-year-old Oracle marketing director says, "but the real value was taking the haggling out of the process." Now that the buyer is in control, you may just be able to persuade the dealer to deliver the car to your door. That way, you can be on the road in a new set of wheels—without ever setting foot in a showroom.

By Larry Armstrong

Study Questions

1. How can various Web sites serve the needs of car buyers?

2. What problems might be encountered when buying a motor vehicle online?

9 THE FINANCES OF HOUSING

Chapter Overview

This chapter provides a complete discussion of selecting housing based on life situation, needs, and personal values along with the related financial aspects of this major expenditure. First presented is material regarding factors related to renting a residence. This is followed by a discussion of buying alternatives and the home buying process, including determining housing needs, evaluating potential homes, and pricing the property. Finally, suggestions for selling a home are offered.

Learning Objectives

After studying this chapter, you will be able to:

Obj. 1 Evaluate available housing alternatives.

Obj. 2 Analyze the costs and benefits associated with renting.

Obj. 3 Implement the home-buying process.

Obj. 4 Calculate the costs associated with purchasing a home.

Obj. 5 Develop a strategy for selling a home.

Key Terms

adjustable rate mortgage (ARM)
amortization
appraisal
balloon mortgage
buy down
closing costs
condominium
conventional mortgage
cooperative housing
deed
earnest money
escrow account
graduated payment mortgage
growing equity mortgage
lease
manufactured home
mortgage
payment cap
points
rate cap
refinance
reverse mortgage
second mortgage
shared appreciation mortgage (SAM)
title insurance
zoning laws

Pretest

True-False

T 1. (Obj. 1) Renting tends to be less costly in the short run than buying your place of residence.

T 2. (Obj. 2) A lease is the legal document that sets forth the conditions of a rental agreement.

F 3. (Obj. 2) A security deposit is designed to cover the costs of property taxes when renting a house.

T 4. (Obj. 3) In a condominium, the owner only has title to the individual living unit.

T 5. (Obj. 3) Location is frequently mentioned as the most important factor when selecting a house to purchase.

T 6. (Obj. 4) A high down payment will reduce the amount of the mortgage a person needs to buy a house.

T 7. (Obj. 4) Qualifying for a mortgage is similar to obtaining other types of credit.

F 8. (Obj. 4) As interest rates rise, people are usually able to afford a higher-priced home.

T 9. (Obj. 4) Negative amortization is the result of an increase in the amount owed on a mortgage.

T 10. (Obj. 4) A deed is a document that transfers ownership of property from one party to another.

Self-Guided Study Questions

Obj. 1

Evaluating Housing Alternatives (p. 279)

1. What are the main factors that influence housing selection?

Your Lifestyle and Your Choice of Housing (p. 279)

2. How do personal preferences and financial factors affect housing choice?

Opportunity Costs of Housing Choices (p. 279)

3. What are common trade-offs associated with housing decisions?

Renting versus Buying Housing (p. 280)

4. What personal and financial factors influence a person's choice of renting or buying?

5. When would renting be preferred to buying a home?

Housing Information Sources (p. 280)

6. What information is available to help a person with housing selection?

Obj. 2

Renting Your Residence (p. 283)

7. Why do most people rent their housing at some point in their life?

Selecting a Rental Unit (p. 283)

8. What are the housing types commonly available to rent?

Advantages of Renting (p. 283)

9. What are viewed as the main advantages of renting your place of residence?

Disadvantages of Renting (p. 284)

10. What are common drawbacks of renting?

11. What is the purpose of a lease?

Costs of Renting (p. 286)

12. What costs are commonly associated with renting?

13. What is the purpose of a security deposit?

Obj. 3

The Home-Buying Process (p. 286)

Step 1: Determine Homeownership Needs (p. 286)

14. What are common advantages of owning your own home?

15. What disadvantages are associated with owning your own home?

16. What options are available to a person who wants to purchase housing?

17. How does a condominium differ from cooperative housing?

18. What are the positive and negative aspects of a manufactured (mobile) home?

19. What factors need to be considered before selecting a contractor for building a home?

20. What factors influence the amount a person can spend when buying a home?

21. What features are most commonly desired in a home?

Step 2: Find and Evaluate a Property to Purchase (p. 290)

22. What is the purpose of zoning laws?

23. How does the quality of schools affect the value of all homes in an area?

24. What services can a real estate agent provide?

Step 3: Price the Property (p. 290)

25. What factors influence the price a person might offer for a home for sale?

26. How does a "buyer's" market differ from a "seller's" market when negotiating a price?

Obj. 4

The Finances of Home Buying (p. 293)

Step 4: Obtain Financing (p. 293)

27. How does the amount of money a person has available for a down payment affect financing availability?

28. What qualifications must be met to obtain a mortgage?

29. What factors affect the amount of mortgage a person can afford?

30. How do points affect the cost of a mortgage?

Types of Mortgages (p. 296)

31. What is a conventional mortgage?

32. How do government-guaranteed financing programs assist homebuyers?

33. What are the positive and negative aspects of an adjustable rate mortgage?

34. How do a buy down and a shared appreciation mortgage assist a person when buying a home?

35. What is a second mortgage?

Step 5: Close the Purchase Transaction (p. 301)

36. What are common closing costs associated with finalizing a real estate transaction?

37. What is the purpose of title insurance?

38. What is an escrow account?

Obj. 5

Selling Your Home (p. 303)

Preparing Your Home for Selling (p. 303)

39. What should a person consider doing when preparing a home for selling?

Determining the Selling Price (p. 304)

40. What factors will influence the selling price of a home?

Sale by Owner (p. 304)

41. What are the advantages and disadvantages of selling your own home?

Listing with a Real Estate Agent (p. 304)

42. How can a real estate agent assist you when selling a home?

Post Test

Completion

1. (Obj. 4) Amortization refers to the reduction of a loan balance through payments made over a period of time.
2. (Obj. 3) A(n) condo is an individually owned housing unit in a building with a number of such units.
3. (Obj. 4) A(n) balloon mortgage has fixed monthly payments and a very large final payment.
4. (Obj. 4) The document that transfers ownership or property from one party to another is the deed.
5. (Obj. 2) The legal document that defines the conditions of a rental agreement is a(n) lease.
6. (Obj. 4) Points are prepaid interest charged by a lender.
7. (Obj. 4) A(n) buy down is an interest rate subsidy from a builder or real estate developer that reduces the mortgage payments in the first few years of the loan.
8. (Obj. 4) Money deposited with a financial institution for the payment of property taxes and home insurance is the escrow account.
9. (Obj. 3) Earnest money is a portion of the purchase price that the buyer deposits as evidence of good faith to show the purchase offer is serious.
10. (Obj. 4) closing costs are the fees and charges paid when a real estate transaction is completed.

Multiple Choice

C 1. (Obj. 2) A common advantage of renting a place to live is
   A. the tax advantage.
   B. equity.
   C. mobility.
   D. community pride.

B 2. (Obj. 2) The legal document that defines the conditions of a rental agreement is a
   A. mortgage.
   B. lease.
   C. title.
   D. deed.

A 3. (Obj. 3) Which of the following is a housing arrangement involving membership in a nonprofit organization in which a person may rent a living unit?
A. Cooperative
B. Condominium
C. Conventional mortgage
D. Contingency clause

D 4. (Obj. 3) A common disadvantage of home ownership is
A. limited responsibility.
B. few financial benefits.
C. low initial costs.
D. limited mobility.

C 5. (Obj. 3) The most frequently mentioned factor considered when selecting a home to buy is
A. quality of schools.
B. zoning restrictions.
C. location.
D. condition of the home.

D 6. (Obj. 3) The purpose of zoning laws is to
A. reduce housing costs.
B. improve the quality of schools.
C. maintain public services in a community.
D. restrict how property is used.

B 7. (Obj. 4) Which of the following would increase the amount of mortgage a person could afford?
A. Increased interest rates
B. Decreased interest rates
C. A low down payment
D. A large amount of other debts

B 8. (Obj. 4) A mortgage with a constant interest rate is commonly referred to as a(n) ____________ mortgage.
A. government-guaranteed
B. conventional
C. equity
D. amortized

C 9. (Obj. 4) A home equity loan is also referred to as a
A. buy-down.
B. shared appreciation mortgage.
C. second mortgage.
D. conventional mortgage.

B 10. (Obj. 4) Which of the following items is commonly paid out of an escrow account?
A. Title insurance
B. Property insurance
C. Closing costs
D. Credit report fee

Problems, Applications, and Cases

1. Based on the following information for George and Alicia Peters, would you recommend that they continue to rent an apartment or buy a house?

   monthly rent $650

   monthly mortgage payment $790

   approximate annual mortgage interest $8,900

   annual property taxes $1,575

   estimated annual maintenance $420

   federal income tax rate 28%

   In addition to this analysis, what other factors should George and Alicia consider when deciding whether to rent or buy their housing?

2. Conduct an assessment of two or more apartments that you would consider renting. Refer to text pages 283-286 for additional information on this topic.

3. In an effort to compare different alternatives for purchasing a home, review text pages 288-289. Compare the features of three different types of housing.

4. With the use of Exhibit 9-6 on page 291, conduct an inspection of a home you or a friend might consider buying.

5. For each of the following situations, which type of mortgage discussed on pages 296-300 of the text would be most appropriate?

Situation	Type of mortgage
a. A moderate income family with limited funds available for a down payment	
b. An individual who believes interest rates are quite high and believes he will be able to refinance at a lower rate in three to five years	
c. A person who wishes to use current equity in her home to finance a son's college education	
d. A family desires a fixed-rate loan with a constant level of payments	
e. A person desires low mortgage payments at present, but will be able to afford higher payments in future years	

Supplementary Case 9-1: Hunting for a Home

Topic: Housing Choices

Text Reference: pp. 279-303

Dan and Lia Schultz were recently married and are looking for a permanent residence. Dan, a computer operator, is learning programming as a part-time student. Lia works part-time as a receptionist and is taking courses toward a degree in health care administration. They have $2,000 in a savings account.

Dan and Lia are considering renting an apartment that has a monthly rent of $575 and requires a $600 security deposit. They are also looking into a condominium that they can buy with a $2,300 down payment and monthly mortgage payments of $730.

Case Questions

1. What personal and household factors should Dan and Lia consider before choosing their housing?
2. What positive and negative aspects of the two housing alternatives mentioned above should Dan and Lia consider?
3. Besides the two housing alternatives mentioned above, what other alternatives might be available to Dan and Lia?
4. What future events might affect the current choice made by Dan and Lia?
5. What should Dan and Lia do?

Supplementary Case 9-2: Move or Remodel?

Topic: Changing Homes

Text Reference: pp. 286-296

Pat and Marci Koswall have lived in their current home for three years. The house is located within a half hour of each of their places of employment. With declining interest rates, the Koswalls are considering a larger home.

Most of the available homes they like are located in a different area, farther from work. However, these homes provide many features that appeal to Pat and Marci.

To keep the conveniences of their current location, the Koswalls are considering a major upgrade of their current home. This work would include a new kitchen floor and cabinets, a remodeled bathroom, and the addition of a bedroom (which could be used as an office).

Case Questions

1. How might Pat and Marci assess their alternatives about buying a different house or remodeling their current one?
2. What financial factors should they consider?
3. What action would you recommend for the Koswalls?

Supplementary Case 9-3: Refinance versus Home-Equity Loan

Topic: Mortgages

Text Reference: pp. 293-300

Ben and Jan Wooden recently encountered some unexpected medical bills and need to obtain cash for that purpose. Since interest rates have recently declined, they could refinance their mortgage. By taking out a slightly larger mortgage, the Woodens could obtain the needed cash and their monthly payments would stay at the same level.

Several financial institutions are offering home-equity loans with no closing costs. This would allow the Woodens to borrow against the equity in their home. The rates for these loans are slightly higher than the rate for refinancing—however, remember there are no closing costs.

Case Questions

1. What factors should be considered before selecting one of the two alternatives?
2. How can the Woodens evaluate the financial benefits and cost of each situation?
3. What action would you recommend for the Woodens?

Supplementary Reading 9

Ellen Hoffman, "Let Your Keyboard Do the House-Hunting, Would-be buyers can see homes near and far on the Web" *Business Week*, October 18, 1999, p. 215.

Let Your Keyboard Do the House-Hunting

Would-be buyers can see homes near and far on the Web

LaRae Maruyama, controller for the U.S. Olympic Committee, sifted through about 300 Colorado Springs (Colo.) real estate listings and looked at 60 houses over five months before she found one with the formal living and dining room and mountain view she wanted. But her search might have taken even longer were it not for the latest time-saving tool for buying and selling real estate—the Internet.

Especially helpful to Maruyama was a custom Web page, updated daily with new listings by Jennifer and Joe Boylan, agents for Prudential Professional Realtors. She came across the Boylans because their name was on a sign posted in front of a house that interested her. Their Web-based service alerted her to the home she ultimately bought. Using the Internet "helped me eliminate properties that did not meet my specifications, and compare attributes of the houses, such as the type of building construction," she says.

Maruyama is in the forefront of a fast-growing trend. Save for closing your deal, you can now go through every stage of a home search without leaving your desk. Some 23% of buyers now use the Net as a search tool, up from only 2% in 1995, says the National Association of Realtors. By providing 24-hour access to information, listings, and financing options, the Net expedites what is often a time-consuming and frustrating process.

If you are a buyer thinking of following in Maruyama's path, you might first check Web sites with sections that can demystify the process. Microsoft's homeadvisor.msn.com provides tips on how you can determine whether you're paying the right price. The Housing & Urban Development Dept.'s site (www.hud.gov/conright.html) covers such topics as the role of brokers, anti-discrimination laws, and explanations of the fees you will be charged.

Once you launch a search in earnest, you'll find most sites allow you to create a profile of the home you want, from its location and price to the number of bathrooms. But the resulting listings vary greatly in comprehensiveness. For instance, some listings aren't updated regularly. And some national sites, such as online auctioneer Homebid.com, lack listings for entire cities and states. That's why it helps to search for Web sites of local real-estate agents.

PANORAMA. I conducted a trial search and found that one of the best—or at least the most comprehensive—sources for listings is the NAR's Realtor.com. My goal was a home in the Minneapolis suburb of Golden Valley, with at least three bedrooms and two bathrooms, 2,000 to 3,000 square feet, and a price range of $100,000 to $400,000. Realtor.com, whose database contains 1.3 million properties collected from Multiple Listing Services, an information-sharing system used by agents, yielded the largest list of homes for sale, with 36 properties that met my specifications. Homeadvisor.msn.com and Homebid.com showed nothing at all. Homes.com had no listings for Golden Valley, but it yielded six for the county it is in, Hennepin, which encompasses numerous suburbs. On Cyberhomes, I found 20 properties, but details on them were not as extensive as on Realtor.com.

If you are on the other side of the transaction, the Internet gives you the option of selling your home through an agent, who posts the listing, or by yourself. To avoid paying an agent's commission, look into "sale by owner" sites. Owners.com—whose sales, says Chief Executive Hans Koch, have totaled $30 billion since its launch in May, 1996—currently lists 20,000 homes for sale. It offers sellers two three-month "listing packages," one for $139 that allows you to post five pictures on the Net and the other for $89.95 that shows one photo. You will also get, by mail, some traditional marketing tools, including a sign for your front yard and a book on how to sell your own home. You can list on Owners.com for free, but you only get one picture. This one-month listing, like the paid listings, also is distributed through Yahoo! and some other Net browsers. Online realtor PrivateForSale.com will list your house, including up to six photos, for $39.95 per month or $99.95 for four months. To help you determine a price for your property, HomeGain.com offers an instant valuation and a list of recent sales of comparable houses in your neighborhood.

Whether you are selling on your own or via a broker, check if your chosen site offers a moving, virtual tour of your house. Developed by bamboo.com, the tour consists of a sweeping view of a home's exterior and interior areas, such as bedrooms, living room, and kitchen. While the shots can be somewhat distorted, the tour allows potential buyers to see more of the house than any two-dimensional picture could. Dana Weiler, partner and senior sales consultant at Pacific Union Residential Brokerage in Danville, Calif., credits the trendy visual with closing a $599,000 sale of a Walnut Creek home. A couple had liked the house, but the rest of the family was in Southern California. So the absent members got on the Net to have a look. "They all said, 'You have to buy it,'" says Weiler.

BANNER ADS. Almost every real-estate Web site can connect you with someone selling mortgages. In some cases, banner ads link you to a bank or mortgage company. In others, a click will bring you to a site, such as mortgage.com's or E-Loan's, that allows you to sort through current rates and types of loans, apply for a mortgage, and receive approval through the Net. These online mortgages can be cheaper than the conventional variety.

Through mortgage.com, which is a lender, and E-Loan, which gives you a choice of loans from more than 70 mortgage companies, you can submit much of your financial data through the Internet and talk with an associate on a toll-free number. To close, buyers are referred to local offices of lawyers, title companies, and business affiliates.

Online mortgages can suffer from snags. Air Force Lieutenant Colonel Tim Printzenhoff of Colorado Springs got a 6.625%, three-year adjustable rate mortgage from E-Loan, a lower rate than from a local lender. But when he arrived at the title company for settlement, he found his documentation—which he had sent to E-Loan 60 days earlier—had not arrived. He had to fax documents on his investments back to E-Loan before the settlement could occur, four hours late. He also was charged a $675 underwriting fee instead of the $300 quoted. When he objected, Printzenhoff received a $250 rebate.

Despite such hassles, real estate cybershopping is providing tremendous savings of time and money to homebuyers and sellers alike. Sure, if you're a buyer, you'll eventually need to walk through the door of your dream home and see if that great room really is as spacious as the pictures you saw on your monitor. But think of how much easier the Net made it for you to locate that home in the first place.

By Ellen Hoffman

Study Questions

1. What online information sources are available to homebuyers?

2. What are the limitations of using the Internet when buying a home?

3. How can the Internet assist people selling their home?

10 HOME AND AUTOMOBILE INSURANCE

Chapter Overview

Adequate financial protection of property is a vital component of financial planning. This chapter covers the fundamental aspects of risk management, along with home and auto insurance. Discussed are coverages available to homeowners and renters, along with information on the types of policies and the factors that affect the cost of home insurance. The second major aspect of the chapter involves a presentation of the importance, types of coverages, and cost factors of automobile insurance.

Learning Objectives

After studying this chapter, you will be able to:

Obj. 1 Develop risk management plan using insurance.

Obj. 2 Discuss the importance of property and liability insurance.

Obj. 3 Explain the insurance coverages and policy types available to homeowners and renters.

Obj. 4 Analyze the factors that influence the coverage amount and cost of home insurance.

Obj. 5 Identify the important types of automobile insurance coverages.

Obj. 6 Evaluate the factors that affect the cost of automobile insurance.

Key Terms

actual cash value (ACV)
assigned risk pool
bodily injury liability
coinsurance clause
collision
comprehensive physical damage
driver classification
endorsement
financial responsibility laws
hazard
homeowners insurance
household inventory
insurance
insurance company
insured
insurer
liability
medical payments coverage
negligence
no-fault system
peril
personal property floater
policy
policyholder
premium
property damage liability
pure risk
rating territory
replacement value
risk
self-insured
speculative risk
strict liability
umbrella policy
uninsured motorists protection
vicarious liability

Pretest

True-False

F 1. (Obj. 2) Vicarious liability refers to a failure to take ordinary or reasonable care in a situation.

T 2. (Obj. 3) Personal property refers to furniture, appliances, clothing, and other personal belongings.

T 3. (Obj. 3) An umbrella policy provides additional liability coverage for an individual or family.

F 4. (Obj. 3) Flood insurance is included in the broad form of homeowners policy.

F 5. (Obj. 4) A coinsurance clause requires the insured to pay the first $50 or $100 of a claim.

T 6. (Obj. 4) The actual cash value claim method is based on current replacement cost.

F 7. (Obj. 5) Financial responsibility laws require that drivers have comprehensive physical damage insurance coverage.

T 8. (Obj. 5) People injured in your car in an accident would be covered by medical payments coverage.

T 9. (Obj. 5) Comprehensive physical damage provides coverage from losses from fire, theft, or vandalism to your vehicle.

F 10. (Obj. 6) Most automobile insurance companies charge the same amount for coverage regardless of your place of residence.

Self-Guided Study Questions

Obj. 1

Insurance and Risk Management: An Introduction (p. 311)

What Is Insurance? (p. 311)

1. What is insurance?

2. What is an insurance company?

3. What are the financial trade-offs of not obtaining the right amount and type of insurance?

Types of Risk (p. 311)

4. What are the three types of risks?

5. What is pure risk?

6. What is a speculative risk?

Risk Management Methods (p. 312)

7. What is risk management?

8. What are the various methods of managing risk?

9. What is self-insurance?

Planning an Insurance Program (p. 313)

10. What personal factors are important in setting your insurance goals?

11. What questions must you ask when planning to reach your insurance goals?

12. How do you carry out your plan?

13. What questions must you answer when evaluating your insurance plan?

Obj. 2

The Role of Property and Liability Insurance in Your Financial Plan (p. 317)

Potential Property Losses (p. 317)

14. What are the two main risks faced by property owners?

Liability Protection (p. 318)

15. What is meant by the term liability?

16. How does negligence differ from vicarious liability?

Obj. 3

Principles of Home and Property Insurance (p. 318)

Homeowners Insurance Coverage (p. 318)

17. What are the basic coverages of a homeowner's insurance policy?

18. What is the purpose of additional living expenses?

19. What is a personal property floater?

20. Why is a home inventory important to a homeowner or renter?

21. What types of potential losses are covered by the personal liability component of home insurance?

22. What is the purpose of medical payments coverage?

23. What types of natural disasters require special insurance coverage?

Renters Insurance (p. 322)

24. What coverages are provided in a renter's property insurance policy?

Home Insurance Policy Forms (p. 322)

25. What are the main differences between the different forms of home insurance policies?

26. What is the main purpose of a modified coverage form home insurance policy?

Obj. 4

Home Insurance Cost Factors (p. 323)

How Much Coverage Do You Need? (p. 324)

27. What factors affect the amount of home insurance coverage a person needs?

28. What is the purpose of a coinsurance clause in home insurance policies?

29. How do the two methods used to settle claims differ?

Factors That Affect Home Insurance Costs (p. 325)

30. What influences the amount paid for home insurance?

31. What are common home insurance discounts?

Obj. 5

Automobile Insurance Coverages (p. 326)

32. What is the purpose of financial responsibility laws?

Motor Vehicle Bodily Injury Coverages (p. 327)

33. How does bodily injury coverage differ from medical payments coverage?

34. What is the purpose of uninsured motorists protection?

35. Why have no-fault insurance systems not been as successful as expected?

Motor Vehicle Property Damage Coverages (p. 329)

36. What is the main purpose of property damage liability insurance?

37. How does collision coverage differ from comprehensive physical damage?

Other Automobile Insurance Coverages (p. 330)

38. What is the purpose of wage loss insurance?

Obj. 6

Automobile Insurance Costs (p. 331)

Amount of Coverage (p. 331)

39. What factors should a person consider when determining the amount of automobile insurance?

Automobile Insurance Premium Factors (p. 331)

40. What factors influence the cost of automobile insurance?

41. What factors are used to create driver classification categories?

42. What is an assigned risk pool?

Reducing Automobile Insurance Premiums (p. 332)

43. What actions can a person take to lower the cost of auto insurance?

Post Test

Completion

1. (Obj. 5) Comprehensive physical damage protects an automobile owner from financial loss from such risks as fire, theft, glass breakage, falling objects, and vandalism.
2. (Obj. 4) Under the actual cash value method of settling claims, the payment you receive is based on the current replacement cost of a damaged or lost item, less depreciation.
3. (Obj. 5) Property damage liability protects you against financial loss when your car damages the property of others.
4. (Obj. 2) Vicarious liability is present when a person is held responsible for the actions of another person.
5. (Obj. 6) Driver classification is a category based on the driver's age, sex, marital status, driving record, and driving habits used to determine automobile insurance premiums.
6. (Obj. 4) Financial responsibility law is state legislation that requires drivers to prove their ability to cover the cost of damage or injury caused by an automobile accident.
7. (Obj. 2) Failure to take ordinary or reasonable care is referred to as negligence
8. (Obj. 5) Collision insurance pays for damage to your automobile when it is involved in an accident, regardless of who is at fault.
9. (Obj. 3) A(n) umbrella policy supplements your basic personal liability coverage.
10. (Obj. 5) medical payments covers the costs of health care for people who were injured in your automobile, including yourself.

Multiple Choice

C 1. (Obj. 2) Vicarious liability refers to
  A. vandalism.
  B. failure to take ordinary and reasonable care.
  C. a person being held responsible for the actions of another.
  D. property damage caused by natural disasters.

C 2. (Obj. 3) Which of the following would be an example of personal property?
  A. Trees and shrubs
  B. A garage
  C. Furniture
  D. A house

B 3. (Obj. 3) The purpose of an umbrella policy is to
A. provide coverage against loss from earthquakes.
B. supplement personal liability coverage.
C. provide insurance coverage while on vacation.
D. reduce the cost of amounts paid for home insurance.

322

A 4. (Obj. 3) The ___________ form of home insurance provides the most extensive coverage.
A. special
B. basic
C. tenants
D. broad

C 5. (Obj. 4) The ___________ value method of settling claims involves receiving the full cost of repairing or replacing a damaged or lost item; depreciation is not considered.
A. actual cash
B. full cost
C. replacement
D. coinsurance

B 6. (Obj. 5) People Injured in another car in an accident for which you were at fault would be covered by
A. medical payments.
B. bodily injury liability.
C. wage loss insurance.
D. collision insurance.

D 7. (Obj. 5) The 50 in 100/300/50 refers to __________ coverage.
A. collision
B. comprehensive physical damage
C. bodily injury liability
D. property damage liability

C 8. (Obj. 5) Damage to your car caused by wind or hail would be covered by
A. property damage liability.
B. collision.
C. comprehensive physical damage.
D. no-fault insurance.

C 9. (Obj. 6) Rating territory for a driver is based on
A. age.
B. driving record.
C. place of residence.
D. year, make, and model of vehicle.

332

A 10. (Obj. 6) What is the purpose of an assigned risk pool?
A. To help people with poor driving records to get insurance
B. To obtain insurance for young drivers
C. To offer discounts to safe drivers
D. To implement a no-fault insurance program

Problems, Applications, and Cases

1. Prepare an inventory of your belongings that could serve as proof of value in case of damage or loss. Refer to text pages 319-320 for information.

2. Talk to an insurance agent to determine the types and amounts of automobile insurance coverages that he or she would recommend.

3. For each of the following situations, indicate the type of auto insurance coverage that would be involved.

   a. A friend is injured while riding in your car. medical payments

   b. You damage a neighbor's mailbox while driving in a snowstorm. property damage liabili[illegible]

   c. A person in another vehicle is holding you responsible for injuries. bodily injury liability

   d. Your automobile is damaged by a large tree branch in a snowstorm. Comprehensive physical damage

   e. Members of your family are injured in an accident with another driver who doesn't have insurance. Uninsured motorist prot[illegible]

   f. You need to have your car repaired after accidentally hitting a tree. Collision

Supplementary Case 10-1: The Importance of Planning Ahead

Topic: Developing an Insurance Plan

Text Reference: pp. 313-316

Michael Beale works in a gift shop in the city where his take-home pay is about $1,600 a month. He has a four-year old son, and he and his wife are expecting another child. Last year, during a review of his policy, Michael told his insurance agent that he felt his family was sufficiently protected with a $40,000 life insurance policy and a hospital expense health insurance policy.

Michael's shop is successful, so he feels that additional protection is not necessary. Besides, he knows that he will have plenty of time to save for his children's education.

Two weeks ago, however, Michael was injured when he fell from a ladder, leaving him disabled and unable to work. Now, Michael is concerned that his family will not have enough income to meet their monthly living expenses.

Case Questions

1. Did Michael have the right kind of insurance protection for his family? How will his disability affect the welfare of his growing children?
2. What are some ways in which Michael's insurance program could have been improved?
3. Should Michael have considered loss of income insurance? Why or why not?

Supplementary Case 10-2: Household Insurance Decisions

Topic: Home and Auto Insurance Coverages

Text Reference: pp. 318-325

Doug and Brenda Patterson have two children, Heidi, 22, and Chuck, 17. They have basic home insurance coverage on their house, and they are considering additional coverage since they collect antiques and have four rare items as well as a number of other pieces.

The Patterson's dog, Ruffy, is one of the most popular pets in the neighborhood. Ruffy can be seen playing with children almost every day.

Heidi shares an apartment with a friend, Ruth Bowman. Since Heidi and Ruth don't have much furniture or other belongings, they decided not to get insurance. Although they are assuming some risks, they are also saving the cost of insurance.

Chuck Patterson drives to school each morning, then to his part-time job. He also uses his car for social trips on evenings and weekends. He has the minimum amount of automobile liability insurance required by the state.

As you can see, the Pattersons have some financial risks that they could reduce with insurance. Damage to their home and property, harm done by their pet, injuries to people in their dwelling, and automobile accidents causing property damage and injuries are a few of the areas in which the Pattersons might consider purchasing additional insurance. Striking the proper balance between too much insurance and not enough insurance is a difficult financial decision. Knowing the risks and the available coverages related to your home and your automobile can help you make your property and liability insurance choices.

Case Questions

1. What additional insurance coverages might the Pattersons consider obtaining?
2. What factors should the Pattersons consider in deciding whether they require additional coverages?

3. How could the Pattersons' home and auto insurance coverages affect other aspects of their financial planning?
4. What efforts can the Pattersons make to reduce the amount they pay for property and liability insurance?

Supplementary Case 10-3: Can You Prove It?

Topic: Home Insurance Claim

Text Reference: pp. 318-325

Barry Kendall lives in an apartment with his seven-year-old daughter. While they were gone for the day, burglars stole a television, a portable CD player, a notebook computer, and some rare coins.

Fortunately, Barry had renters insurance for his personal property. However, Barry's insurance agent told him that the company would only pay a portion of what Barry thought the items were worth. The items were several years old and his policy included actual cash value coverage. In addition, the insurance company would not pay for any of the rare coins since Barry could not prove he had owned these items.

Case Questions

1. What action did Barry take to protect his personal property from financial loss?
2. What weakness did Barry have in his renters insurance coverage?

Supplementary Case 10-4: So You Claim!

Topic: Auto Insurance Coverage

Text Reference: pp. 326-331

Catharine Wood was driving home one evening during a rainstorm. As a result of oil on the pavement, her automobile skidded into a cement barrier on the side of the highway. Catharine was not hurt, but the accident caused extensive damage to her three-year-old car.

Auto repair experts estimated it would cost more than $10,000 to get the vehicle back in proper running condition. Since the insurance company estimated the car was worth only $8,500, that was the amount Catharine was offered to settle the claim. However, to buy a comparable car, Catharine would have to spend of $10,000.

Case Questions

1. What actions might Catharine have taken before buying auto insurance to prevent this situation?
2. Should Catharine accept the claim settlement from the insurance company? What additional actions may be appropriate for Catharine to take?

Supplementary Reading 10

Susan J. Marks, "Cybersettle: Staking a Claim to the Online Mediation Market, Two personal injury lawyers have found a way to streamline dispute resolution via the Net," *Business Week Online: Business Week e.biz: Company Closeup*, March 14, 2000.

Cybersettle: Staking a Claim to the Online Mediation Market

Two personal injury lawyers have found a way to streamline dispute resolution via the Net

Move over Judge Judy. Insurance companies and their customers have begun using the Net to settle claims and other minor disputes faster and for a lot less cost than the traditional courtroom way. Just ask James D. Burchetta and Charles S. Brofman, two Manhattan personal injury lawyers, who traded in the grind of civil court to co-found cybersettle.com, an online dispute resolution service that offers companies the chance to save dozens of hours of courtroom time and mega-bucks in potentially costlier settlements.

How much faster and cheaper? It can take two to five years in some cases for a personal injury case to go to trial, says Burchetta. The property and casualty insurance industry spent $37 billion last year on lawyers, settlements, and courtroom time, says A.M. Best, a leading provider of information and ratings on insurance companies. With cybersettle.com a claim can be settled online for just $300 in fees for the insurer and $200 for the claimant—that $500 total is a fraction of the thousands of dollars it traditionally costs. And the process can be wrapped up in a matter of hours, not weeks or months.

SPLIT THE DIFFERENCE. Here's how it works: Parties in a case click onto cybersettle.com, fill out a registration form, and type in their passwords. Each participant is then asked to submit a settlement offer, or demand, which is revealed only to Cybersettle's electronic system. If the difference between what each side wants falls within an agreed-upon range, usually 30%, or $5,000, the claim is settled instantly for the median amount. If the offers and demands are vastly different, then it's on to another round. For example, say you demand $250,000 from your auto insurance company to resolve an accident claim, and your insurer offers to settle for $40,000. Negotiations would continue into a second round—and a third, if necessary. Say, on the other hand, your insurance company enters $80,000 and you want $100,000. Cybersettle's system would end the negotiating, split the difference, and you'd end up getting $90,000.

How does Cybersettle make money? After all, lawyers are lawyers—online and off. Burchetta says Cybersettle gets $25 from the insurance company to upload a claim, then another $75 when a claimant clicks on for online dispute resolution. Each side then pays Cybersettle an additional $200 each if their dispute is settled. If disputes can't be settled online, Cybersettle still makes money. And since bidding is nonbinding if a settlement isn't reached and confidential, parties in a dispute can always take their case to court should online wrangling fail to settle it.

The idea for the company was discovered almost by accident. Burchetta and Brofman got their concept for Cybersettle, aptly, in court—while on opposite sides of a case. The two decided to write down, on separate pieces of paper, the bottom-line settlement each was willing to accept, then gave them to a court clerk as a neutral third party. Were they close enough to avoid trial? "We were $1,000 apart," Burchetta recalls. "We split the difference and went and had coffee. We literally settled the case in 10 minutes. It would have, otherwise, taken four or five weeks of trial." One drawback: It might be more difficult to go out for coffee after you settle your case online.

Sure, in some cases, you might have been able to get more money if you'd taken your case to court. But if time and cost are important, says Burchetta, it's a risk worth taking. And there are other advantages: Online dispute resolution lets you conquer geographical distances and minimizes the chance that emotions will get in the way of a good settlement.

So far, clients love it. Since its first claim was settled in August, 1998, the New York-based startup has helped to resolve more than 15,000 claims involving more than $30 million in awards in the U.S. and Canada. Clients include Travelers Property Casualty, American International Group (AIG), Kemper Insurance, and Sears Roebuck. Another big fan is Bobby Wallach, president and CEO of New York's Robert Plan, a leading servicer and underwriter of automobile insurance. Cybersettle has helped his company shave 60% to 70% off the average cost of settling a claim.

At least one member of the traditional legal establishment is taking the idea seriously. William E. Hornsby Jr., a staff counsel and the lawyer coordinating online trade dispute matters for the American Bar Assn., says the ability to use a third party for dispute resolution, and to do it online, is a boon to the legal industry. "Third-party dispute resolution is the core of our system of litigation. The great majority of courts have systems of pretrial conferences, where offers are made and accepted or rejected. The difference here is that it's done behind the electronic curtain—and can be done much faster.

MAJOR CLAIM CASES. Not all types of cases can be settled online, says Richard Sutton, a personal injury and medical malpractice attorney with Sutton Overholser & Schaffer in Dayton, Ohio. Sutton used Cybersettle to intervene in an auto accident case, and the case was settled for $10,000 in 10 minutes—impressive to Sutton. But Sutton says he's not sure he would use Cybersettle in a major claim case, where there is permanent injury, since the liability in such cases isn't always so clear-cut and it's tougher to valuate damages and injuries. Says ABA's Hornsby: "If there are things other than dollars and cents involved, face-to-face forums might be far better for resolution over the long term."

Still, Cybersettle has plans for expansion. This spring, Burchetta plans to roll out Claim Court, a virtual court that will target business-to-business disputes and one-to-one personal disputes. The company will offer a database containing similar court cases, to help parties set values on claims. For example, if you broke your leg in an auto accident, you could tap into Cybersettle's databank and get an idea of what kinds of settlements have been reached in similar cases. Next up: Starting on Apr. 15, Cybersettle will serve Europe. Burchetta says Cybersettle's system can handle a million claims a day in any currency from anywhere in the world.

To be sure, Burchetta and Brofman face challenges. Competitors are entering the fray, including Resolute Systems, Settleonline, SettlementNow, and National Arbitration & Mediation Corp.'s ClickNsettle. Still, Burchetta thinks Cybersettle will remain a leader in online mediation because of its unique double-blind, real-time bidding technology—which keeps bidding confidential so parties can take their cases to court, should online mediation fail. A patent is pending on that technology. Cybersettle says its system is faster than ClickNsettle's, which allows users to make bids over a two-month period. But ClickNsettle boasts a 60% settlement rate, compared with a 40% rate for Cybersettle.

Can Cybersettle succeed in the long-term? The jury's still out. For now, though Cybersettle's bid to be a leader in online dispute resolution has gotten off to a wining start.

By Susan J. Marks

Study Questions

1. What benefits are associated with selling insurance claims online?

2. What are possible drawbacks with this system?

11 HEALTH AND DISABILITY INSURANCE

Chapter Overview

Planning a health insurance program needs careful study, because the protection should be shaped to the needs of the individual or the family. However, the task is simplified for many families because a foundation for their coverage is already provided by group health insurance at work. We begin the chapter explaining why the costs of health insurance and health care have been increasing. Then we define health insurance and disability income insurance, and explain their importance in financial planning. Next, we explore the sources of the disability income insurance requirement. Then we analyze the benefits and limitations of the various types of health insurance coverages. Private sources of health insurance and health care are presented next, with a complete coverage of health maintenance organizations (HMOs). Finally, we discuss the sources of government health programs, such as Medicare and Medicaid.

Learning Objectives

After studying this chapter, you will be able to:

Obj. 1 Explain why the costs of health insurance and health care have been increasing.

Obj. 2 Define health insurance and disability income insurance and explain their importance in financial planning.

Obj. 3 Recognize the need for disability income insurance.

Obj. 4 Analyze the benefits and limitations of the various types of health care coverage.

Obj. 5 Evaluate private sources of health insurance and health care.

Obj. 6 Appraise the sources of government health programs.

Key Terms

basic health insurance coverage
Blue Cross
Blue Shield
coinsurance
comprehensive major medical insurance
coordination of benefits (COB)
copayment
deductible
disability income insurance
exclusive provider organization
health maintenance organization (HMO)
hospital expense insurance
hospital indemnity policy
long-term care insurance
major medical expense insurance
managed care
Medigap insurance
physician expense insurance
point-of-service plan
preferred provider organization
stop-loss
surgical expense insurance

Pretest

True-False

T	1.	(Obj. 1) The United States has the highest per capita medical expenditures of any industrialized country in the world.
T	2.	(Obj. 1) The best way to avoid the high cost of sickness is to stay well.
F	3.	(Obj. 2) Almost all people in the United States have health insurance.
T	4.	(Obj. 2) The coordination of benefits (COB) is a method of integrating the benefits payable under more than one insurance plan.
pg. 346 F	5.	(Obj. 3) There is a standard definition of disability.
T	6.	(Obj. 3) Like Social Security benefits, workers' compensation benefits are determined by your earnings and your work history.
pg. 351 T	7.	(Obj. 4) Major medical expense insurance protects against the large expenses of a serious injury or a long illness.
F	8.	(Obj. 4) Dread disease and cancer policies are usually good values.
pg. 359 T	9.	(Obj. 5) Managed care refers to prepaid health plans that provide comprehensive health care to members.
F	10.	(Obj. 6) Medicaid is a federal health insurance program for people 65 or older.

Self-Guided Study Questions

Obj. 1

Health Care Costs (p. 339)

1. What are the four sources of health insurance available to individuals?

① PRIVATE INSURANCE COMPANIES
② SERVICE PLANS
③ HEALTH MAINTENANCE ORGANIZATIONS
④ GOVERNMENT PROGRAMS

High Medical Costs (p. 339)

2. What was the average per capita spending on health care in 1999?

$4,340

3. How do administrative costs in the United States compare with those in Canada?

26% healthcare dollars consumed by administrative costs compared Canada only 1%.

4. Currently how many Americans are uninsured or underinsured?

285 million people - 42 million have no insurance.

Why Does Health Care Cost So Much? (p. 341)

5. What factors have contributed to the high and rising costs of health care?

technology/sophisticated
people living longer.
Doctors fee's going up

6. Why do hospitals, doctors, and patients often lack the incentive to make the most economical use of health care services?

What Is Being Done About the High Costs of Health Care? (p. 342)

?

7. How is the private sector coping with the cost of health care?

HMO
PPO

What Can You do to Reduce Health Care Costs? (p. 343)

8. What steps can you take to reduce your health care costs?

? Stay in good health

Obj. 2

Health Insurance and Financial Planning (p. 343)

9. Why have a growing number of college students been uninsured?

Due to the growth of the older student population not covered by family policies. Today 40% of college students are over the age of 25.

What Is Health Insurance? (p. 343)

10. What is the purpose of health insurance?

Health insurance is a protection against the financial burden of illness or accident.

Group Health Insurance (p. 344)

11. What is group health insurance?

12. What is the Health Insurance Portability and Accountability Act of 1996?

13. What are Medical Savings Accounts (MSAs)?

Individual Health Insurance (p. 344)

14. What is individual health insurance?

Supplementing Your Group Insurance (p. 344)

15. What are some reasons to supplement your group insurance?

16. What is a coordination of benefits (COB) provision?

Medical Coverage and Divorce (p. 345)

17. What is the importance of discussing medical coverage of nonworking spouses when couples divorce?

18. What is the purpose of the Consolidated Omnibus Budget Reconciliation Act of 1986?

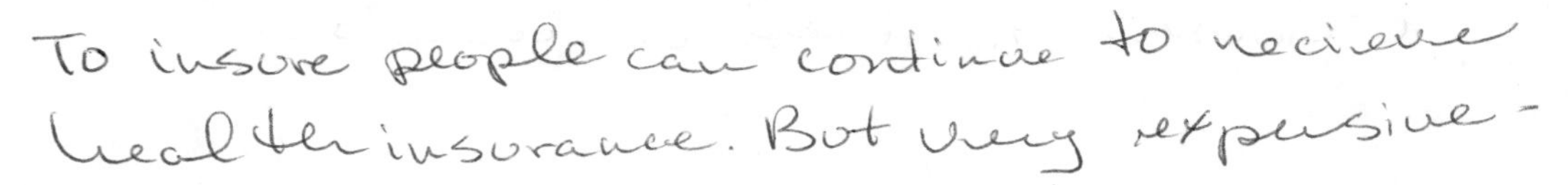

Obj. 3

Disability Income Insurance (p. 345)

19. Why is disability often called the living death?

Definition of Disability (p. 346)

20. Why are there different definitions of disability?

21. What are the features of a good disability plan?

Disability Insurance Trade-Offs (p. 346)

22. What trade-offs should you consider when purchasing disability income insurance?

23. Why should you ask for non-cancelable and guaranteed renewable disability income insurance?

(?) So insurance company ~~won't~~ can't drop you.

Sources of Disability Income (p. 347)

24. What are the various sources of disability income?

social security
workman's comp

25. How are worker's compensation benefits determined?

(?) By hours and time at job.

Determining Your Disability Income Insurance Requirement (p. 348)

26. How do you calculate your disability income insurance requirement?

gross × 7 (years) × 70%

Obj. 4

Types of Health Insurance Coverages (p. 349)

? 27. What should a good health insurance plan cover?

BASIC Coverage

Hospital Expense Insurance (p. 350)

28. What is hospital expense insurance?

Insurance that covers hospital room, board and

Surgical Expense Insurance (p. 351)

29. What is surgical expense insurance?

Insurance that covers surgery

Physician Expense Insurance (p. 351)

30. What is physician expense insurance?

Insurance that covers check-ups and Doctor visits, X-rays

Major Medical Expense Insurance (p. 351)

? 31. What is major medical expense insurance?

Is hospital, surgery and physician coverage (basic) but more coverage for long term.

32. What is a deductible provision in a health insurance policy?

the amount of money the insured must pay before the insurance company will pay.

? 33. What is a coinsurance clause?

The insurer and insured share the cost of coverage. the insured covers approx. 20% the insurer 80% approx.

34. What is a stop-loss provision in a health insurance policy?

the insured person pays a certain amount of money (1000.00 etc) and the insurer pays 100% after that.

35. Why do some major medical policies contain a stop-loss provision?

Comprehensive Major Medical Insurance (p. 351)

36. How does major medical expense insurance differ from comprehensive major medical insurance?

comprehensive has lower deductible

Hospital Indemnity Policies (p. 351)

37. Why do some people buy a hospital indemnity policy?

38. Is a hospital indemnity policy a good buy?

Dental Expense Insurance (p. 352)

39. What is dental expense insurance?

coverage for X-rays, cleaning, exams

Vision Care Insurance (p. 352)

40. What should good vision care insurance cover?

Other Insurance Policies (p. 352)

41. What are dread disease and cancer insurance policies?

coverage for specific diseases (cancer etc.)

42. Who should buy dread disease and cancer insurance policies?

No-one really

Long-Term Care Insurance (p. 352)

43. What is long-term care insurance?

Major Provisions in a Health Insurance Policy (p. 354)

44. What are major provisions in a health insurance policy?

45. What is a copayment?

Which Coverage Should You Choose? (p. 356)

46. How do you decide which health insurance coverage you should choose?

Health Insurance Trade-Offs (p. 357)

47. How do you tackle the trade-offs between the costs and benefits of health insurance coverages?

48. What is the difference between a reimbursement policy and an indemnity policy?

Health Information Online (p. 357)

49. What are a few good sources of healthcare Web sites on the Internet?

Obj. 5

Private Sources of Health Insurance and Health Care (p. 358)

Private Insurance Companies (p. 358)

50. How many private insurance companies sell health insurance?

Hospital and Medical Service Plans (p. 359)

51. What benefits are provided by Blue Cross/Blue Shield?

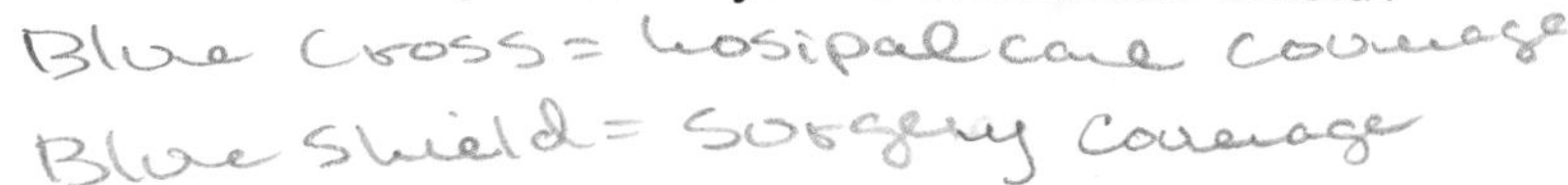

52. What is the meaning of managed care?

prepaid

53. Who provides managed care?

Health Maintenance Organizations (HMOs) (p. 359)

54. How do health maintenance organizations (HMOs) operate?

55. What services should be included with your membership in a typical HMO?

Preferred Provider Organizations (PPOs) (p. 360)

56. What are preferred provider organizations (PPOs)?

57. What is an exclusive provider organization (EPO)?

58. What are point-of-service plans?

59. How do PPOs and HMOs differ?

Home Health Care Agencies (p. 362)

60. How does a health association differ from a home health agency?

Employer Self-Funded Health Plans (p. 362)

61. What is an employer self-funded health plan?

Obj. 6

Government Health Care Programs (p. 363)

Medicare (p. 363)

62. What are the two sources of government health insurance?

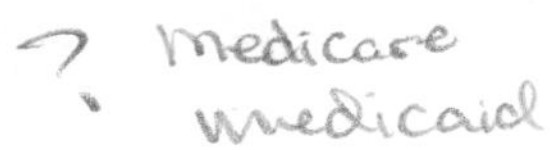

63. What hospital insurance benefits are provided through Medicare?

64. What medical insurance benefits are provided through Medicare?

65. What services are not covered by Medicare?

Medigap (p. 366)

66. What is Medigap or MedSup insurance?

It is a supplementary insurance to pay for what medicare doesn't

67. Who needs Medigap insurance?

Medicaid (p. 367)

68. What is Medicaid?

69. Who administers Medicaid programs?

70. How is Medicaid financed?

71. Should people who have Medicaid coverage purchase supplemental insurance?

Fight Against Medicare/Medicaid Fraud and Abuse (p. 367)

72. What is the Medicare/Medicaid Anti-Waste, Fraud, and Abuse Act?

Government Consumer Health Information Web Sites (p. 367)

73. What are major Health and Human Services (HHS) Web sites?

Post Test

Completion

1. (Obj. 1) The best way to avoid the high cost of sickness is to ____________ ____________.
2. (Obj. 2) The purpose of ____________ ____________ is to alleviate the financial burdens suffered by individuals because of illness or injury.
3. (Obj. 3) ____________ ____________ ____________ benefits provide regular cash income lost by employees as the result of accident, illness or pregnancy.
4. (Obj. 4) ____________ ____________ ____________ pays part or all of hospital bills for room, board and other charges.
5. (Obj. 4) ____________ ____________ ____________ pays part or all of a surgeon's fee for an operation.
6. (Obj. 4) ____________ ____________ ____________ helps pay for physician's care that does not involve surgery.
7. (Obj. 5) ____________ ____________ plans provide hospital care benefits on essentially a "service-type" basis.
8. (Obj. 5) ____________ ____________ plans provide benefits for surgical and medical services performed by physicians.
9. (Obj. 6) ____________ is a federal health insurance program for people 65 and older.
10. (Obj. 6) ____________ is administered by each state within certain broad federal requirements and guidelines.

Multiple Choice

______ 1. (Obj. 1) In 1999, the average per capita spending on health care totaled about ____________ a year.
   A. $900
   B. $1,900
   C. $3,800
   D. $4,340

______ 2. (Obj. 2) Which type of insurance protects your most valuable asset—your ability to earn income?
   A. Disability income
   B. Life
   C. Liability
   D. Dread disease

D 3. (Obj. 2) Group health insurance plans comprise more than ______ percent of all the health insurance issued by life insurance companies.
A. 25
B. 45
C. 65
D. 85

C 4. (Obj. 3) If your take-home pay is $500 a week, you could be eligible for disability insurance of about __________ a week.
A. $600-$650
B. $500-$600
C. $350-$400
D. $200-$300

C 5. (Obj. 4) Which type of health insurance pays part or all of hospital bills for room, board, and other charges?
A. Physician expense
B. Surgical expense
C. Hospital expense
D. Major medical expense

A 6. (Obj. 4) Which type of health insurance helps pay for a physician's care that does not involve surgery?
A. Physician expense
B. Surgical expense
C. Hospital expense
D. Major medical expense

B 7. (Obj. 4) Which type of health insurance pays part or all of the surgeon's fee for an operation?
A. physician expense
B. surgical expense
C. hospital expense
D. major medical expense

59 A 8. (Obj. 5) What statewide hospital and medical service plan provides health care benefits on essentially a "service-type" basis?
A. Blue Cross
B. Blue Shield
C. HMO
D. Home Health Agency

9 B 9. (Obj. 5) What statewide hospital and medical service plan provides benefits for surgical and medical services provided by physicians?
A. Blue Cross
B. Blue Shield
C. HMO
D. Home Health Agency

C 10. (Obj. 6) The Social Security Act provides for a program of medical assistance to certain low-income individuals and families. The program is called
A. Blue Cross.
B. Blue Shield.
C. Medicare.
D. Medicaid.

Problems, Applications, and Cases

1. The protection provided by individual and group insurance varies from plan to plan. List advantages and disadvantages of each plan.

Group insurance

Individual insurance

2. Whether you want to evaluate your present policies or purchase new insurance, there are some key points to explore in any health insurance. Based on what you have learned so far, decide what kinds of benefits and costs you would look for in purchasing a policy. Put this sheet aside to use in the next part of this section.

Services I would want in a health insurance policy

3 = essential 2 = not important 1 = don't need

	Now	In 5 years	In 10 years
Hospital services			
Diagnostic tests			
Prescription drugs			
Out-patient care			
Private nursing			
No limit on consecutive days hospitalization			
No limit on total number of days per year			
Small deductible			
Large percentage of major medical coverage			
No exclusions for: private nursing homes Medicare occupational hazards			
Non-cancelable			
Premium can't be increased			
Maternity benefits			
Short waiting period for pre-existing conditions			
Home health care			
Second opinion surgery			
Pre-admission testing			

Courtesy of Health Insurance Association of American, Washington, D.C.

3. There are many considerations in meeting cost containment objectives. If containing costs was your responsibility, which of the following ideas would you select?

Yes	No	Not sure	
			• reduce benefits so premiums would be lower
			• provide benefits for medical care outside of the hospital
			• provide benefits for medical care in the home
			• develop a mechanism toward keeping doctors' charges reasonable
			• cancel policies where large amounts have been paid in claims
			• provide benefits for physical examinations to encourage prevention of medical care, disability, and premature death
			• discourage benefits for other than hospital confinement and doctor expense, so that the number of claims would be reduced
			• set specific rates for surgical procedures
			• work to have all insurers—private and government—reimburse for actual expenses
			• encourage the development of wellness programs (exercise, nutrition, weight control)

Courtesy of Health Insurance Association of America, Washington, D.C.

4. For each of the following situations, select the type of health insurance coverage that would be involved.

Basic protection	Disability income
Major medical protection	Supplemental policies

a. coronary artery by-pass surgery Major medical protection
b. emergency appendectomy Basic protection
c. stroke that demands rehabilitation Basic + Major medical protection + Di
d. broken arm Basic protection
e. removal of impacted wisdom tooth Supplemental policies (dental
f. birth of a baby Basic protection

5. Larry and Liz are a young couple both working full time and earning about $35,000 a year. They recently purchased a house and have taken out a large mortgage. Since both of them work, they own two cars and are still making payments on them. Liz has major medical health insurance through her employer, but Larry's coverage is inadequate. Currently they do not have any children, but they hope to start a family in about three years. Liz's employer provides disability income insurance, but Larry's employer does not.

   Analyze the need for health and disability insurance for Liz and Larry.

6. Pam is 31 and recently divorced, with children ages 3 and 6. She earns $18,000 a year as a secretary. Her employer provides her with basic health insurance coverage. She receives child support from the children's father, but he misses payments often and is always behind in payments. Her ex-husband, however, is responsible for the children's medical bills.

   Analyze the need for health and disability insurance for Pam.

Supplementary Case 11-1

Topic: Here's How to Cut Insurance Costs

Text Reference: pp. 339-343

Although it's true that insurance companies place people into groups to classify their risk potential, individual actions still make a big difference. It's "all for one, and one for all." What one policyholder does affects all policyholders.

Take auto insurance: the volume of claims and the severity of loss or injury directly affect premium charges. If the number of accidents and the extent of loss or injury in those accidents can be reduced, insurance costs will also decline. Drinking and driving is a major cause of accidents and rising costs. Someone's car is stolen in the country every 19 seconds. Policyholder premiums had to foot the $8 billion bill that insurers paid out for vehicle thefts during 1991.

Only tax evasion ranks above insurance scam as America's favorite fraud. Nationally, policyholders paid $17.5 billion for false or inflated claims during 1991. Insurance fraud ranges from professional criminal rings to basically honest people who rationalize that it's okay to falsify an insurance application or to pad a claim.

Auto insurance isn't the only area where policyholders can hold down costs. Homeowners who use safety and antitheft devices to prevent and control losses are curtailing insurance costs—as are life and health insureds who don't smoke, and who exercise, control their weight, reduce stress, and get periodic physical checkups.

The fact is, many costs that influence what we pay for insurance can be controlled and even reduced if each of us is good to our fellow policyholders.

Case Questions

1. How can individual actions make a big difference for all policyholders?
2. How can you reduce the premiums on automobile insurance?
3. Why is the insurance scam one of America's favorite frauds?
4. What can homeowners do to curtail home insurance costs?

Source: Nationwide Insurance Annual Report/1991, Columbus, Ohio, p. 23.

Supplementary Case 11-2

Topic: Buying Adequate Insurance Coverage

Text Reference: pp. 349-356

Kathy Jones was a junior at Glenbard High School. She had two younger brothers. Her father, the manager of a local supermarket, had take-home pay of $2,000 a month. He had a small group health insurance policy and a $20,000 life insurance policy. He said that he could not afford to buy additional insurance. All of his monthly salary was used to meet current expenses, including car and house payments, food, clothing, transportation, children's allowances, recreation and entertainment, and vacation trips.

One evening, Kathy was talking with her father about insurance, which she was studying in an economics course. She asked what kind of insurance program her father had for their family. This question started Mr. Jones thinking about how well he was planning for his wife and children. Since the family had always been in good health, Mr. Jones felt that additional health and life insurance was not essential. Maybe after he received a raise in his salary and after his daughter was out of high school, he could afford to buy more insurance.

Case Questions

1. Do you think Kathy's father was planning wisely for the welfare of his family? Can you suggest ways in which this family could have cut monthly expenses and thus set aside some money for more insurance?
2. Although Mr. Jones's salary was not big enough to buy insurance for all possible risks, what protection do you think he should have had at this time?
3. Suppose Mr. Jones had been seriously injured and unable to work for at least one year. What would his family have done? How might this situation have affected his children?

Supplementary Case 11-3

Topic: Health Care Benefits for Live-In Mates

Employers are starting to consider providing benefits to unmarried mates of employees, but the practice faces financial, tax, and insurance problems. Moreover, the employers face political opposition from conservative groups that see homosexuals as the main beneficiaries.

Still in an embryonic state, partner benefits and policies have been adopted in recent years by almost a dozen employers. Such cities as Madison, Wisconsin, and Berkeley, California, have led the way in awarding sick and bereavement leave to workers with unmarried mates.

The impetus behind the drive is simple. Of an average worker's total annual compensation, 40 percent will be paid out in benefits next year, up from 35.4 percent in 1975, according to Hewitt Associates, a benefits consulting firm. And with health care costs surging, health coverage is an especially coveted benefit for unmarried partners who don't already have it.

The lack of health care benefits is nettlesome to Alix Olson and Martha Popp. Ms. Olson, a city police detective, can't get health coverage for Ms. Popp, her companion of 13 years, or Ms. Popp's two children. "We take our kids to school, we pay our taxes," says Ms. Popp, a substitute teacher without health coverage. "Then to turn around and not be allowed to have benefits—it wears away on you."

Case Questions

1. Do you think employers should provide health care benefits to live-in mates? Why or why not?
2. Why are health care benefits especially coveted by employees?
3. Why is the lack of health care benefits nettlesome to Alix Olson and Martha Popp?

Supplementary Case 11-4

Topic: Disability Income Insurance

Text Reference: pp. 345-349

Gene and Dixie are parents of a two-year-old girl. They live in an apartment in a small city in Illinois, where Gene, 24, earns $18,000 a year as a salesman. His monthly take-home pay is $1,180. Dixie has given up her job as a secretary to take care of their daughter. Gene has no prior military or civil service that might qualify him for government disability programs. Since Gene and Dixie rent an apartment, they have no mortgage disability insurance to cover basic housing costs in case of a disability. Unexpectedly, Gene suffers increasingly serious emotional and mental crises. He is unable to function at his job, and a psychiatrist declares him totally disabled.

Gene's employer provides a long-term disability benefit that pays 50 percent of the average earnings of the prior three years. Since Gene did not work long enough to qualify for full coverage, his benefit is based on an assumed average salary of only $10,000, rather than the $18,000 he actually earned. He is ineligible for Social Security disability benefits because he hadn't been working in covered employment long enough. He is also ineligible for worker's compensation because the disability is not job-related.

The long-term disability policy provided by his employer will pay Gene $417 a month. But Gene and Dixie now have to pay monthly premiums of $100 to continue their group life and medical insurance. While Gene was working, these premiums were paid by his employer. Therefore, Gene, Dixie, and their daughter must now live on a monthly replacement income of only $317.

If Gene and Dixie had realized the inadequacies of Gene's disability income coverage, due partly to the fact that he was relatively new in his job, they could have purchased an individual policy for a nominal fee. A consultation with their agent would have helped them build the income coverage they needed to protect them against the financial disaster they now face.

Case Questions

1. What, if anything, can Gene and Dixie do to alleviate their present problems?
2. Why do you think Gene did not take advantage of the additional disability insurance that he could have purchased at work?
3. What advice would you offer to someone in Gene's situation? Why?

Supplementary Reading 11-1

Lorraine Woellert, with Phoebe Eliopoulos, "Suddenly, A Healthy Shot at Health-Care Reform," *Business Week*, February 7, 2000, p 53.

Suddenly, A Healthy Shot at Health-Care Reform

Edited by John Carey

As 1999 drew to a close, health care was on life support. Congress was at an impasse over allowing patients to sue their health-maintenance organizations and reforming Medicare. And while lawmakers in both parties deplored the plight of the 44 million uninsured, no one was doing anything about it. Meanwhile, a Presidential election season was kicking into high gear, leaving Washington little time or political will to tackle health care.

What a difference a month—and a flurry of public-opinion polling—can make. As Congress returned to work on Jan. 24, health care leaped to the top of the agenda. House Majority Leader Dick Armey (R-Tex.) is predicting that a patients'-rights measure will land on President Clinton's desk by spring. House Republicans are planning to give prescription-drug benefits to low-income seniors, and they promise to beef up medical privacy protection. On Jan. 19, Clinton previewed a hallmark of his Jan. 27 State of the Union Address: a massive $110 billion, 10-year plan to expand health-care coverage for the uninsured.

Why the sudden interest? One factor is the high visibility that Democratic Presidential candidates Al Gore and Bill Bradley are giving the issue. While voter unhappiness had been building for years, Hill Republicans weren't spurred to action until pollsters warned that they may pay a steep price come November. "Republicans are beginning to recognize that they can't be silent on health care," says Scott Reed, chairman of the Republican

Leadership Coalition, a group formed to woo minorities to the GOP. Another reason: the hot economy. With a projected $1.9 trillion surplus over 10 years, polls are betting that generosity is a surefire way to win votes.

A Jan. 19 poll by the Kaiser Family Foundation and the Harvard School of Public Health found that 54% of voters want the government to spend part of the surplus on seniors' prescription drugs. The same percentage said Medicare was a top priority. "There's a resurgent interest in health," says Kaiser Foundation President Drew E. Altman.

Now, health-care companies, like some Republicans on the Hill, are backing off their hard line. The drug industry promises to work with Clinton on a prescription-drug benefit for seniors. And on Jan. 19, the Health Insurance Association of America (HIAA) resurrected the famous TV duo of Harry and Louise, who helped kill Clinton's 1992 health-care plan. Only this time, Harry and Louise are bemoaning the plight of the uninsured—in part to mute the call for HMO reform. "By 2001, it's a sure thing something will happen," predicts HIAA President Charles N. Kahn III.

Fallout Control. Meanwhile, chief executives at 15 of the nation's largest managed-care outfits have been meeting regularly since last fall to explore ways to improve their companies' battered image. They are considering a $30 million to $40 million campaign that will paint a kinder, gentler insurance industry—and help limit fallout if a patients'-rights bill passes. "You need to have public approval and public trust," says Roger Bolton, a senior vice-president at Aetna Inc.

The first item on Congress' health-care agenda should be the patients' bill of rights. The sticking point—whether to let patients sue their HMOs—is likely to be resolved by allowing some access to federal courts for patients' grievances. And the Hill next may find a way to provide a limited Medicare drug benefit. While Clinton's proposal to provide coverage to the uninsured is the least likely to see action this year, who knows? Other health-care measures are making miraculous recoveries.

Lorraine Woellert, with Phoebe Eliopoulos

Study Questions

1. Why was health-care reform on life support as 1999 drew to a close??

2. What are house Republicans' agenda to reform the health-care system?

3. Do you believe patients should be able to sue their HMOs? Explain.

Supplementary Reading 11-2

By Ellen Licking in New York, "Health Care," *Business Week*, January 10, 2000, p. 114.

Health Care

Psychiatrists examining the U.S. health-care system might make the following diagnosis: split personality or manic depression. In one corner, managed-care companies in 2000 will struggle to maintain earnings while net margins languish at just 2% to 3%, on average. In the other corner, Internet-based health concerns will be on a tear. More than 100 e-health-care companies were launched in 1999—and several are very healthy indeed. Sixteen high-profile initial public offerings and two successful secondary offerings have amassed more than $1 billion in new capital.

In the sick corner, health-maintenance organization stocks lost an estimated 14% of their value in 1999.

With enrollment in employer managed-care plans at almost 90% nationwide, untapped markets are scarce at best. "Earlier in this decade, managed care was a growing industry and everyone could thrive," says H. Gregory Solomon, an analyst at J.P. Morgan Securities Inc. "But the low-hanging fruit is gone."

In addition to slowing growth, the industry is plagued by rising medical costs and an uncertain regulatory climate. In December, 1998, most companies confidently estimated medical cost increases of 3% to 5% for the coming year. But as the months waned, companies quietly began reporting upward trends of 5% to 6%—and in August, CIGNA Corp. reported 6.5% to 7%. One reason for the increases: the cost of prescription drugs, which rose 15% to 25% in 1999. Banc of America Securities analyst Todd B. Richter expects health-care costs will continue to increase. "The debate will shift from how to control health-care costs to how to finance them," he says.

Those efforts may be stymied by an ever more vocal public that is demanding greater access and flexibility in health-care plans. "The only way to succeed is to assuage the customer," says Solomon. That, he says, is what inspired United Health Group's November decision to give doctors final authority over patient care. Whether it boosts the bottom line for United, the decision has been a public-relations coup, garnering lavish praise from Congress and the American Medical Assn.

For now, the health-care industry is pinning its hope on consolidation and premium hikes. Deals such as the recent Aetna Inc.-Prudential HealthCare Group Inc. merger allow organizations to trim costs, exploit economies of scale, and gain leverage with providers. Insurers have also started raising premiums. The average cost of employer-sponsored health plans jumped 7.3% in 1999— nearly three times the rate of general inflation, according to consultants William M. Mercer Cos. In 2000, price hikes may be still higher, topping 9%. But as Banc of America Securities' Richter points out, when medical costs skyrocket, "premium increases stop being beneficial to insurers and become necessary to prevent profit losses."

E-health may be just what the managed-care organizations ordered. According to credit Suisse First Boston, at least 18¢ of every health-care dollar is eaten up by administration costs. A recent study by Northwest Healthcare Network shows how the Internet can streamline such inefficiencies: It found that electronic referrals cost health-care companies one-tenth as much as paper referrals. Many insurers, including Aetna and Oxford Health Plans, are looking to beef up their Internet programs. Aetna already has two major Web initiatives: Ezenroll, which allows consumers to sign up online, and E-pay, where physicians submit claims electronically and are guaranteed payment within 15 days. Such programs make life easy both for consumers and their physicians. Oxford, meanwhile, plans to use the Net to promote its disease management programs.

E-health is still new and relatively untested in the minds of many physicians. But as managed-care companies continue to search for new ways to reduce expenses, the Internet may provide some of the medicine so badly needed by the health-care industry.

By Ellen Licking in New York

Study Questions

1. "Earlier in the 1990s, managed care was a growing industry and everyone could thrive. But the low-hanging fruit is gone." Explain.

2. What is plaguing the health-care industry?

3. How can the Internet streamline the rising health-care costs?

Supplementary Reading 11-3

Joshua Kendall, "Elective Surgery How to trim health-care costs? A "split funding" strategy may be just what the doctor ordered," *Business Week Frontier*, March 27, 2000, p. F.12.

Elective Surgery How to trim health care costs?
A "split funding" strategy may be just what the doctor ordered

IF YOUR HEATH PLAN isn't making you queasy, you probably have a strong stomach. For companies with fewer than 50 employees, premiums soared an average of 14% in 1999, according to employee benefits consultant William M. Mercer, and other analysts project a 20% jump this year. That means businesses now paying an average of $3,800 per employee will see increases of $760 a head.

Numbers of this magnitude put small companies in a bind. With unemployment at a 30-year low, cutting back on coverage or passing the higher costs on to employees isn't realistic. But neither is absorbing a big hit to the bottom line. So what's an entrepreneur to do? In the desperate scramble to cut costs, some are switching to the strategy of "split funding."

Think of it as partial self-insurance. You select a plan similar to what you have, only opt for bigger deductibles and higher out-of-pocket maximums. Those adjustments will save your company 15% to 35% on premiums. Next, promise workers that you will pick up the tab whenever it exceeds the old deductibles or out-of-pocket limits. Presto: lower costs for you, and no additional burden for your employees. And you don't have to worry that any single claim will bankrupt you. That's because catastrophic coverage kicks in once the caps are reached.

You're essentially betting that the savings in premiums will exceed additional out-of-pocket expenses for care. It could be a gamble worth taking. But because the strategy is new, your local broker may not know about it. If not, your best bet is to find a benefits consulting firm that specializes in small companies.

It worked for Kness Mfg. Co., a mousetrap maker with 48 employees, in Albia, Iowa. Last January, the company was hit with a 23% hike in premiums. "We thought we would have to drop coverage altogether," says Milly Eastlick, general manager at Kness. Instead, the company switched to split funding, raising deductibles and out-of-pocket maximums. Employees were responsible for costs up to the old levels; then Kness pitched in. The result: Premiums dropped 26%, from $323,000 to $238,000. Total health-care costs fell by 3%.

Split funding can clip future increases, too, because premiums for high-deductible plans are rising much more slowly than for other plans—about 60% slower, says Bill Lindsay, a Denver benefits consultant.

On average, only about 25% of employees hit their maximums in any given year. Still, Larry A. Levitt, a policy analyst at the Henry J. Kaiser Family Foundation, warns that "a minority of small firms with an older or sicker workforce could get hurt" by split funding. It isn't for everyone. But for many small outfits, the plan could save employees a few bucks—and their employers a splitting headache.

Joshua Kendall

For more tips on coping with health-care costs, click OnLine Extras at frontier.businessweek.com

Study Questions

1. What is "split funding." Why are small business owners employing this technique?

2. Is "split funding" a gamble worth taking? Explain.

3. Who could get hurt by split funding?

12 LIFE INSURANCE

Chapter Overview

In this chapter, we explain the meaning of life insurance, outline its history, and describe its purpose. We show how the principle of home insurance discussed in Chapter 12 can be applied to the lives of persons. We also stress the importance of determining life insurance needs and estimating life insurance requirements. Next, we identify the two types of life insurance companies—mutual and stock—and distinguish between participating and non-participating life insurance policies. Then we describe types of life insurance policies: Term life, whole life, modified life, variable life, adjustable life, and endowment policies are discussed in detail. In addition, newer types of life insurance policies such as universal life, group life, home service life, and credit life insurance are also covered. Next, we focus on major and important provisions contained in a life insurance contract. We emphasize the need for comparing insurance policy costs and examining a policy before and after the purchase. Various settlement options are also presented in this section. Finally, we conclude the chapter with a discussion on how annuities provide security to individuals.

Learning Objectives

After studying this chapter, you will be able to:

Obj. 1 Define life insurance and describe its purpose and principle.

Obj. 2 Determine your life insurance needs.

Obj. 3 Distinguish between the two types of insurance companies and analyze the various types of life insurance policies issued by these companies.

Obj. 4 Select important provisions in life insurance contracts.

Obj. 5 Create a plan to buy your life insurance.

Obj. 6 Recognize how annuities provide financial security.

Key Terms

annuity
beneficiary
cash value
chartered life underwriter
double indemnity
incontestability clause
interest-adjusted index
nonforfeiture clause
nonparticipating policy
participating policy
rider
suicide clause
term insurance
universal life
whole life policy

Pretest

True-False

F 1. (Obj. 1) Life insurance is mysterious and difficult to understand.

_____ 2. (Obj. 1) Life expectancy tables do not indicate the age at which a person has the highest probability of dying.

F 3. (Obj. 2) Everyone needs life insurance.

F 4. (Obj. 2) The easy method of determining life insurance is almost useless.

_____ 5. (Obj. 3) Term insurance is protection for a specified period of time.

F 6. (Obj. 3) Whole life insurance does not have a cash value.

_____ 7. (Obj. 4) A beneficiary is a person who is designated to receive something, such as life insurance proceeds, from the insured.

_____ 8. (Obj. 4) The accidental death benefit is often called double indemnity.

F 9. (Obj. 5) The price of life insurance policies does not vary among life insurance companies.

?, T 10. (Obj. 6) A prime reason for buying an annuity is to give you retirement income for the rest of your life.

Self-Guided Study Questions

Obj. 1

Life Insurance: An Introduction (p. 375)

1. How has consumer awareness of life insurance changed over the years?

What Is Life Insurance? (p. 375)

2. What is the meaning of life insurance?

The Purpose of Life Insurance (p. 376)

3. What is the purpose of life insurance?

4. How may life insurance proceeds be used?

The Principle of Life Insurance (p. 376)

5. What is the principle of life insurance? Give an example.

How Long Will You Live? (p. 376)

6. What is the purpose of the table of mortality?

Obj. 2

Determining Your Life Insurance Needs (p. 377)

7. What five factors must be considered before buying life insurance?

Do You Need Life Insurance? (p. 377)

8. How do you determine if you need life insurance?

Determining Your Life Insurance Objectives (p. 377)

9. What three factors should be considered in determining your life insurance objectives?

Estimating Your Life Insurance Requirements (p. 378)

10. How do you estimate your life insurance requirements?

11. What is the easy method of estimating your life insurance requirements?

12. What is the DINK method of estimating your life insurance requirements?

13. What is the "non-working spouse" method of estimating life insurance requirements?

14. What is the "family need" method of estimating your life insurance requirements?

Obj. 3

Types of Life Insurance Companies and Life Insurance Policies (p. 380)

Types of Life Insurance Companies (p. 380)

15. What are participating and nonparticipating policies?

16. What are the differences between mutual and stock insurance companies?

Types of Life Insurance Policies (p. 380)

17. What are two basic types of life insurance policies?

Term Life Insurance (p. 380)

18. What is term life insurance?

19. Why is term insurance sometimes called temporary life insurance?

20. What is meant by a renewability option in term insurance?

21. What is convertible term insurance?

22. What is decreasing term insurance?

Whole Life Insurance (p. 383)

23. What is the whole life, straight life policy, or an ordinary life policy?

24. For what kind of people do cash value policies make sense?

25. What is cash value?

26. What is a nonforfeiture clause?

27. What type of policy has constant premiums throughout one's life?

28. What is a limited payment policy?

29. Why are annual premiums higher for a limited payment policy?

30. What is a variable life insurance policy?

31. Who assumes the risk of poor investment performance in a variable life policy?

32. What is an adjustable life insurance policy?

33. What is a universal life insurance policy?

34. How is universal life insurance different from whole life insurance?

35. What are the key distinguishing features of universal life policies?

Other Types of Life Insurance Policies (p. 386)

36. What is a group life insurance policy?

37. Usually, who pays the cost of group insurance premiums?

38. Is group life insurance always a good deal?

39. Who needs credit life insurance?

40. What might be a better alternative to credit life insurance?

41. What type of insurance is a good substitute for credit life insurance?

42. How often should you reevaluate your insurance coverage?

Obj. 4

Important Provisions in a Life Insurance Contract (p. 389)

43. What are some of the most common provisions in a life insurance policy?

Naming Your Beneficiary (p. 389)

44. What is a beneficiary?

The Grace Period (p. 390)

45. What is the grace period?

Policy Reinstatement (p. 390)

46. What is a policy reinstatement provision?

47. Is there a time limit on policy reinstatement?

Incontestability Clause (p. 390)

48. What is the incontestability clause?

Suicide Clause (p. 390)

49. What is a suicide clause?

Automatic Premium Loans (p. 390)

50. What is an automatic premium loan option?

Misstatement of Age Provision (p. 391)

51. What is a misstatement of age provision?

Policy Loan Provision (p. 391)

52. What is a policy loan provision?

53. Does a policy loan reduce the death benefit if the loan is not repaid?

Riders to Life Insurance Policies (p. 391)

54. What is a rider?

55. What is a waiver of premium disability benefit?

56. Under what circumstance should you not buy the waiver of premium rider?

57. What is an accidental death benefit clause?

58. Why is the accidental death benefit often called double indemnity?

59. What is a guaranteed insurability option?

60. When is a guaranteed insurability option desirable?

61. What is the purpose of cost of living protection?

62. What are accelerated or living benefits?

Obj. 5

Buying Life Insurance (p. 392)

63. What factors must you consider before buying life insurance?

From Whom to Buy? (p. 393)

64. Why should you choose carefully when deciding on an insurance company or an insurance agent?

65. What are several private and public sources of life insurance?

66. How are insurance companies rated for their financial strength?

67. Who rates insurance companies?

68. How do you go about choosing your insurance agent?

69. Who is a chartered life underwriter (CLU)?

70. Who is designated as a chartered property and casualty underwriter (CPCU)?

Comparing Policy Costs (p. 394)

71. How do you compare policy costs?

72. What is an interest-adjusted index?

Obtaining a Policy (p. 395)

73. What are the two parts in a life insurance policy?

Examining a Policy (p. 396)

74. How do you examine an insurance policy before and after the purchase?

Choosing Settlement Options (p. 397)

75. How do you choose settlement options?

76. What is a lump-sum payment option?

77. What is a limited installment payment option?

78. What is a life income option?

Switching Policies (p. 398)

79. Should you switch policies?

Obj. 6

Financial Planning with Annuities (p. 399)

80. What is an annuity?

81. What are the two kinds of annuities?

Why Buy Annuities? (p. 399)

82. Why do people buy annuities?

Tax Considerations (p. 400)

83. How are annuities taxed?

Post Test

Completion

1. (Obj. 1) Covering the financial need arising from the risk of untimely death is a function of ____________ ____________.
2. (Obj. 2) The ____Easy____ ____Method____ of estimating life insurance requirements is based on the insurance agent's rule of thumb that a "typical family" will need about 70 percent of your salary for seven years before it adjusts to the financial consequences of your death.
3. (Obj. 3) A(n) ____Participating policy____ has somewhat higher premiums than a nonparticipating policy.
4. (Obj. 3) ____Term____ ____Life____ is life insurance protection for a specified period of time.
5. (Obj. 3) The premium for the ____whole____ ____Life____ insurance policy stays the same for the rest of your life.
6. (Obj. 3) A(n) ____Group____ ____________ plan insures a large number of persons under the terms of a single policy without medical examinations.
7. (Obj. 4) A(n) ____________ is a person who is designated to receive life insurance proceeds from the insured.
8. (Obj. 5) ____________ ____________ index is a method of evaluating the cost of life insurance by taking into account the time value of money.
9. (Obj. 6) A(n) ____________ is a financial contract written by an insurance company to provide you with a regular income.
10. (Obj. 6) A fixed ____________ is a contract stating that the annuitant will receive a fixed amount of income over a certain period or for life.

Multiple Choice

B 1. (Obj. 1) Which one of the following statements regarding life insurance is correct?
- A. Consumers eagerly purchase life insurance.
- B. Consumer awareness of life insurance has changed very little.
- C. Consumers are rebelling against life insurance companies.
- D. Consumers believe that life insurance companies are taking an unfair advantage of policyholders.

B 2. (Obj. 2) If you have no dependents and your spouse earns as much or more than you do, you may consider which of the following methods to estimate your life insurance needs?
- A. Easy
- B. DINK
- C. "Non-working spouse"
- D. Thorough

A 3. (Obj. 3) If you wish to pay exactly the same premium each year, you should choose what type of life insurance policy?
- A. Nonparticipating
- B. Participating
- C. Term
- D. Universal

D 4. (Obj. 3) The most common type of permanent life insurance is the ___________ life policy.
- A. variable
- B. universal
- C. term Tempory
- D. whole Permanate

C 5. (Obj. 3) Which life insurance provision allows you not to forfeit all accrued benefits?
- A. Incontestability clause
- B. Forfeiture clause
- C. Nonforfeiture clause
- D. Suicide clause

A 6. (Obj. 3) Which type of life insurance plan insures a large number of persons under the terms of a single policy without medical examination?
- A. Group
- B. Whole
- C. Modified
- D. Variable

B 7. (Obj. 4) Which life insurance provision permits the owner of the policy to borrow any amount up to the cash value of the policy?
A. Double indemnity
B. Policy loan provision
C. Incontestability clause
D. Nonforfeiture clause

C 8. (Obj. 4) Which life insurance provision allows you to buy specified additional amounts of life insurance at stated intervals without the proof of insurability?
A. Double indemnity
B. Policy loan
C. Guaranteed insurability option
D. Incontestability

p. 395 D 9. (Obj. 5) Which is a method of evaluating the cost of life insurance by taking into account the time value of money?
A. Consumer price index
B. Cash value index
C. Insurance cost index
D. Interest-adjusted index

p. 402 A 10. (Obj. 6) Some of the recent growth in the use of annuities can be attributed to the passage of the
A. Employment Retirement Income Security Act.
B. Occupational Safety and Health Act.
C. Fair Labor Standards Act.
D. National Labor Relations Act.

Problems, Applications, and Cases

1. Review the sources of life insurance. Investigate the sources of life insurance available in your community for you and your family. Make a list of the pros and cons of each.

2. Contact your State Insurance Department to get information about whether interest-adjusted-cost disclosure is required in your state. Obtain any appropriate literature for your use.

3. Each of the three basic types of life insurance policies (term, straight life, and limited payment) has special features designed to serve specific purposes. For each situation described below, indicate which basic type would be most suitable.

   a. A high school student who has no insurance

   b. The head of a family who has borrowed a large sum of money which must be repaid over the next five years

   c. A professional man, age 45, whose children are grown and who earns a large income and who is more interested in protection for his wife than in retirement for himself

   d. A man, age 30, who already has $20,000 of straight life and who has just bought a home with a $10,000 mortgage on it

4. Examine your (or your parents') life insurance policy. Prepare an outline for a report describing the purposes and provisions of the policy. Consider the following questions when preparing your report. The questions are not listed in any logical order. Some questions may not apply and you will undoubtedly think of other questions that are important.

   a. What is the general title of the policy?
   b. What type or types of protection does the policy provide?
   c. How long does the policy continue?
   d. Is the policy renewable? Explain.
   e. Specifically, what is not covered by the policy?
   f. What happens if the premiums are not paid?
   g. How should claims be presented?
   h. What are the maximum benefits?
   i. What are the premium rates for this policy?
   j. Is it a participating or nonparticipating policy?
   k. What are your options if you decide not to continue paying premiums?
   l. Who is the beneficiary?
   m. What is the grace period?
   n. Is there a suicide clause?
   o. Is there an automatic premium loan provision?
   p. Is there a waiver of premium disability benefit?
   q. Is there an accidental death benefit?
   r. Do you have a guaranteed insurability option?

5. Mike is single, 21, and a college senior. He has no dependents and does not plan to marry soon. He is working part-time to supplement his college grant in order to meet school and living expenses. He is independent and does not receive any financial support from his widowed mother, who works and just meets her own living costs.

   Analyze Mike's need for life insurance.

6. Mary and Barry have two children, ages 2 and 4. Mary does not work outside the home and has no marketable job skills. Mary and Barry are planning to buy their first house. They have discussed the fact that if something happens to either of them (death or disability), the surviving spouse will stay in the house to rear the children. Barry has $30,000 worth of term insurance through his employer. Barry has been earning about $30,000 per year. His employer provides basic health insurance with an option of HMO or fee-for-service.

   Analyze the need for life insurance for this family.

Supplementary Case 12-1

Topic: Identifying the Need for and Amount of Life Insurance

Text Reference: pp. 378-379

Joanne Kitsos was a 27-year-old single parent. She and her four-year-old son, Brad, lived in a small two-bedroom apartment. Since graduating from high school, Joanne had been employed as a secretary for an insurance company. Brad stayed at a day-care center while Joanne worked.

Joanne found it very difficult to maintain a home for herself and her son on her $13,000 salary. She was often forced to borrow money from her parents. She had a small Christmas savings account in her company's credit union, a $5,000 term life insurance policy, and a $2,000 debt with a local furniture store.

Joanne's two major goals were: (1) to increase her income and (2) to protect her income should she become unable to work. She approached her employer to find out how she could progress in her company. She learned that the company had an upward mobility program for employees with at least five years seniority. Interested employees were given company-paid, on-the-job training and college courses to learn one of several jobs. Joanne quickly applied for admission to the program. Within several months, she was able to secure an entry-level position as a computer operator and an accompanying salary raise.

Joanne then turned her attention toward protecting her income and providing for Brad's future education. She bought a $25,000 term life insurance policy on herself; the policy had a disability rider under which she would be paid if she became disabled and could not work. Joanne had always been unable to stick to a savings plan—withdrawing money as quickly as she deposited it. So she took out a $5,000 endowment policy on Brad that would come due when he was 18 and contribute to his college education. The policy also gave him life insurance protection as long as the premiums were paid.

Case Questions

1. Was purchasing term insurance and an endowment policy the right decision for Joanne? Why?
2. Did Joanne need additional life insurance? Why?

Supplementary Case 12-2

Topic: Young Marrieds' Life Insurance

Text Reference: pp. 379-386

Jeff and Ann are both 28 years old. They have been married for three years, and they have a son who is almost two. They expect their second child in a few months.

Jeff is a teller in a local bank. He has just received a $30-a-week raise. His income is $480 a week, which after taxes, leaves him with $1,648 a month. His company provides $20,000 of life insurance, a medical/hospital/surgical plan, and a major medical plan. All of these group plans protect him as long as he stays with the bank.

When Jeff received his raise, he decided that part of it should be used to add to his family's protection. Jeff and Ann talked to their insurance agent, who reviewed the insurance Jeff obtained through his job. Under Social Security, they also had some basic protection against the loss of Jeff's income if he became totally disabled or if he died before the children were 18.

But most of this protection was only basic, a kind of floor for Jeff and Ann to build on. For example, monthly Social Security payments to Ann would be approximately $1,250 if Jeff died leaving two children under age 18. Yet the family's total expenses will soon be higher after the birth of the second baby. Although the family's expenses would be lowered if Jeff died, they would be at least $250 a month more than Social Security would provide.

Case Questions

1. What type of policy would you suggest for Jeff and Ann? Why?
2. In your opinion do Jeff and Ann need additional insurance? Why or why not?

Supplementary Reading 12

Christopher Farrell, "The Fifth-Best Option," *Business Week*, May 8, 2000, p. 166.

The Fifth-Best Option

As baby boomers search for tax-sheltered ways to save for retirement and benefit from the runup of stock prices over the past few years, sales of variable annuities are flourishing. Last year, nearly $121 billion worth were sold, 10 times 1990's volume. But it's hard to make a case that variable annuities are a good buy.

Despite their popularity, variable annuities have a number of drawbacks, including steep fees, limited financial flexibility, and the transformation of low-tax capital gains into high-tax ordinary income. "They are the fifth-best option for retirement planning, behind everything else," says Ross Levin, president of Accredited Investors, an Edina (Minn.) financial-planning firm. So if you feel you must have one, focus only on those with the lowest expenses.

A variable annuity is essentially a mutual fund wrapped in a tax-deferred insurance firm account. Individuals buy variable annuities with after-tax dollars, but earnings compound tax-deferred until retirement, when any gains are taxed as ordinary income. Another part of variable annuities' appeal is their death benefit. When the owner of an annuity dies, the estate or beneficiary gets back the original investment, plus some guaranteed minimum return. So, if a variable-annuity owner invests $25,000 and dies when the investment shows a paper loss of $5,000, the estate or beneficiary still gets $25,000 and, depending on the contract, any guaranteed minimum return. If the owner dies during a bull market and the original $25,000 investment is worth $60,000, heirs get the $60,000. While the death benefit is clearly comforting, it isn't worth anywhere near the price most insurers charge. A recent study by Moshe Arye Milevsky of Canada's York University and Steven Posner of Goldman Sachs concludes consumers are being charged as much as 5 to 10 times the economic value of the guarantee. A variable-annuity holder pays an annual fee for the death benefit, labeled the mortality and expense risk charge, or "M&E" fee. The average M&E fee last year was 1.14% according to Variable Annuity Research & Data Service (VARDS) in Marietta, Ga. Morningstar, meanwhile, estimates the median M&E at 1.25% per annum. But how much is the death benefit really worth? Not much, says Milevsky.

SLIM ODDS. For one thing, the benefit probably doesn't make much sense for long-term investors. Market history suggests the odds are slim that the dollar value of an investment account will shrink over 10 to 30 years. For a more methodical and rigorous analysis, Milevsky and Posner use modern option-price theory and standard assumptions about such variables as interest rates and stock market volatility. Their estimate of the economic value of the death benefit appears in their study *The Titanic Option: Valuation of the Guaranteed Minimum Death Benefit in Variable Annuities.* The study is available at www.yorku.ca/faculty/academic/milevsky/.

Their study says a typical 50-year-old male who buys a variable annuity with a simple return-of-premium guarantee should be charged a maximum of 3.5 basis points annually. As women live longer than men, a female buying a similar policy should pay only 2 basis points. A variable-annuity contract with a 4% interest-rate guarantee, which is obviously worth more, should charge a 50-year-old male 20 basis points and a 50-year-old female 12 basis points. That is about one-fifth to one-eighth the industry average for the M&E fee. Worse yet, companies typically tack on other fees. The average expense on a variable annuity is 2.23%, according to VARDS.

Since life insurers generally pay salespeople hefty commissions, most variable annuities carry surrender charges if you decide to bail out during the first several years of a contract. Surrender charges can be as high as 7% in the first year, 6% in the second, and so on during the first 5 to 10 years of the contract. And many salespeople persuade customers to place variable annuities in tax-deferred retirement accounts, a waste of the tax-shelter features of the insurance.

Many financial planners suggest consumers would be better off investing for retirement in a 401(k) or Roth IRA plan and putting any leftover cash in an equity mutual fund. For one thing, withdrawals from a variable annuity are treated as ordinary income, while some of any returns from a mutual fund may be taxed at the lower capital-gains rate. Indeed, many studies show that the breakeven point between investing in the equity account of a variable annuity and an equity mutual fund is between 15 and 25 years, a long time to lock yourself into one contract.

Anyone stuck in a high-fee product should consider a tax-free transfer of their money into a lower-cost alternative—assuming they're past any surrender charges. Vanguard Group, for example, offers variable annuities with no sales load or commission charges, an average expense ratio of 0.69%, and no surrender charges. Increased competition in the variable annuity business is bringing such thrifty alternatives about. But a lot more progress is needed.

By Christopher Farrell

Study Questions

1. Despite their popularity, what are drawbacks of variable annuities?

2. What should you look for if you must invest in a variable annuity?

3. What is the mortality and expense risk charge or "M&E" fee?

4. What is the average expense on a variable annuity?

13 INVESTING FUNDAMENTALS

Chapter Overview

This chapter is the first chapter in Part Five—Investing Your Financial Resources. We begin our discussion by stressing the importance of preparing for an investment program. Next, we examine how the factors of safety, risk, income, growth, and liquidity affect investment programs. Then, we provide an overview of different investment alternatives available to individuals. We also study methods that investors can use to reduce investment risk. Included in this section on reducing risks is a discussion of the role of financial planners and material on the importance of the individual's role in the investment process. Finally, we discuss sources of investment information, which include the Internet and online computer services, newspapers, business periodicals and government publications, corporate reports, statistical averages, and investor services and newsletters.

Learning Objectives

After studying this chapter, you will be able to:

Obj. 1 Explain why you should establish an investment program.

Obj. 2 Describe how the factors of safety, risk, income, growth, and liquidity affect your investment decisions.

Obj. 3 Identify the major types of investment alternatives.

Obj. 4 Recognize the role of the professional financial planner and your role in a personal investment program.

Obj. 5 Use the various sources of financial information that can reduce investment risks.

Key Terms

corporate bond
diversification
dividend
emergency fund
equity capital
government bond
line of credit
liquidity
mutual fund
speculative investment

Pretest

True-False

T — 1. (Obj. 1) Investment goals must be specific, measurable, and tailored to your particular financial needs.

F — 2. (Obj. 1) A good rule of thumb is to limit installment payments to 30 to 40 percent of your net monthly pay after taxes.

T — 3. (Obj. 1) The amount of money that should be salted away in an emergency fund varies from person to person. 3-9 mon. of living expen

F — 4. (Obj. 2) The safety and risk factors are unrelated to each other.

F — 5. (Obj. 2) The ease with which an asset can be converted to cash without substantial loss in dollar value is called the income factor.

F — 6. (Obj. 3) A corporation is obligated to repay equity capital sometime in the future.

T — 7. (Obj. 3) A corporate bond is a corporation's written pledge that it will repay a specified amount of money, with interest.

T — 8. (Obj. 3) Professional management and diversification are the two primary reasons why investors choose mutual funds.

T — 9. (Obj. 4) A qualified planner has had at least two years of training in securities, insurance, taxes, real estate, and estate planning, and has passed a rigorous examination.

F — 10. (Obj. 5) The fees for investor services generally range from $5 to $30 per year.

Self-Guided Study Questions

Obj. 1

Preparing for an Investment Program (p. 409)

1. Why is the decision to start an investment program important?

Establishing Investment Goals (p. 410)

2. Why should investment objectives be specific and measurable?

3. What kinds of questions can be used by individuals to establish valid investment objectives?

4. What is the difference between a short-term objective, an intermediate objective, and a long-term objective?

Performing a Financial Checkup (p. 410)

5. Why is it necessary for an individual to make sure that his or her personal financial affairs are in order before beginning an investment program?

6. How can individuals spend more than they make on a regular basis?

7. What steps should be taken to reduce installment purchases and the resulting installment payments?

8. What types of insurance coverage do individuals need to examine before beginning an investment program?

9. What is an emergency fund?

10. Why is it a good idea to establish a line of credit at a commercial bank, savings and loan association, or credit union?

Getting the Money Needed to Start an Investment Program (p. 411)

11. What are four specific suggestions that were presented in this chapter that may help you obtain the money needed for a successful investment program?

The Value of Long-Term Investment Programs (p. 412)

12. How does the time value of money affect a long-term investment program?

Obj. 2

Factors Affecting the Choice of Investments (p. 414)

Safety and Risk (p. 414)

13. What is the relationship between safety and risk when choosing an investment?

14. What investments fall into the conservative category? What investments fall into the speculative category?

Components of the Risk Factor (p. 416)

15. What are the five component factors that make up the risk factor?

Investment Income (p. 419)

16. What types of investments provide a steady flow of predictable income?

17. What investments offer little, if any, potential for regular income?

Investment Growth (p. 419)

18. What sacrifice must investors make when purchasing growth stocks?

19. What types of investments offer growth potential?

Stocks

20. What types of investments offer less growth potential?

Savings acct.

Investment Liquidity (p. 420)

21. How would you define liquidity?

an investment easily turned into cash.

22. How does the concept of liquidity affect an individual's investment decision?

Obj. 3

An Overview of Investment Alternatives (p. 420)

23. After you have considered the risks, established your emergency fund, and accumulated some money for investment purposes, what is the next step when establishing an investment program?

Stock of Equity Financing (p. 420)

24. What are the two factors an investor should consider before investing in stock?

25. What is the difference between common stock and preferred stock?

Corporate and Government Bonds (p. 421)

26. How would you define a corporate bond? How would you define a government bond?

Corporate bond = a corporations written pledge to repay a specified amount of money w/ interest

Government bond = a written pledge to repay a specific sum of money w/ interest by the government or municipality.

27. What two major questions should an investor consider before investing in corporate or government bonds?

? pay @ maturity

Mutual Funds (p. 421)

28. What is a mutual fund?

? a pool of investors managed by a financial planner

29. What are two major reasons why investors choose mutual funds?

diverse investment and personal manager

Real Estate (p. 422)

30. What questions should an investor ask before investing in real estate?

31. What are the disadvantages of real estate investments?

Other Investment Alternatives (p. 422)

32. In your own words, what is a speculative investment?

High Risk - GROWTH investment

33. What types of investments are included in the speculative category?

Some stocks (high risk - growth)

? gold

Summary of Factors that Affect Investment Choices (p. 423)

34. How would you define diversification?

Spreading investments around from safe risk to very risky.

35. Why is diversification important?

So you don't lose entire amount invested. — Lose some and gain some.

A Personal Plan of Action for Investing (p. 424)

36. What are the steps required for an effective personal investment plan of action?

37. Under what circumstances would an investor need to change investment goals?

Obj. 4

Factors that Reduce Investment Risk (p. 426)

The Role of a Financial Planner (p. 426)

38. What qualifications does a true financial planner have?

2 yrs. in real estate, securities, taxes, insurance and estate planning and a 10 hr. rigorous test

39. What do the abbreviations CFP and ChFC stand for?

Certified Financial Planner

Chartered Financial Consultant

Your Role in the Investment Process (p. 427)

40. Why is it necessary for investors to monitor the value of their investments?

41. Why is maintaining accurate and complete records related to an investment extremely important?

Tax Considerations (p. 428)

42. What is the difference between tax-exempt income and tax-deferred income?

43. How are dividends, interest income, rental income, capital gains, and capital losses taxed?

44. For an investor in the 28 percent tax bracket, what is the current tax rate for a long-term capital gain?

45. How much of a capital loss can be used to offset ordinary income?

Obj. 5

Sources of Investment Information (p. 430)

The Internet and Online Computer Services (p. 430)

46. What type of investment information is available to investors who use the Internet?

47. How would you access information about investments on the Internet?

48. Name four commercial online companies that provide investors with a broad range of information on a variety of topics as well as a connection to the Internet.

Newspapers (p. 430)

49. What types of financial information is contained in newspapers?

Business Periodicals and Government Publications (p. 431)

50. What are five periodicals that would contain information that could be used by an investor to investigate investment alternatives?

51. Name five magazines that provide information on personal finance topics.

52. What type of publications are available from the federal government?

Corporate Reports (p. 431)

53. What type of information is contained in corporate reports?

Statistical Averages (p. 432)

54. How can investors gauge the value of their investments by following statistical averages?

Investor Services and Newsletters (p. 432)

55. What type of fees do investor services charge?

56. What are the three widely accepted services for investors who specialize in stocks?

57. What are two widely accepted services for investors who specialize in mutual funds?

Post Test

Completion

1. (Obj. 1) Before beginning an investment program, most financial planners recommend establishing an emergency fund that is equal to at least __3 - 9__ month's of living expenses.
2. (Obj. 2) __Safety__ and __RISK__ are two sides of the same coin.
3. (Obj. 2) The __Interest__ __Rate__ risk associated with a fixed return investment in a preferred stock or a government or corporate bond is the result of changes in the interest rates in the economy.
4. (Obj. 2) __LIQUIDITY__ is the ease with which an asset can be converted to cash without a substantial loss in dollar value.
5. (Obj. 3) A share of __Common__ __stock__ represents the most basic form of corporate ownership.
6. (Obj. 3) The most important priority an investor in __preferred__ __Stock__ enjoys is receiving cash dividends before common stockholders are paid any cash dividends.
7. (Obj. 3) The maturity dates for bonds range between __1__ and __30__ years.
8. (Obj. 3) A(n) __mutual__ __Fund__ is an investment alternative available to individuals who pool their money to buy stocks, bonds, and other securities selected by financial managers who work for an investment company.
9. (Obj. 4) A qualified __financial__ __Planner__ has had at least two years of training in securities, insurance, taxes, real estate, and estate planning, and has passed a rigorous examination.
10. (Obj. 5) Dividends are taxed as __Ordinary__ income.

Multiple Choice

__B__ 1. (Obj. 1) A short-term loan that is approved before the money is actually needed is called a(n)
   A. emergency fund.
   B. line of credit.
   C. corporate obligation.
   D. equity capital.

__B__ 2. (Obj. 2) Which of the following investments would offer the greatest potential for predictable income?
   A. Negotiable accounts
   B. Government bonds
   C. Antique collectibles
   D. Stocks

B 3. (Obj. 2) Which of the following investments would offer the greatest potential for growth?
A. Government bonds
B. Stocks
C. Gemstones
D. Commodities
E. Options

D 4. (Obj. 2) Which of the following investments would be considered the most liquid?
A. Gemstones
B. Commodities
C. Corporate bonds
D. Checking accounts

D 5. (Obj. 3) Money obtained from the owners of a business is called
A. corporate obligations.
B. certificates of deposit.
C. NOW financing.
D. equity capital.

C 6. (Obj. 3) Which of the following statements is not true?
A. As a rule, real estate increases in value, but there are no guarantees.
B. Real estate investments, like all investments, must be carefully evaluated.
C. Location is not important when selecting a piece of real estate in a metropolitan area.
D. Finding a buyer can be difficult if loan money is scarce.

B 7. (Obj. 3) Which of the following is not classified as a speculative investment?
A. Derivatives
B. Savings accounts
C. Call option
D. Put option

B 8. (Obj. 3) Diversification is
A. not a concern for small investors.
B. the process of spreading your assets among several types of investments.
C. only practical for investors who choose speculative investments.
D. the ease with which an investment can be converted to cash.

C 9. (Obj. 4) Which of the following statements is false?
A. Successful investors continually monitor the value of their investments.
B. Accurate recordkeeping can help you spot opportunities.
C. Tax deferred and tax-exempt mean the same thing.
D. Interest income is taxed at the federal level.

A ~~B~~ 10. (Obj. 5) A(n) ____________ is a requirement for corporations selling a new issue of securities.
A. prospectus
B. annual report
C. Form 10k
D. Federal Investor Report

Problems, Applications, and Cases

1. Objectives are classified as short-term, intermediate, or long-term according to the amount of time required to accomplish each type of objective. List two or three personal financial objectives for each of the three categories below. Make your goals practical, measurable, and realistic in terms of what you really think you can accomplish.

Type of objective	Personal financial objectives
Short-term objectives (two years or less)	
Intermediate objectives (two to five years)	
Long-term objectives (more than five years)	

2. Complete the "Personal Plan of Action for Investing" that is provided with this exercise. Assume that you have been out of college for two years and are earning $28,000 a year. Your take-home pay is $1,750 per month. Your living expenses come to about $1,350. You have no family responsibilities, so you must decide what to do with the extra money.

Step 1
My investment goals are:

Step 2
By ___________, 20___,
I will have obtained
$____________.
Signed,

Step 3
I have ________________
available for investment purposes.
Date: ________________

Step 4
Possible investment alternatives:
a.
b.
c.
d.
e.

Step 5-A
Examination of risk factor for each alternative:
a.
b.
c.
d.
e.

Step 5-B
Evaluation of projected return for each alternative:
a.
b.
c.
d
e.

Step 6
Investment decision based on the top three:
1.
2.
3.

Step 7
Final decision based on re-evaluation of top three:
1.
2.

Step 8
Continued evaluation of your investment choices

3. Using the information provided in this chapter, describe the advantages and disadvantages of each investment alternative presented below.

Investment alternative	Advantages	Disadvantages
1. Common stock		
2. Preferred stock		
3. Corporate bonds		
4. Government bonds		
5. Mutual funds		
6. Real estate		
7. Commodities, options, and precious metals		

Supplementary Case 13-1: Basic Rules for Investing

Topic: Preparing for an Investment Program

Text Reference: pp. 409-414

Bob Martin, 48 and single, had never thought much about saving money or establishing an investment program. He had always enjoyed life and spent everything he could lay his hands on. He always had a new car, bought designer clothes, enjoyed dating, and went on nice vacations. He had almost $3,000 in a savings account, which he thought should be enough to get him through any emergency. In his own words, he was looking forward to the future because he seemed to be on the right track.

But something happened last week that made Bob sit back and take a long, hard look at the track he was really on. Alex Newton, one of his best friends had decided to take their firm's early retirement option. The fact that Alex was going to retire was upsetting, but even more upsetting was the fact that Alex was only two years older than Bob. How could he afford to retire at 50?

Alex had started saving money when he graduated from college. Later, he began investing in what he referred to as quality, long-term stocks, and mutual funds. Early retirement had been one of his long-term goals. He wanted to travel now and eventually open a small ski-repair business in the Colorado Rockies.

Alex's retirement made Bob sit back and examine his own financial condition. He knew he would never be able to retire unless he changed his lifestyle. That's why he made an appointment with a financial planner who worked for Barns and Barnett Investment Consultants. After a two-hour exploratory meeting, he left the consultant's office with some basic ideas on how to get started. According to the consultant, Bob had to take some logical steps if he was going to change his current financial picture. The consultant made the following suggestions:

1. *Plan Your Financial Future.* Determine short-term and long-term financial objectives that are important to you.
2. *Learn to Budget.* Most people spend money without thinking. A better approach is to determine which expenditures are important and which are unnecessary.
3. *Keep Accurate Records.* A good recordkeeping system lets you see where your money is going. Most experts believe that establishing such a system is one of the most important steps in financial planning.
4. *Take Advantage of Windfalls.* You should use unexpected inheritances, tax refunds, bonuses, and other windfalls to achieve the long-term investment goals of your financial plan.
5. *Reevaluate Your Investment Plan.* Your financial goals and objectives may change over time. You should be able to change your investment plan to meet revised goals and objectives.

Although Bob realized that his financial planning was long overdue, he felt encouraged after his conversation with the consultant. He was excited by the prospect of achieving added security through an increase in his savings and of fulfilling some of his long-term financial objectives through the purchase of quality investments.

Case Questions

1. Why did Bob Martin become upset when he learned that one of his friends had decided to take their firm's early retirement option?
2. Based on the information presented in this case, what type of financial plan would you recommend for Bob Martin?

Supplementary Case 13-2: An Obvious Need for Financial Planning

Topic: Preparing for an Investment Program

Text Reference: pp. 409-414

Mike Denton, 36, was a chemical engineer employed by Exxon Corporation. During 2000, he earned $62,000. Julie, his wife, earned $32,000 a year as a medical technician for a local hospital. Since their marriage, three years ago, they had purchased two new BMWs and a new home in an exclusive Houston suburb. They each had American Express and VISA credit cards, which they used to purchase almost anything they wanted. According to Mike, everything seemed to be right on track.

One year later, everything was off track. It all started when Mike lost his job—he simply got the boot. Since he had always taken his well-paying job for granted, he and Julie had never thought much about money. Now that he was unemployed, they were suffering because they had not done any financial planning. He was trying not only to find another job but also to pay the monthly bills on a lot less money.

When Mike lost his job, the Denton's had $2,800 in the bank, and their monthly expenses totaled more than $4,500. Until Mike found a new job, they had to find a way to live on Julie's $32,000 salary. First, they sold one of the BMWs. Next, they took out a bank loan to pay off their credit card debts. Finally, they put their home up for sale, but they were unable to sell it because of the depressed home prices in their suburb. Eventually, they lost their home when the mortgage company foreclosed on it. They then moved to a one-bedroom apartment.

Fifteen months after losing his job at Exxon, Mike Denton got another engineering job and he and Julie began to rebuild their lives. They both vowed to develop a financial plan. They had learned their lesson well, and they didn't want to make the same mistakes again.

Case Questions

1. During 2000 Julie and Mike Denton earned close to $100,000. And yet, their financial affairs were thrown into a tailspin when Mike suddenly lost his job. What went wrong?
2. Fifteen months after losing his job, Mike got another engineering job. Not wanting to make the same mistakes again, Mike and Julie Denton ask for your help. What would you tell them?

Supplementary Reading 13

Heather Timmons, "For An Expert, Click Here," *Business Week*, May 15, 2000, pp. 184, 186.

For An Expert, Click Here

They're the Web children of talk radio's investor call-in programs: online sites that offer free or low-cost personalized advice on taxes, investments, and financial planning. If you're financially savvy, these online advisers can help you make decisions without a trip to the accountant, attorney, or broker.

At Quicken.com, free message boards on personal finance are patrolled by prescreened moderators. Paid a nominal hourly rate, they start discussions and offer answers to questions on anything from saving for college to capital-gains taxes. Brian Borawski, a certified public accountant in Detroit who has been a Quicken moderator for a year, says he signed on because he was thinking of starting his own practice and thought he might drum up some business. He has taken a corporate job since joining Quicken. But he says he has stuck with the site because it "keeps me on my toes." In one posting entitled "My granddad is a sugar daddy now," one person asks what could happen to his grandfather's estate now that he's remarried to a woman 25 years his junior. A Quicken moderator with the handle QcomMiriam tells him that as long as his grandfather has not remade his will since his remarriage, his estate most likely will go to his offspring.

If message boards aren't your style, Errold Moody Jr., a financial planner and former University of California professor, has set up a virtual library and free advice service. At www.efmoody.com, you'll find around 1,000 pages of financial information, links, financial quizzes, and investment calculators, sprinkled with heavily opinionated advice to consumers. "There never has been, nor is there currently, any reason for ever buying an investment or insurance at a bank," he writes in one essay. Moody, who says he "doesn't think much of most financial planners," set up the site to "point people in the right direction" and "make them read and think." The ex-professor answers specific e-mailed questions on 401(k)s and other financial topics. But he declines to give specific investment recommendations unless you become a paying customer of his financial-planning practice. "I won't give investment advice to anyone I don't know," he says.

E-mail is also at the heart of Expertcentral.com, where nearly 700 finance experts are available, and answers are provided overnight. Users rate the experts' answers on a scale of one to five, and the site has 6,300 more professionals advising on everything from pit bulls to prostate cancer.

Specific questions are answered for free—though responses may differ if you ask more than one expert. I asked three-top-rated advisers: "What's a safe five-year investment that can be cashed out at the end for a home down payment?" One recommended a Janus or Fidelity stock-mutual fund, the second a stock-and-bond fund, and the third suggested savings bonds. And each one provided detailed reasons. If you want more complicated advice, say, on writing a will, Expertcentral's advisers may charge you a fee. But the charge generally will be lower what they would charge clients in person.

Expertcentral CEO Greg Schmergel, a former Bain & Co. strategy consultant, says some of his online experts have signed up to gain exposure for their businesses. But a "surprising" number sign on for "purely altruistic reasons," such as a retired Internal Revenue Service agent who now gives tax advice. Although the site screens experts' resumes, it doesn't do more thorough background checks.

As with any planner or accountant, there's always a risk that you could get the wrong advice. To reassure questioners that they're talking to a professional, most of the advisers at Expertcentral and Quicken provide real names and a summary of their professional experience. But will sites like these ultimately reduce the need for in-person financial consulting? Not necessarily, says Jeanne A. Robinson, a Doylestown (Pa.) certified financial planner. She says that with "so much information out there," some clients still need help sorting it out. But for anyone who is past the sorting-out stage, these sites can cut down on the need to pick up the phone or get in the car. And they're a lot easier on your wallet.

Heather Timmons

Free Advice from Knowledgeable Folks

SITE (WWW)	WHAT IT OFFERS	FOUNDER'S PHILOSOPHY
expert-central.com	700 certified financial planners and accountants answer questions via e-mail	"We want to give users direct, specific answers"
efmoody.com	1,000 pages of info and advice from a former professor at the Univ. of Calif.	"I'm trying to get people to read and think"
quicken.com	Message board for financial and tax advice staffed by many pros	"We're providing general financial advice"

Study Questions

1. Many people believe that "you get what you pay for." With that fact in mind, would you consult a Web site that offers free personal finance advice? Explain your answer.

2. What type of questions would you ask an online personal finance expert?

3. What type of questions would you want to discuss in person with a financial planner?

14 INVESTING IN STOCKS

Chapter Overview

Initially, this chapter describes both common and preferred stock as investment alternatives. We discuss the topics of why corporations sell common stocks, and why investors purchase those stocks. Next, we examine the major differences between common stock and preferred stock. We also describe the cumulative, participation, and conversion features that can make a preferred stock a more attractive investment. Methods that investors can use to evaluate stock investments are presented. The steps involved in buying and selling stocks are described. We also provide an overview of security regulation at the state and federal levels. Then we explain the long-term techniques of buy and hold, dollar cost averaging, direct investment, and dividend reinvestment plans. Also, the speculative techniques of selling short, margin transactions, and stock options are discussed.

Learning Objectives

After studying this chapter, you will be able to:

Obj. 1 Identify the most important features of common stock.

Obj. 2 Discuss the most important features of preferred stock.

Obj. 3 Explain how you can evaluate stock investments.

Obj. 4 Describe how stocks are bought and sold.

Obj. 5 Explain the traditional trading techniques used by long-term and short-term speculators.

Key Terms

account executive
annualized holding period yield
bear market
beta
blue-chip stock
book value
bull market
callable preferred stock
capitalization
churning
cumulative preferred stock
current yield
cyclical stock
defensive stock
direct investment plan
discretionary order
dividend reinvestment plan
dollar cost averaging
earnings per share
efficient market theory
fundamental theory
growth stock
income stock
initial public offering (IPO)
investment bank
large-cap stock
limit order
margin
market order
Nasdaq
odd lot
option

over-the-counter (OTC) market
par value
penny stock
preemptive right
price-earnings ratio
primary market
proxy
record date
round lot
secondary market
securities
securities exchange
selling short
small-cap stock
specialist
stock split
stop order
technical theory
total return

Pretest

True-False

T 1. (Obj. 1) A public corporation is a corporation whose stock is traded openly in stock markets and may be purchased by any individual.

T 2. (Obj. 1) The record date is the date when a stockholder must be registered on the corporation's books in order to receive dividends.

F 3. (Obj. 2) Common stockholders receive cash dividends before preferred stockholders are paid cash dividends.

F 4. (Obj. 2) Cumulative preferred stock is preferred stock that can be exchanged, at the stockholder's option, for a specified number of shares of common stock.

F 5. (Obj. 3) *The Wall Street Journal* is published weekly.

T 6. (Obj. 3) An income stock is a stock that pays higher than average dividends.

F 7. (Obj. 4) A market order is a request that a stock be bought or sold at a specified price.

T 8. (Obj. 4) For stock transactions, the commission charged is based on the number of shares transacted and the value of those shares.

F 9. (Obj. 5) Dollar-cost averaging is a short-term investment technique.

T 10. (Obj. 5) Selling short is selling stock that has been borrowed from a stockbroker and must be replaced at a later date.

Self-Guided Study Questions

Obj. 1

Common Stock (p. 441)

1. In your own words, define the term securities.

Investments

2. What are the long-term returns for stocks, corporate bonds, and U.S. treasury bills?

Why Corporations Issue Common Stock (p. 442)

3. What are the two classifications of corporations?

2 common + preferred

4. What are two reasons why corporations sell common stock?

① Don't have to pay dividends

②

5. What is the difference between a proxy and a preemptive right?

6. What do stockholders vote on?

Why Investors Purchase Common Stock (p. 443)

7. What are three reasons why investors purchase common stock?

8. Why is the record date important?

9. Why do corporations split their stock?

Obj. 2

Preferred Stock (p. 447)

10. What is the most important priority that an investor in preferred stock enjoys?

11. How is the dividend on preferred stock determined?

12. Why do corporations issue callable preferred stock?

The Cumulative Feature of Preferred Stock (p. 448)

13. What is the advantage for the investor of purchasing cumulative preferred stock?

The Participation Feature of Preferred Stock (p. 448)

14. Why would investors purchase preferred stock with a participation feature?

The Conversion Feature of Preferred Stock (p. 448)

15. Why would investors purchase convertible preferred stock?

Obj. 3

Evaluation of a Stock Issue (p. 449)

16. What are the most available sources of investment information?

17. How often are *The Wall Street Journal* and *Barron's* published?

Classification of Stock Investments (p. 449)

18. What is a blue-chip stock?

19. What is an income stock?

20. What is a growth stock?

21. What is a cyclical stock?

22. What is a defensive stock?

23. What is a large-cap stock?

24. In your own words, define capitalization.

25. What is a small-cap stock?

26. What is a penny stock?

How to Read the Financial Section of the Newspaper (p. 450)

27. How are stocks listed in the newspaper?

28. What do the letters "pf" indicate?

The Internet (p. 451)

29. What type of information is available on a corporation's home page?

30. What type of information is available on Web sites like Yahoo and other search engines?

31. Name three professional advisory services that provide information on stocks to Internet users.

Stock Advisory Services (p. 453)

32. What type of information is provided by investor services like Standard & Poor's, Value Line, and Moody's?

Corporate News (p. 455)

33. What type of information is contained in a corporation's prospectus? In an annual report?

34. How can you obtain a corporation's annual report?

35. Name some business and personal finance magazines that could help you evaluate a corporation and its stock issues.

Factors that Influence the Price of a Stock (p. 457)

36. What is the difference between a bull market and a bear market?

37. How would you define book value?

38. What is the formula for calculating current yield?

39. How do you calculate the total return for a stock investment?

40. What does the annualized holding period yield calculation measure?

41. Why would an investor want to know the amount for earnings per share?

42. How do you calculate earnings per share?

43. What is the price-earnings ratio?

44. Why would an investor be concerned with the beta for a specific stock?

45. What is the fundamental theory of investment?

46. What is the technical theory of investing in stocks?

47. What is the efficient market theory?

Obj. 4

Buying and Selling Stocks (p. 462)

48. What is the difference between the primary market and the secondary market for stocks?

49. What is the role of an investment bank?

50. In your own words, define IPO.

Primary Market for Stocks (p. 462)

51. How would you sell $100 million worth of common stocks or preferred stocks if you were a financial manager for a large corporation?

Secondary Market for Stocks (p. 463)

52. What is a securities exchange?

53. What does a specialist do?

54. Before a corporation is approved for listing on the New York Stock Exchange, what five conditions must be met?

55. How does the over-the-counter market differ from a securities exchange?

56. How is an order to buy or sell stock executed in the Nasdaq market?

Brokerage Firms and Account Executives (p. 465)

57. What is churning?

58. If you wanted to buy or sell stocks, would you use a full-service or discount brokerage firm? Explain your answer.

59. What is the difference between a market order, a limit order, a stop order, and a discretionary order?

60. What steps are required to buy or sell stock on an organized exchange?

61. In what ways could a computer help you invest in stock?

62. How are commissions for stock transactions determined?

63. What is the difference between a round lot and an odd lot?

64. Why does a full-service broker charge more commission than a discount broker?

Securities Regulation (p. 470)

65. What is the purpose of state securities legislation?

66. What is the purpose of the Securities Act of 1933?

67. What is the purpose of the Securities Exchange Act of 1934?

68. What is the purpose of the following federal acts?

    a. The Maloney Act of 1938

    b. The Investment Company Act of 1940

    c. The Investment Advisers Act of 1940

    d. The Federal Securities Act of 1964

    e. The Securities Investor Protection Act of 1970

    f. The Securities Acts Amendments of 1975

    g. The Insider Trading Sanctions Act of 1984

    h. The Insider Trading Act of 1988

    i. The Financial Services Modernization Act of 1999

Obj. 5

Long-Term and Short-Term Investment Strategies (p. 471)

Long-Term Techniques (p. 471)

69. What is the difference between a long-term investment and a speculative investment?

70. In what three ways could an investor profit by using a buy and hold technique?

71. What usually happens to the value of a stock when a stock split occurs?

72. How would you describe dollar cost averaging?

73. What is a direct investment plan? How does it differ from a dividend reinvestment plan?

Short-Term Techniques (p. 472)

Buying Stock on Margin (p. 472)

74. Why would an investor buy stock on margin?

75. When an investor purchases stock on margin, what is the danger?

Selling Short (p. 474)

76. Why would an investor use the selling short investment technique?

77. How could an investor lose money using the selling short technique?

Trading in Options (p. 474)

78. Why would an investor use options?

Post Test

Completion

1. (Obj. 1) A(n) Proxy is a legal form that lists the issues to be decided in a stockholders' meeting and requests that stockholders transfer their voting rights to some individual or individuals.
2. (Obj. 1) A(n) Stock Split is a procedure in which the shares of common stock owned by existing stockholders are divided into a larger number of shares.
3. (Obj. 2) Cumulative preferred stock is stock that a corporation may exchange, at its option, for a specified amount of money.
4. (Obj. 3) A(n) defensive stock is a stock that remains stable during declines in the economy.
5. (Obj. 3) The ______________-____________ ratio is the price of a share of stock divided by the corporation's earnings per share of stock outstanding over the last 12 months.
6. (Obj. 3) The Fundamental theory is based on the assumption that a stock's intrinsic or real value is determined by the future earnings of the company.
7. (Obj. 4) A(n) __________________ ________________ is a marketplace where member brokers who are representing investors meet to buy and sell securities.
8. (Obj. 4) A(n) account executive, or stockbroker, is a licensed individual who buys or sells securities for his or her clients.
9. (Obj. 5) A(n) _______________ ______________ plan allows stockholders to purchase stock directly from a corporation without having to use an account executive or a brokerage firm.
10. (Obj. 5) A(n) _______________ gives an investor the right to buy or sell shares of a stock at a predetermined price during a specified period of time.

Multiple Choice

D 1. (Obj. 1) Corporations issue common stock because
A. it is a form of equity financing.
B. dividends are not mandatory.
C. the money obtained from this type of financing does not have to be paid.
D. All of the above.

C 2. (Obj. 2) A preferred stock issue whose unpaid dividends accumulate and must be paid before any cash dividend is paid to the common stockholders is called ______________ preferred stock.
A. callable
B. cumulative
C. convertible
D. participating

B 3. (Obj. 2) A preferred stock issue that allows preferred stockholders to share in the corporation's earnings is called ______________ preferred stock.
A. callable
B. cumulative
C. convertible
D. participating

_____ 4. (Obj. 3) A stock issued by a corporation that has the potential to earn above average profits when compared to other firms in the economy is called a(n) ______________ stock.
A. blue-chip
B. income
C. growth
D. cyclical

A 5. (Obj. 3) A theory based on the assumption that stock price movements are purely random is called the ______________ theory.
A. fundamental
B. technical
C. efficient market
D. primary

B 6. (Obj. 4) A market for existing financial securities that are currently traded between investors is called the ______________ market.
A. primary
B. secondary
C. efficient
D. fundamental

B 7. (Obj. 4) The largest securities exchange in the U.S. is the ________ Exchange.
A. American
B. New York Stock
C. Boston
D. Midwest

______ 8. (Obj. 4) A request that a stock be purchased or sold at the current market price is called a ____________ order.
A. market
B. limit
C. stop
D. restricted

______ 9. (Obj. 4) The first state law regulating securities was enacted in 1911 by
A. Ohio.
B. New York.
C. New Jersey.
D. Kansas.

______ 10. (Obj. 5) An investor who thinks the market price of a stock will decrease during a short period of time may decide to use the ____________ technique.
A. buy
B. dividend reinvestment
C. selling short
D. the margin

Problems, Applications, and Cases

1. Choose one stock that is listed on the New York Stock Exchange (NYSE) or Nasdaq. Then go to the library or the Internet to find the necessary information to complete the form below. *Standard & Poor's Register of Corporations, Directors and Executives*, *Value Line,* and *Moody's Handbook of Common Stocks* should be helpful.

Company Information Sheet

Name	Industry
Products and services	
Location of headquarters	
Incorporation date	State where incorporated
Number of stockholders	
Subsidiaries	
Would this company be a good investment at this time?	
Why?	
What have you learned about this company?	

2. Assume that you own 125 shares of common stock in American Chemical Company. You receive a copy of the firm's annual report. After examining the financial statements that were included in the annual report, you determine that the firm has reported assets of $17 million, liabilities of $6 million, after-tax earnings of $4 million, and 1,250,000 outstanding shares of common stock.

   a. Calculate the book value of a share of American Chemical.

   b. Calculate the earnings per share of American Chemical's common stock.

   c. Assuming that a share of American Chemical's common stock has a market value of $46, what is the firm's price-earnings ratio?

3. Assume that you purchased 100 shares of General Retail Store's common stock for $88 a share, that you received an annual dividend of $3 per share, and that you sold your General Retail stock for $96 a share at the end of two years. (Ignore commissions for this problem.)

   a. At the end of the two-year period, calculate the current yield for your General Retail common stock.

   b. Calculate the total return on your General Retail investment.

   c. Calculate the annualized holding period yield of your General Retail investment at the end of two years.

4. You notice that Watson Plastics, Inc. has a price-earnings ratio of 20 to 1, while the average price-earnings ratio for firms in the same industry is 14 to 1. Given these facts, is Watson Plastics a good investment? Why?

Supplementary Case 14-1: Choosing an Account Executive

Topic: Brokerage Firms and Account Executives

Text Reference: pp. 447-449

A good investment program should start before you choose an account executive. First of all, you must establish financial goals and objectives to meet your individual needs. Then you must accumulate enough money to get started. Most authorities suggest maintaining an emergency fund, equal to at least three months' living expenses. Once you have accumulated funds in excess of the emergency fund, it's time to decide if you want to use a full-service or discount brokerage firm or trade stocks online.

If You Choose a Full-Service Brokerage Firm, You Will Need To Choose an Account Executive

Many investors begin their search for an account executive by asking friends or business associates for recommendations. This is a logical starting point, but remember that some account executives are conservative, while others are risk oriented. It is quite common for investors to test an account executive's advice over a period of time. Then, if the account executive's track record is acceptable, his or her investment suggestions can be taken more seriously. At this point, most investors begin to rely more heavily on the account executive's advice and less on their own intuition and research.

Why You Need an Account Executive

Basically, your account executive sees that your order to buy or sell stocks, bonds, or other securities is correctly executed. Your account executive should also be able to provide you with current financial information about the stocks, bonds, mutual funds, or other securities in which you are interested. There are no guarantees that the securities you buy on the basis of your account executive's recommendations will increase in value, but he or she should help in the evaluation process.

A Final Word of Caution

Before choosing an account executive, you should ask a few questions to determine whether you and the account executive are on the same wavelength with regard to investment goals and objectives. Don't be surprised if your account executive wants to ask you a few questions too. In order to provide better service, he or she must know what type of investment program you want to establish. If, after a reasonable period of time, you become dissatisfied with your investment program, do not hesitate to discuss your dissatisfaction with the account executive. You may even find it necessary to choose another account executive if your dissatisfaction continues.

Case Questions

1. Would you use a full-service or discount brokerage firm or trade stocks online? Explain your answer.
2. Many investors "just choose an account executive" and let that person make all the decisions. Why can this approach lead to problems for the investor?
3. Assume that you are in the process of choosing an account executive. Prepare a list of ten questions that you could use to interview a stockbroker or account executive.
4. As part of the interview process, the account executive would probably want to ask you some questions before completing the first transaction. What type of information would an account executive want to know about you?

Supplementary Case 14-2: Research Information for Stock Investments

Topic: Evaluation of a Stock Issue

Text Reference: pp. 449-462

In Chapter 14, (Investing in Stocks), we have stressed the importance of evaluating potential investments. Now it's your turn to try your skill at evaluating a potential investment in The Coca-Cola Company. Assume that you could invest $20,000 in common stock of this company. To help you evaluate this potential investment carefully examine the research reports available in your college library or public library provided in *Moody's Handbook of Common Stock, Standard and Poor's Stock Guide, Value Line*, or information available on the firm's home page on the Internet.

Case Questions

1. Based on your research, would you buy Coca-Cola common stock? Justify your answer.
2. What other investment information would you need to evaluate this company's stock? Where would you obtain this information?
3. On Monday, June 5, 2000, Coca-Cola's common stock was selling for $58 a share. Using a recent newspaper or the Internet, determine the current price of a share of Coca-Cola common stock. Based on this information, would your investment have been profitable if you had purchased Coca-Cola stock for $58 a share? Why or why not?

Supplementary Reading 14

Christopher Farrell, "Online or Off, the Rules Are the Same," *Business Week*, May 22, 2000, pp. 148-149.

Online or Off, the Rules Are the Same

Low-cost online trading has opened the world of equities to millions of people who might not have otherwise considered playing the stock market. More than half of American households now own stocks, and about one-fifth of them made their first investment during the past four years, when online trading became a national pastime. But investors haven't always jumped in with sufficient knowledge. "The lure of online trading seems to be that here is something you can do with no skill, no knowledge, and yet you can make tons of money," says Meir Statman, chairman of the finance department at Santa Clara University's Leavy School of Business.

But the past few weeks have been sobering. Nasdaq is down a sickening 31% from its March high. Thousands of dot-com companies are losing altitude fast. Even blue-chip Lucent Technologies, America's most widely held stock, is down about 17% since early March. True, the stock market has usually rallied after its steepest declines. But after several years of historically low volatility, choppy markets have returned with a vengeance in recent months. "The technology to do trades online, combined with so many inexperienced investors at the leading edge of market activity, underscores the dangerous nature of the market bazaar today, says James Griffin, a senior vice-president and corporate economist at Aeltus Investment Management in Hartford.

If you're a recent convert to online investing, you may have learned your first real object lessons. No one is saying you should shut down that E*Trade account—heck, even Merrill Lynch and its full-service rivals are rolling out online-trading accounts these days. But if the past few months can teach us online traders anything at all, it's that we need to remember some of the basic rules of investing—the ones that long predate the Web:

• Frequent trading can be costly. The average online transaction fee was $23.35 in March, according to Stephen Franco, an equity analyst at U.S. Bancorp Piper Jaffray. That may be cheap compared with traditional broker fees, but it adds up quickly even if you're trading as infrequently as five times a week. Then, too, there are income taxes triggered by profits from active trading. On a quick trade, you'll pay as much as 39.6% of your profits to Uncle Sam. Buy and hold for just one year, however, and you'll qualify for the lower capital-gains rate of 20%. "Very active trading will be very unlikely to beat a buy-and-hold strategy," says Burton Malkiel, the Princeton University finance economist and author of *A Random Walk Down Wall Street* (Norton, $29.95 cloth, $15.95 paper).

• Frequent trading may be hazardous to your wealth. The ease of trading with the click of a mouse tempts many people to do it more often. Yet it's tough to beat the market—that's certainly what seasoned hedge-fund operator Julian Robertson discovered recently.

Economists Brad Barber and Terrance Odean at the University of California at Davis studied the stock-trading behavior and investment performance of 1,607 investors who switched from phone-based to online trading from 1992 to 1995. The study, available at www.gsm.ucdavis.edu/~odean, found that individuals who made the switch traded more actively and more speculatively than before. And guess what? Their returns went from beating the market by an average of 2% to lagging it by more than three points annually.

•Buying stock with borrowed money can be perilous. Many investors who were caught up in the online-buying frenzy resorted to margin debt or borrowing money from their broker and using their investments as collateral. The level of margin debt surged to record levels over the past year, and profits from margin lending padded the earnings of online brokers such as E*Trade Group, Ameritrade, and TD Waterhouse Group.

When the market is going up, buying on margin lets you build your investment position quickly. But in volatile markets, you may be required to put up additional cash or securities to cover any losses. The brokerage firm can even dump your stock to meet a margin call, as many investors have learned to their chagrin. They should have read the fine print in their margin agreements that gave their brokers permission to sell them out. "The past several weeks have been a lesson in leverage when things go awry," says Henry Hu, a professor of banking and finance law at the University of Texas School of Law.

• Being in the right place at the right time doesn't mean you're a brilliant investor. Many of us attribute too much of our investing successes and failures to our own behavior. We feel smart when the market is going up, so we're tempted to trade more and take on riskier positions. We feel stupid when the market is going down, and less sure about our stock picks.

• Know what you are buying. Unless you enjoy gambling on a hunch, you need to delve into fundamentals and try to answer the question: "What is this stock worth?" This means not automatically latching onto a stock simply because it's going up. Serious, successful investors still want to know about profitability, management strategy, capital investments, and market share.

If you don't have the inclination to educate yourself about individual stock picks, stick with index funds. At least you'll match the market's performance and pay razor-thin fees. Even Warren Buffett, the renowned stock-picker, advocates index funds for anyone unwilling to delve deeply into the economics of a particular business. "By periodically investing in an index fund, for example, the know-nothing investor can actually outperform most investment professionals," wrote the Wizard of Omaha in Berkshire Hathaway's 1993 annual report. "Paradoxically, when 'dumb' money acknowledges its limitations, it ceases to be dumb."

• Use the Internet wisely. Bulletin boards and chat rooms with their illusion of easy money and susceptibility to manipulation, are notorious sources of bad information. At least try to verify information from them before you act on it. You may be better off at the sites of major mutual-fund companies, brokerage houses, business and finance publications, and academically oriented finance Web sites. All offer sophisticated insights into the markets, plus a vast array of educational tools.

• Manage your portfolio around the concept of risk. The trick is to mix and match major financial assets to create a well-diversified portfolio with the highest expected return for the amount of risk you are comfortable taking. The Internet offers plenty of tools to help you do that. "Figure out what you are trying to do, and then find an investment strategy to deal with it," says Griffin.

The online world allows individuals to participate in the stock market with unprecedented speed. But speed alone is no guarantee of success. Despite all the hoopla over day trading, there is still no evidence to suggest that trigger-happy traders will ever outperform investor who simply buy and hold.

Christopher Farrell

Study Questions

1. According to this article, more than half of American households now own stocks, and more than one-fifth of them made their first investment during the past four years. Why do you think stocks have become so popular?

2. Although the low commissions offered by online brokers are appealing, online trading is not for everyone. Describe the type of investor who can benefit from online trading?

3. From an investor's standpoint, what factors can help insure success when trading stocks online or by more traditional methods?

15 INVESTING IN BONDS

Chapter Overview

This chapter describes bonds as an investment alternative. Initially, we examine important characteristics that pertain to bond investments. Then, we discuss the topics of why corporations sell bonds and why investors buy those bonds. The differences between corporate and government bonds and the factors that investors use to evaluate bond investments are presented.

Learning Objectives

After studying this chapter, you will be able to:

Obj. 1 Describe the characteristics of corporate bonds.

Obj. 2 Discuss why corporations issue bonds.

Obj. 3 Explain why investors purchase corporate bonds.

Obj. 4 Discuss why federal, state, and local governments issue bonds and why investors purchase government bonds.

Obj. 5 Evaluate bonds when making an investment.

Key Terms

bearer bond
bond indenture
call feature
convertible bond
corporate bond
current yield
debenture
face value
general obligation bond
maturity date
mortgage bond
municipal bond
registered bond
registered coupon bond
revenue bond
serial bonds
sinking funds
subordinated debenture
trustee
yield
yield to maturity
zero-coupon bond

Pretest

True-False

_______ 1. (Obj. 1) The usual face value for a corporate bond is $5,000.

_______ 2. (Obj. 1) The trustee is an independent firm that acts as the bondholder's representative.

_______ 3. (Obj. 2) A debenture bond is a bond that is secured by various assets of the issuing corporation.

_______ 4. (Obj. 2) The conversion feature of a convertible bond allows investors to enjoy the low risk of a corporate bond, but also to take advantage of the speculative nature of common stock by exercising their right of conversion.

_______ 5. (Obj. 3) To collect interest on a registered coupon bond, bondholders must clip a coupon and then redeem it by following the procedures outlined by the issuer.

_______ 6. (Obj. 3) When a bond is selling for more than its face value, it is said to be selling at a priority price.

_______ 7. (Obj. 4) Treasury bills are issued in minimum units of $10,000, with maturities that range from 13 weeks to 52 weeks.

___T___ 8. (Obj. 4) The purchase price for Series EE Savings Bonds is one half of their maturity value.

___F___ 9. (Obj. 5) The highest bond rating assigned by Standard & Poor's is BBB.

_______ 10. (Obj. 6) The current yield is determined by dividing the dollar amount of annual dollar interest by its face value.

Self-Guided Study Questions

Obj. 1

Characteristics of Corporate Bonds (p. 483)

1. In your own words, how would you define a corporate bond?

2. What is the usual face value of a corporate bond?

3. What is the range of maturity dates for corporate bonds?

4. What is included in a bond indenture?

5. What does a trustee do?

Obj. 2

Why Corporations Sell Corporate Bonds (p. 485)

6. How does a corporate bond differ from common stock or preferred stock?

Types of Bonds (p. 486)

7. What is the difference between a debenture bond, a mortgage bond, and a subordinated debenture?

Convertible Bonds (p. 486)

8. How is a convertible bond different from a typical corporate bond?

9. Why would an investor purchase a convertible bond?

10. Why would a corporation issue convertible bonds?

Provisions for Repayment (p. 487)

11. Why would a corporation issue a bond that is callable?

12. How would you explain the two methods that corporations use to redeem a bond issue at maturity?

Obj. 3

Why Investors Purchase Corporate Bonds (p. 489)

13. What are the three reasons why investors purchase corporate bonds?

Interest Income (p. 489)

14. What is the annual interest amount for a corporate bond that has a face value of $1,000 and pays 7¼ percent interest a year?

15. What is the difference between a registered bond, a registered coupon bond, a bearer bond, and a zero-coupon bond?

16. What two factors should you consider when investing in zero-coupon bonds?

Dollar Appreciation of Bond Value (p. 490)

17. Explain why a bond's market value may be more or less than its face value.

18. As related to bonds, what do the terms premium and discount mean?

19. What is the formula for determining the approximate market value for a bond?

20. In addition to interest rates, what other factors account for increases and decreases in a bond's value?

Bond Repayment at Maturity (p. 490)

21. When you purchase a bond, what two options do you have?

A Typical Bond Transaction (p. 491)

22. In a bond transaction illustrated in Exhibit 15-3 on page 491, the investor experienced a total return of $1,251. In your own words, explain why the bondholder received $1,251.

23. If the company in this example—Borden, Inc.—had experienced financial problems before the bond's maturity, what would have happened to the value of this bond?

The Mechanics of a Bond Transaction (p. 491)

24. What steps are involved in a typical bond transaction?

25. What are the typical commissions for bond transactions?

Obj. 4

Government Bonds and Debt Securities (p. 493)

Treasury Bills, Notes, and Bonds (p. 493)

26. Why does the federal government sell bonds and securities?

27. What is the difference between a treasury bill, a treasury note, and treasury bond?

28. How does a Series EE savings bond differ from a Series HH bond?

Federal Agency Debt Issues (p. 495)

29. Which federal agencies issue bonds in order to obtain financing?

State and Local Government Securities (p. 495)

30. How would you describe the difference between a general obligation bond and a revenue bond?

31. Why must an investor evaluate an investment in a specific municipal bond?

32. Why are municipal bonds attractive investments for investors in a higher income tax bracket?

33. What is the formula for determining the tax-equivalent yield on a municipal bond?

Obj. 5

The Decision to Buy or Sell Bonds (p. 497)

How to Read the Bond Section of a Newspaper (p. 498)

34. In bond quotations, prices are given as a percentage of the face value, which is usually $1,000. With this fact in mind, what is the selling price for a bond that is quoted at 90?

35. For a government bond, what is the difference between the bid price and the asked price?

Annual Reports (p. 499)

36. Why must bondholders be concerned about the financial health of a corporation or government unit that issues bonds?

37. How can you obtain an annual report from a corporation that has issued bonds?

The Internet (p. 499)

38. How could you obtain financial information about bonds by accessing the Internet?

Bond Ratings (p. 501)

39. How important are the bond ratings provided by Moody's and Standard & Poor's?

40. As illustrated in Exhibit 15-6, what is the highest rating according to Moody's? According to Standard & Poor's?

41. As illustrated in Exhibit 15-6, what is the lowest rating according to Moody's? According to Standard & Poor's?

Bond Yield Calculations (p. 502)

42. How do you calculate the current yield for a bond?

43. What factors does the yield to maturity take into account?

44. How do you calculate the yield to maturity?

Other Sources of Information (p. 503)

45. What two additional sources of information can you use to evaluate a bond investment?

Post Test

Completion

1. (Obj. 1) A(n) ____________ ____________ is a corporation's written pledge that it will repay a specified amount of money, with interest.
2. (Obj. 1) The ____________ ____________ of a corporate bond is the date on which the corporation is to repay the borrowed money.
3. (Obj. 2) A(n) ____________ ____________ is a bond that gives bondholders a claim secondary to that of other debenture bondholders with respect to both income and assets.
4. (Obj. 2) A fund to which deposits are made each year for the purpose of redeeming a bond issue is called a(n) ____________ fund.
5. (Obj. 3) Investors purchase corporate bonds for three reasons: (1) ____________ income, (2) possible increase in ____________, and (3) ____________ at maturity.
6. (Obj. 3) A(n) ____________ bond is a bond whose ownership is registered by the issuing company.

7. (Obj. 4) Treasury bonds are issued in minimum units of ____________ with 10- to 30-year maturities.
8. (Obj. 4) A bond backed by the full faith, credit, and unlimited taxing power of the government that issued it is called a(n) ____________ ____________ bond.
9. (Obj. 5) The first price quotation, or the ____________ price, is the highest price that a dealer is willing to pay for a government security.
10. (Obj. 5) A bond's current yield is determined by dividing the dollar amount of annual interest by its current ____________ value.

Multiple Choice

______ 1. (Obj. 1) The legal document that details all of the conditions relating to a bond issue is called a
A. trustee agreement.
B. bond indenture.
C. subordinated agreement.
D. mortgage agreement.

______ 2. (Obj. 2) A bond that is backed only by the reputation of the issuing corporation is called a
A. debenture bond.
B. mortgage bond.
C. subordinated debenture.
D. convertible bond.

______ 3. (Obj. 2) Bonds of a single issue that mature on different dates are called
A. trust bonds.
B. convertible bonds.
C. indentured bonds.
D. serial bonds.

______ 4. (Obj. 3) What is the annual interest for a $1,000 bond that pays 8 ½ percent?
A. $75
B. $85
C. $90
D. $117

______ 5. (Obj. 3) Assume that you purchase a corporate bond that pays 8 ¼ percent interest based on a face value of $1,000. Also assume that new corporate bond issues of comparable quality are currently paying 11 percent. What is the approximate market value for the XYZ corporate bond?
A. $750
B. $800
C. $825
D. $1,000
E. $1,100

______ 6. (Obj. 4) A security issued by the federal government in $1,000 units with a maturity of more than 1 year but not more than 10 years is called a
   A. treasury bond.
   B. treasury note.
   C. savings note.
   D. savings bond.

______ 7. (Obj. 4) A bond that is repaid from the income generated by the project it is designed to finance is called a
   A. general obligation bond.
   B. revenue bond.
   C. certified bond.
   D. coordinated bond.

______ 8. (Obj. 5) A corporate bond that has a face value of $1,000 and is quoted as 85 ½ in *The Wall Street Journal* has a selling price of
   A. $85 ½
   B. $85.50
   C. $850.00
   D. $855.00
   E. $1,000

______ 9. (Obj. 5) For municipal bonds maturing in three years or less, the highest rating given by Standard & Poor's is
   A. SP-1.
   B. SP-2.
   C. SP-3.
   D. SP-4.
   E. Municipal bonds with short maturities are not rated by Standard & Poor's because they are considered risk-free.

______ 10. (Obj. 6) What is the current yield for a bond that pays $75 annual interest and has a market value of $900?
   A. 7.5 percent
   B. 7.75 percent
   C. 8.33 percent
   D. 10 percent
   E. With the above information, it is impossible to determine the current yield.

Problems, Applications, and Cases

1. To determine the quality and risk associated with bond issues, investors rely on the bond ratings provided by Moody's Investor's Service and Standard & Poor's Corporation. For each bond rating listed below, provide a brief description of the type of bonds included in that category.

	Rating	*Description*
Standard & Poor's	AAA	
Standard & Poor's	BBB	
Standard & Poor's	B	
Standard & Poor's	CCC	
Standard & Poor's	D	
Moody's	Aaa	
Moody's	A	
Moody's	Caa	
Moody's	C	

2. One of the most important features of municipal securities is that they may be exempt from federal taxes. When evaluating this type of investment, it is necessary to determine the taxable equivalent yield. Using the formula presented in this chapter, determine the taxable equivalent yield for the problems below.

Tax-exempt yield	*Applicable tax rate*	*Taxable equivalent yield*
5%	28%	a. ______________
6%	28%	b. ______________
6.5%	28%	c. ______________
7.5%	28%	d. ______________
8%	28%	e. ______________

3. Using a recent newspaper or the Internet, fill in the following table for selected corporate bonds.

Company	***Interest rate***	***Maturity date***	***Current yield***	***Volume***	***Close price***	***Net change***
a. ATT 7 ½ 06						
b. Cleveland El 8 ¾ 05						
c. IBM 7 ½ 13						
d. Zenith 6 ¼ 11						

4. Choose one of the corporate bonds listed in Exercise 3. Then use Moody's Industrial Manuals (available at your college or public library) to answer the following questions on this bond issue.
   a. What is Moody's rating for this issue?
   b. What is the purpose of this issue?
   c. Does the issue have a call provision?
   d. Who is the trustee for the issue?
   e. What collateral, if any, has been pledged as security for the issue?
   f. Based on the information you have obtained, would the bond be a good investment for you? Why?

5. The yield to maturity is a yield calculation that takes into account the relationship among a bonds' maturity value, the time to maturity, the current price, and the dollar amount of interest. For the problems below, determine the yield to maturity.

Face value (par value)	***Coupon interest rate***	***Annual interest***	***Time to maturity***	***Current market value (price)***	***Yield to maturity***
$1,000	6%	$60	5 years	$900	a. _________
$1,000	7%	$70	5 years	$1,100	b. _________
$1,000	8%	$80	8 years	$800	c. _________
$1,000	9%	$90	8 years	$900	d. _________
$1,000	10%	$100	10 years	$700	e. _________

Supplementary Case 15-1: The ABCs of Bond Ratings

Topic: Bond Ratings

Text Reference: pp. 501-502

Are bonds safer than common or preferred stock? The answer to that question depends on such factors as the conditions contained in the bond agreement and the likelihood of repayment at maturity. Most investors rely on two financial services, Standard & Poor's, to provide ratings for bonds. Standard & Poor's bond ratings range from AAA (highest) to D (the lowest). Moody's bond ratings range from Aaa (the highest) to C (the lowest). For most investors, a bond rated A or better is probably safe as a blue-chip stock, while a C-rated bond could be as risky as the most speculative stock.

Recently, a number of corporate bond issues whose Standard & Poor's ratings are lower than A have been sold in the bond market. The reasons for the lower ratings vary. A bond may have been assigned a low rating because the corporation that issued it has long-term debt that is too high or earnings that are too low, or because changing economic conditions may make payment of bond interest or repayment of the bond principal doubtful. Whatever the reasons, the corporations issuing the low-rated bonds had to increase the interest rate on them in order to attract purchasers. As a result, the bonds offer extremely attractive current yields to investors who are willing to take a chance. For example, a $1,000 corporate bond issued by Chiquita Brands is paying 11.875 percent interest until its maturity in 2003. The current market price of this bond is $1,030 which means that the current yield is 11.5 percent. Standard & Poor's rates the bond B.

Case Questions

1. How important are the Moody's and Standard & Poor's bond ratings? What does the Standard & Poor's B rating mean?
2. An 11.5 percent current yield is at least 3 to 4 percent higher than the current yield of more conservative corporate bond issues. Is this additional interest worth the added risks involved in purchasing a bond with lower ratings such as the Chiquita Brands bond?
3. As the maturity date of the Chiquita Brands bond approaches, what should happen to the price of this bond? Why?
4. What other information would you need to evaluate the Chiquita Brands bond? Where would you get this information?

Supplementary Case 15-2: Are Higher Yields on Corporate Bonds Worth the Added Risk

Topic: Why Investors Purchase Corporate Bonds

Text Reference: pp. 489-493

The days of investors putting their money in a certificate of deposit and receiving 10 percent year after year are over. In fact, since the early 1990s, investors in certificates of deposit have seen their returns bottom out at between 3 and 5 percent. These low returns, the lowest in over 30 years, have forced many investors like Barbara Haynes to look for ways to squeeze additional income from their investment portfolios.

Back in 1993, Barbara, then 36 and single, was injured in an automobile accident. After a lengthy court battle with the driver of the other car and his insurance company, Barbara won a $575,000 settlement, of which she paid almost $150,000 to her attorney. She invested the remaining $425,000 in long-term certificates of deposit that earned an average of 8 percent, or about $34,000 a year, over the last seven years. But now the highest CD interest rates she could find are around 6 percent. Faced with the prospects of lower income, she decided it was time to explore other investment options. To accomplish the goal, she made an appointment with Jim Mathis, an account executive with the brokerage firm of Paine Webber.

According to Jim, there were ways to increase the yield on Barbara's investment portfolio, but she would have to assume greater risks. After considering different alternatives, both decided that one option, investing in high-quality corporate bonds with maturities no shorter than 10 years, could increase her income with only a slight to moderate increase in risk. Jim went on to say that the bond market had many high-quality corporate bonds with current yields between 7 and 9 percent. At the conclusion of the meeting, he suggested that she might evaluate bonds issued by American Telephone and Telegraph (AT&T).

A trip to the library yielded some useful information about AT&T bonds. Barbara discovered that the company had many different bond issues, not just one. Most of the bonds were paying between 4 and 5 percent, but some were paying as much as 7 to 9 percent. Since her goal was to increase her investment income, Barbara decided to research the bond with the highest yield. This particular AT&T bond had a maturity value of $1,000, matured in 2031, and paid 8 percent interest each year. Because the bond was currently selling at a discounted price of $975, the current yield had increased to 8.8 percent. That was almost three percentage points higher than her bank was offering on CD renewals. Although Barbara liked the higher income the AT&T bond offered, she wanted to know more about the risks before investing her nest egg.

Case Questions

1. During the year 2000, investors were forced to look for ways to squeeze additional income form their investment portfolios. Do you think investing in corporate bonds is the best way to increase income? Why or why not?

2. What other information could Barbara Haynes use to evaluate this bond issue? Where would you get this information?
3. If you were Barbara Haynes, would you purchase AT&T bonds? If so, how much of her $425,000 nest egg would you invest in this AT&T bond?

Supplementary Reading 15

Joan Warner, "Bond Investors Go to Extremes, Good values lie at both ends of the yield curve," *Business Week*, March 20, 2000, pp. 142+.

Bond Investors Go to Extremes

Good values lie at both ends of the yield curve

Many bond investors are still licking their wounds after one of the worst years in recent memory. Now they may be staring at a window of exceptional opportunity. Federal Reserve Chairman Alan Greenspan is raising short-term interest rates to cool a torrid economy. Normally, that pushes up long-term rates, too. But because the government is using its budget surpluses to buy back long-term debt, yields on 10- to 30-year Treasury bonds are heading south instead. This phenomenon calls for new and super-selective strategies.

The ideal bond play offers both high income and capital appreciation. And fixed-income experts these days are finding that the best values lie at the extremes of the yield curve. So they recommend structuring your portfolio like a barbell—loading up on short-term bonds on one end and long-term debt on the other. Ken Volpert, a senior portfolio manager who oversees $17 billion in Vanguard Group bond index funds, explains that in terms of total return, a barbell portfolio will beat one concentrated in intermediate debt. That's because when the yield curve is flattening, the yield at "the middle is going to go up more than a blend of the ends." As intermediate yields rise, of course, the bonds' price will fall.

So which bonds do you pick? At the far end of the curve, good old 30-year Treasuries are looking like a better buy every day. You lock in a yield of around 6% from the safest issuer in the world. Meanwhile, as Washington keeps scarfing up these bonds, their value will rise. Volpert expects that because of their "scarcity premium," they'll appreciate more than long-term corporate bonds for several years. If 30-year government yields fall by a percentage point, to 5%, over the next 12 months, the 6% Treasuries you bought today for $5,000 will be worth $6,072.50, for a total return of 8.23%.

The falloff at the far end of the yield curve has created another opportunity: highly rated, tax-exempt, long-term municipal bonds. Like the federal government, the local entities that issue them are cutting back on debt. According to Randy Smolik, chief analyst at Municipal Market Data in Boston, muni borrowing in the first quarter is running about 35% below last year's levels. And on average, AAA munis are paying 96% of Treasury yields, compared with 87% a couple of years ago. The result: A high-grade, long-term muni can offer returns better than those from long Treasuries—without the tax liability. Assuming your tax bracket is 31%, such a muni returns as much as taxable bond yielding nearly 9%.

FINE ART. Short-term rates, meantime, look likely to keep rising, perhaps by 50 basis points in the next few months. But some short-term bonds may offer price appreciation even in the face of that. High-yield debt has been hammered in the last couple of years as investors have moved into tech stocks. So managers are finding value in corporate and municipal junk bonds. For individuals, the safest way to play this market is probably via bond mutual funds, since dissecting the risks and returns of specific issues is a fine art.

Besides being cheap, high-yield bonds have another plus in a barbell portfolio: diversity. Their performance tends to ignore what's happening with government interest rates, because their yields depend almost entirely on default risk. Says Brad Tank, director of fixed income and portfolio manager at Strong Funds in Milwaukee: "High-yield securities often demonstrate incredible insensitivity to what's going on in the Treasury market."

It's not that hard to narrow the junk field. One no-load choice that's diversified and has beat the odds in a tough environment is the Columbia High Yield Fund. With an average current yield of 8.51%, the fund boasts an annualized average three-year total return of 6.06% through Mar. 3. Manager Jeff Rippey's biggest holding is Unisys junk bonds paying 11.75%—and he is adding to his position.

Many short-term junk funds focus on munis—naturally, since local governments and agencies that need to raise quick cash often get below-investment-grade ratings for their debt. After months of neglect, "we're seeing really good demand from retail investors," says Wayne Godlin, whose $1.45 billion Van Kampen High-Yield Muni A fund in January won Morningstar's Fund of the Decade Award in its category. Godlin specializes in tax-free munis rated BB or lower, with average yields of 6.48%. He has packed his fund with such issues as Richmond (Va.) development bonds paying 8.75% and Alexandria (Va.) debt paying 6.375%.

Another fund attracting attention from value investors is Heartland Short-Duration High-Yield Muni, which wins the unusual description of "high return/low risk" by looking for rich tax-free income but balancing its junk bonds with slightly higher graded munis. Its managers like so-called lifecare bonds—from developers of retirement communities in Texas, for example—paying upward of 8%. The fund's .062% expense ratio makes it one of the better picks in the high-yield muni group, and its modest total return of 0.03% in 1999 beat the Lehman Brothers' Muni Index by more that three percentage points.

Aficionados of convertible bonds are sniffing value, too. Convertibles are relatively short-term investments by definition—most have three-year maturities. Typically issued by growth companies, these bonds allow investors to exchange them for stock. In return for an income stream from the debt, you give up some appreciation potential on the equity.

BACKSEAT NO LONGER. Like munis, convertibles took a backseat to stocks when the equity bulls were running their hardest. Now, demand is picking up. One top performer is the Pilgrim Convertible A fund, which gave its investors a 50.63% return in 1999. Its managers' strategy: Focus on bonds paying in the neighborhood of 6% from fast-growth media companies such as Qualcomm and MediaOne Group.

Of course, if you mainly look to short-term interest rates for yield, the simplest investments may be the most attractive. Regional commercial banks, ever eager for new customers, are taking advantage of the uptick in short-term rates to tickle savers' fancy. The latest wrinkle in marketing bank certificates of deposit is the online auction, in which banks let investors bid for CD rates. For example, Pittsburgh's PNC Bank is offering three-month CDs at www.pnc.com. Visitors plug in how much they want to buy and the lowest annual percentage rate they're willing to accept. The bank is currently setting 10% as the maximum yield. The lowest APR submitted wins—even if it's higher than the current 6.03% national average for three month CDs.

What happens to your strategy if the odd-shaped yield curve doesn't flatten any further? More experts are saying it's a good time to get back into bonds anyway. The Fed seems set on taking more wind out of the stock market's sails. And New Economy-type equities are so expensive that bonds represent good value by comparison. "Smart money now might want to take a few chips off the technology [stock] sector and reassign assets into the fixed-income market," says Van Kampen's Godlin. That's probably good advice even if you don't manage to make your holdings a perfectly shaped barbell.

By Joan Warner

Study Questions

1. Historically, stocks have been the investment of choice for most people, but now some investors are taking another look at bonds. What factors account for this renewed interest in bond investments?

2. Given the fact that the Federal Reserve is raising short-term interest rates and the Federal government is using budget surpluses to buy back long-term bonds, is this a good time to invest in bonds? If so, what type of bonds offer the most potential?

3. Today, you can purchase individual bonds or invest in a bond fund. What advantages does a bond fund offer when compared to purchasing individual bonds?

16 INVESTING IN MUTUAL FUNDS

Chapter Overview

This chapter examines the topic of mutual funds—an investment alternative chosen by individuals who pool their money to buy stocks, bonds, and other securities selected by professional managers who work for an investment company. In this chapter, we consider why individuals invest in mutual funds. We also look at the unique characteristics of different mutual fund investments. Then, we discuss how mutual funds are classified according to the investment objective of the fund. Finally, we consider different methods that investors can use to evaluate mutual funds and the methods of buying and selling shares in a mutual fund.

Learning Objectives

After studying this chapter, you will be able to:

Obj. 1 Describe the characteristics of mutual fund investments.

Obj. 2 Classify mutual funds by investment objective.

Obj. 3 Evaluate mutual funds for investment purposes.

Obj. 4 Describe how and why mutual funds are bought and sold.

Key Terms

capital gains distribution
closed-end fund
contingent deferred sales load
family of funds
income dividends
investment company
load fund
market timer
mutual fund
net asset value (NAV)
no-load fund
open-end fund
reinvestment plan
12b-1 fee

Pretest

True-False

T 1. (Obj. 1) The major reasons why investors purchase mutual funds are professional management and diversification.

F 2. (Obj. 1) A closed-end fund is a mutual fund whose shares are issued and redeemed by the investment company at the request of investors.

F 3. (Obj. 1) Current research indicates that load funds outperform no-load funds.

T 4. (Obj. 1) A 12b-1 fee is charged by some investment companies to defray the costs of marketing and distributing a mutual fund.

F 5. (Obj. 2) A growth fund invests in common stocks of companies in the same industry.

T 6. (Obj. 2) A family of funds exists when one investment company manages a group of mutual funds.

F 7. (Obj. 3) *Kiplinger's Personal Finance Magazine* and *Business Week* provide professional advisory research reports.

F 8. (Obj. 3) An investment company sponsoring a mutual fund must give investors a prospectus each calendar quarter.

T 9. (Obj. 4) Income dividends are the earnings that a fund pays to shareholders after it has deducted expenses from its dividend and interest income.

T 10. (Obj. 4) Because closed-end funds are listed on securities exchanges, it is possible to sell shares in such a fund to another investor.

Self-Guided Study Questions

1. In your own words, define the term mutual fund.

Obj. 1

Why Investors Purchase Mutual Funds (p. 513)

2. What are the two major reasons why investors purchase mutual funds?

3. Since investment companies have professional portfolio managers with years of experience, is it still necessary for investors to evaluate mutual funds? Why?

4. Why does diversification of mutual funds spell safety?

Characteristics of Investment in Mutual Funds (p. 514)

5. How does *Barron's Dictionary of Finance and Investment Terms* define an investment company?

6. What is the difference between a closed-end fund and an open-end fund?

7. How is the net asset value (NAV) for a share in a mutual fund determined?

8. What is the difference between a load fund and a no-load fund?

9. What do several major research studies indicate about the performance of funds that charge commissions compared to funds that don't charge commissions?

10. What is the typical management fee for a mutual fund?

11. What is the typical contingent deferred sales load?

12. What is the typical 12b-1 fee?

13. Why do investment companies charge 12b-1 fees?

14. What is the difference between Class A, Class B, and Class C shares?

Obj. 2

Classifications of Mutual Funds (p. 519)

Stock Funds (p. 519)

15. What types of securities are included in an aggressive growth fund?

16. What types of securities are included in an equity income fund?

17. What types of securities are included in a global stock fund?

18. What types of securities are included in a growth fund?

19. What types of securities are included in a growth and income fund?

20. What types of securities are included in an index fund?

21. What types of securities are included in an international fund?

22. What types of securities are included in a mid-cap fund?

23. What types of securities are included in a regional fund?

24. What types of securities are included in a sector fund?

25. What types of securities are included in a small-cap fund?

26. What types of securities are included in a utility fund?

Bond Funds (p. 521)

27. What types of securities are included in a high-yield (junk) bond fund?

28. What types of securities are included in an insured municipal bond fund?

29. What types of securities are included in an intermediate corporate bond fund?

30. What types of securities are included in an intermediate U.S. bond fund?

31. What types of securities are included in a long-term corporate bond fund?

32. What types of securities are included in a long-term (U.S.) bond fund?

33. What types of securities are included in a municipal bond fund?

34. What types of securities are included in a short-term corporate bond fund?

35. What types of securities are included in a short-term (U.S.) government bond fund?

Other Funds (p. 521)

36. What types of securities are included in a balanced fund?

37. What types of securities are included in a money market fund?

38. What types of securities are included in a stock/bond blend fund?

39. In your own words, define a family of funds.

40. What services does a market timer perform?

Obj. 3

How to Make a Decision to Buy or Sell Mutual Funds (p. 522)

41. Why is the decision to buy or sell shares in a mutual fund "too" easy?

How to Read the Mutual Funds Section in the Newspaper (p. 523)

42. What type of information is provided in the mutual fund section of the newspaper?

43. In a newspaper quotation, what do the letters "NL," "p," "r," and "t" mean?

Financial Objectives — Again (p. 524)

44. How do the investor's financial objectives relate to the objectives of a specific mutual fund?

Mutual Fund Prospectus (p. 525)

45. What type of information is contained in the prospectus that investors could use to evaluate a mutual fund investment?

Mutual Fund Annual Report (p. 525)

46. What type of information is contained in a mutual fund annual report?

47. What role does a fund manager play in a mutual fund investment?

Financial Publications (p. 526)

48. What financial publications can investors use to evaluate mutual fund investments?

Professional Advisory Services (p. 528)

49. What type of information is provided by professional advisory services?

The Internet (p. 528)

50. What type of information can be obtained by using the Internet?

Obj. 4

The Mechanics of a Mutual Fund Transaction (p. 531)

Return on Investment (p. 532)

51. What is an income dividend?

52. What is a capital gain distribution?

53. What is the difference between a capital gain distribution and a capital gain?

54. What are the tax implications of investing in mutual funds?

Purchase Options (p. 536)

55. How can an investor purchase shares in a closed-end fund?

56. What are the four options that investors can use to purchase shares in an open-end fund?

57. All four purchase options allow investors to buy shares over a long period of time. How do these options allow investors to use the principle of dollar cost averaging?

Withdrawal Options (p. 537)

58. How can an investor sell shares in a closed-end fund?

59. How can an investor sell shares in an open-end fund?

60. In addition to just selling shares in an open-end fund, what are four options that investors can use to systematically withdraw funds from an open-end fund?

Post Test

Completion

1. (Obj. 1) The two major reasons why investors purchase mutual funds are personal management and diversification
2. (Obj. 1) A(n) ____________-____________ fund is a mutual fund whose shares are issued by an investment company only when the fund is organized.
3. (Obj. 1) The ____________ ____________ ____________ per share is equal to the current market value of the mutual fund's portfolio minus the mutual fund's liabilities divided by the number of shares outstanding.
4. (Obj. 1) A(n) ____________ ____________ ____________ ____________ is a 1 to 6 percent charge that shareholders pay when they withdraw their investment from a mutual fund.
5. (Obj. 2) A(n) ____________ fund invests in stocks and bonds with the objective of conserving principal.
6. (Obj. 2) A(n) ____________ fund invests in lesser known companies that offer high growth potential.
7. (Obj. 3) Morningstar is a(n) ____________-____________ service.
8. (Obj. 4) Generally, a(n) ____________ contains a summary of the fund and information about fees, past financial performance, and the fund's management and is given to potential investors.
9. (Obj. 4) ____________ ____________ distributions are payments made to a fund's shareholders that result from the sale of securities in a fund's portfolio.
10. (Obj. 4) Investors can determine when they experience a(n) ____________ gain.

Multiple Choice

______ 1. (Obj. 1) Which of the following statements is false?
A. Investors purchase mutual funds because they offer professional management.
B. Investors purchase mutual funds because they are diversified.
C. Numerous investment companies have developed elaborate systems and procedures to help their portfolio managers select the right securities.
D. Because of professional management, there is no need for investors to evaluate a mutual fund investment.
E. Investment companies often hire professional managers who have years of investment experience.

______ 2. (Obj. 1) A mutual fund that charges a commission—sometimes as high as 8 ½ percent of the purchase price—is called a(n) ____________ fund.
A. open-end
B. closed-end
C. load
D. redemption

__C__ 3. (Obj. 1) The typical yearly management fee for a mutual fund is ____________ percent of the fund's assets.
A. 0.25 to 0.50
B. 0.25 to 1
C. 1 to 1.50
D. 1.50 to 2
E. 2 to 3

______ 4. (Obj. 1) A fee used to defray the costs of marketing and distributing a mutual fund is a called a ____________ fee.
A. load
B. management
C. redemption
D. 12b-1
E. 44K-3

______ 5. (Obj. 2) A mutual fund that invests in companies expecting higher than average revenue and earnings growth is called a(n) ____________ fund.
A. balanced
B. beta
C. growth
D. industry
E. index

______ 6. (Obj. 2) A mutual fund that invests in stocks of companies throughout the world is called a ____________ fund.
A. balanced
B. family
C. growth
D. global
E. world

_______ 7. (Obj. 3) In a newspaper like *The Wall Street Journal*, which of the following would indicate that a 12b-1 fee is charged?
A. r
B. p
C. NL
D. Q
E. +

_______ 8. (Obj. 4) Earnings that a fund pays to shareholders after it has deducted expenses from its dividend and interest income are called
A. capital gains.
B. capital gain distributions.
C. ordinary distributions.
D. income dividends.
E. fund dividends.

_______ 9. (Obj. 4) Contractual savings plans are sometimes referred to as _______ funds.
A. front-end load
B. prepaid commission
C. no-load
D. Securities and Exchange Commission
E. prepaid purchase

_______ 10. (Obj. 4) Because _______________ funds are listed on securities exchanges, it is possible to sell shares in such a fund to another investor.
A. closed-end
B. load
C. open-end
D. redemption
E. 12b-1

Problems, Applications, and Cases

1. Match each term with the statements that follow.
   a. closed-end fund
   b. open-end fund
   c. net asset value
   d. load fund
   e. Class C shares
   f. no-load fund
   g. management fee
   h. contingent deferred sales load
   i. 12b-1 fee

______ 1. The current market value of the mutual fund's portfolio minus the mutual fund's liabilities divided by the number of shares outstanding.

______ 2. A fee to defray the costs of marketing and distributing a mutual fund.

______ 3. A mutual fund whose shares are issued and redeemed by the investment company at the request of investors.

______ 4. A yearly fee that usually ranges from 0.25 to 1 percent of the fund's total assets.

______ 5. A mutual fund in which investors pay a commission—sometimes as high as 8 ½ percent of the purchase price for investments under $10,000—every time they purchase shares.

______ 6. A mutual fund whose shares are issued by an investment company only when the fund is organized.

______ 7. A mutual fund in which investors pay no commission to buy or sell shares, but higher ongoing 12b-1 fees.

______ 8. A 1 to 6 percent charge that shareholders pay when they withdraw their investment from a mutual fund.

______ 9. A mutual fund in which no sales charge is paid by the individual investor.

2. The managers of mutual funds tailor their investment portfolios to the investment objectives of their customers. The major categories of mutual funds are presented below. In your own words, describe the type of securities that would be found in each type of mutual fund.

Classification of fund	***Type of securities generally included***
Aggressive growth fund	
Global stock fund	
Growth fund	
Growth and income fund	
Small cap fund	
Sector fund	
Utility fund	
High-yield bond fund	
Intermediate corporate bond fund	
Long-term corporate bond fund	
Long-term (U.S.) bond fund	
Municipal bond fund	
Short-term (U.S.) bond fund	
Balanced fund	

3. Choose at least three different mutual funds that could help you meet your personal investment objectives. Then use the mutual fund quotations published in *The Wall Street Journal*, a local newspaper, or the Internet to monitor the value of each fund for a period of four weeks.

Mutual fund	**Week 1** Net asset value Date ________	**Week 2** Net asset value Date ________	**Week 3** Net asset value Date ________	**Week 4** Net asset value Date __________
1.				
2.				
3.				

Based on your findings, answer the following questions to complete Exercise 3.

a. Which of the above mutual funds had the largest dollar amount of change over the four-week period of time?

b. After watching each of the three mutual funds for a period of four weeks, would you want to invest in one of the funds? Why?

c. What other types of information would you use to evaluate the above mutual funds?

4. ABC Growth Fund is an aggressively managed growth fund that invests in small, rapidly growing corporations in the electronics and computer fields. According to the fund's annual report, ABC has $590 million of assets, $1.4 million of liabilities, and 40,124,200 shares outstanding.

   a. What is the net asset value per share?

   b. If this fund charges a 6 percent commission on the total amount invested, how much commission would be paid on an investment of $2,000?

5. Assume that one year ago you bought 200 shares of a mutual fund for $12.25 per share, that you received $0.60 per share income distribution during the past 12 months, and that the market value of the fund is now $10.75 per share.

   a. Calculate the current yield for this investment at the end of the 12-month period.

   b. Calculate the total return for this investment at the end of 12 months.

Supplementary Case 16-1: Are Mutual Funds for You?

Topic: Evaluation of Mutual Funds

Text Reference: pp. 522-530

Today, there are more mutual funds than ever before—all developed to meet the needs of investors like you. And while putting your money in a mutual fund may seem like a carefree method of investing, nothing can be further from the truth.

In evaluating a mutual fund, the first factor you should consider is the fund's investment objectives. Whether you want your money in conservative, long-term government bonds, or in speculative foreign stocks, there is a mutual fund for you. The key question may be, "Do the objectives of a specific mutual fund match your objectives?"

The second factor you should consider is the fund's past performance. It is fairly easy to obtain a comparative performance ranking for periods ranging from the last 10 years to the most recent quarter. Sources of information on mutual funds that are available at most libraries include *Individual Investor's Guide to No-Load Mutual Funds, Business Week, Kiplinger's Personal Finance Magazine, Money,* and *Forbes*. The most comprehensive reference sources on mutual funds are Morningstar, Inc., the Wiesenberger Investment Companies Service, and the reports published by Lipper Analytical Services.

The third factor you should consider is the information available in newsletters on mutual funds. Thanks to the great interest in mutual funds, over 100 newsletters now specialize in this subject. Many of these newsletters have survived the test of time and provide investors with reliable advice for fees ranging from $85 to $300 a year. But some of these newsletters mislead investors by backdating the performance of their suggested investment portfolios—a practice akin to betting on a horse after the race is over.

Two inexpensive directories list mutual funds by investment goals and give details on commission charges. A guide to funds with small or no sales commissions is available from the Mutual Fund Education Alliance (816-454-9422). A similar guide is available from the Investment Company Institute (202-326-5800).

Case Questions

1. Today, mutual funds are one of the most popular investments in the United States. Why do you think mutual funds have become so popular?
2. Since professional management and diversification are characteristics of mutual funds, why must investors still evaluate a mutual fund?
3. Assume that you are interested in a specific mutual fund. What type of information would you need to evaluate this fund?

Supplementary Case 16-2: How Do You Evaluate a Mutual Fund?

Topic: Evaluation of Mutual Funds

Text Reference: pp. 522-530

In Chapter 16 (Investing in Mutual Funds), we have stressed the importance of evaluating potential investments in mutual funds. Now it's your turn to try your skill at evaluating a mutual fund investment. Assume that you have established an emergency fund and have also accumulated $4,000 that you would like to invest in mutual funds. Also, assume that you are a college graduate and have a job that pays $27,000 a year. Finally, assume that you can choose any mutual fund that is reported in *The Wall Street Journal* or your local newspaper.

To help you evaluate "your" mutual fund, you may want to examine issues of *Business Week, Forbes, Kiplinger's Personal Finance Magazine, Fortune*, or *Money*. Also, to help guide your search for a quality investment, you may want to complete a copy of the evaluation form from the "Financial Planning for Life's Situations" boxed insert on page 533 in Chapter 16.

Case Questions

1. Based on your research, would you buy shares in the mutual fund you originally chose?
2. What other investment information would you need to evaluate your mutual fund? Where would you obtain this information?

Supplementary Reading 16

Jeffrey M. Laderman, "Grand Prix's Big Mo," *Business Week*, May 29, 2000, pp. 208-209.

Grand Prix's Big Mo

Bob Zuccaro's investment management shop Target Investors has been around since 1983, but it was only in 1997 that he decided to launch a mutual fund. The obvious name, Target, was already taken, so he and his colleagues batted around other names. "Grand Prix was the 13th name that came up," Zuccaro recalls. "But it was catchy and suggesting something that's fast, symbolic of what we do."

It turns out the name couldn't be more, well, on target. The Wilton (Conn.)-based fund has established an astonishing record in a period when many funds have been posting turbocharged returns. The fund earned 111.8% in 1998, following that up with 147.8% in 1999 (table). This year the fund was up 70% in March, but is now up just 5.4%. Still, that tops the Standard & Poor's 500-stock index and trounces the Nasdaq composite.

NO NEWBIE. Zuccaro is a momentum investor, a sort much maligned of late with the plunge in the Nasdaq and in high-flying technology stocks. Momentum investors have been painted as inexperienced traders who chased hot stocks, bid prices up to absurd levels, and then turned tail and caused the market to plunge. No doubt that description fits some, but certainly not Zuccaro or the Grand Prix Fund. He's 57 years old and has worked in the investment business since 1967. Zuccaro doesn't invest in initial public offerings or in companies that are losing money."

What Zuccaro buys are the stocks that are leading the market in price appreciation and earnings gains. He also invests in those that are surprising Wall Street the most with higher-than-expected earnings gains. In a bull market, Zuccaro's aggressive strategy may seem to be a layup. "You wonder what will happen if earnings and stock prices stop going up," says Edward S. Rosenbaum, research director at mutual-fund research firm Lipper Inc. Zuccaro says he is not fazed by the inevitable downdrafts, since he has invested through six bear markets and five recessions. "There's always some stocks going up," he says.

Before starting the fund, he was a "growth at a reasonable price" investor. He would, for example, buy stocks with 30% earnings growth when they traded at price-earnings ratios of 15. The idea was to sell when a stock hit its target p-e, usually the same as its growth rate. When the performance of that strategy lagged in 1996 and 1997, he realized the stocks making the biggest gains were stocks that he never would have bought based on their p-e's. By conventional yardsticks, they were overvalued to begin with, yet they made big gains because of their momentum.

To pick the fund's investments, Zuccaro screens some 10,000 stocks on price, earnings, and positive earnings surprises, and looks for those that are in the top 10% on all three criteria. That process alone winnows the pool to under 100. Then he ranks each by criterion, and the 25 with the highest combined scores—the fund is a concentrated, or focus, fund with just 25 stocks—go in the portfolio.

One result is that Grand Prix is usually buying a stock when it's making a new high. Indeed, on May 16 he bought Quest Diagnostics Inc., a medical service company, and Three-Five Systems Inc., which makes display modules for cell phones and other electronic devices, as the two shot up to new highs. "It sounds counterintuitive, but it's not," says Zuccaro. "If a stock makes a new high, most of the shareholders are making money, are not looking to sell, and there's less resistance to it going up." If you buy a stock near its low, he explains, shareholders are probably waiting to sell as it gets near to the price they paid. Those sellers can be a big drag on the stock.

Kari Bayer, a quantitative analyst at Merrill Lynch & Co., says investing by price momentum is a proven strategy. It beat the S&P 500 in all but three of the last 12 years, with an average annual return of 25.3%, vs. 16% for the S&P over the period. In Merrill's studies, earnings momentum and earnings surprise strategies clocked returns close to the S&P. Merrill's work, however, uses the S&P 500 stocks. With a broader universe that includes faster-growing companies, earnings momentum strategies should be more rewarding.

Perhaps where Zuccaro adds the most value is with his sell discipline. Should a stock fall 10% from its high, out it goes. That limits the downside. Over the past year, Zuccaro dumped Legato Systems at 69 (it's now at 14), Emulex at 160 (now 54), and Charles Schwab at 63 (now 45). One change Zuccaro made of late is that when the Nasdaq becomes especially volatile and many stocks move down more than 10% in a day, he sells only a portion of his position. "Otherwise, I would end up with half the fund in cash, and that's not appropriate for an equity fund," says Zuccaro. A high cash position would put the fund at a disadvantage on the rebounds. "I've seen the fund come back 20% in two days," he says. "That wouldn't happen if you had a lot of cash." He now has 12% in cash.

The 10% rule accounts for many but not all of the portfolio's sales. For instance, Zuccaro sells if there's negative news from a company. And as earnings season approaches, he compares his own profit forecasts with the Street's. "If we don't see a positive earnings surprise of at least 5%, we sell." Finally, sometimes a stock is sold to make room for one with a higher score.

BIG SPREAD. All of this makes for lots of trading. During 1999, the fund had 764% turnover, which means the average holding period for a stock was around six to seven weeks, vs. a little less than a year for the average U.S. equity fund. Frequent trading could also result in a lot of short-term capital gains distributions. That hasn't happened yet, mainly because asset growth—from $0 to $500 million in a little more than two years—has allowed the fund to spread the gains over more assets. But as the fund matures, the hyperactive trading may prove troublesome to taxable investors.

Still, if Grand Prix continues to win the performance races, shareholders may not mind. After taxes, he might still be way out in front.

By Jeffrey M. Laderman in Wilton, Conn.

OUTPACING THE COMPETITION

	Total Return*		
	1998	**1999**	**2000****
GRAND PRIX FUND (CLASS A)	111.8%	147.8%	5.4%
LARGE-CAP GROWTH FUNDS	34.1	39.5	0.6
S&P 500	28.6	21.0	0.1
NASDAQ COMPOSITE	39.6	89.6	–8.6

* Appreciation plus reinvestment of dividends and capital gains
**Through May 16

DATA: MORNINGSTAR INC.

Study Questions

1. In 1998, the Grand Prix Fund earned 111.8 percent. In 1999, the fund earned 147.8 percent. While everyone would like returns like these, what are the drawbacks to investing in a fund like Grand Prix?

2. What methods does Bob Zuccaro, the fund manager, use to choose the fund's investments?

3. To generate big returns, Zuccaro trades stocks on a regular basis. In fact, the fund's average holding period for a stock was around six to seven weeks vs. a year for the average U.S. equity fund. From a taxation standpoint, what problems could this create for individual investors?

17 Real Estate And Other Investment Alternatives

Chapter Overview

Traditionally, Americans have invested in real estate. We begin this chapter by classifying types of real estate as direct and indirect investments. We analyze the investment potential of commercial property and show one method that may be used to calculate the expected profitability of commercial properties. Indirect real estate investments such as real estate syndicates or limited partnerships, real estate investment trusts, first and second mortgages, and participation certificates are discussed in depth. Then we present advantages and disadvantages of real estate investments. We close the chapter with investments in precious metals, gems, and other collectibles. Investing in gold, gold bullion, gold bullion coins, gold stocks, gold futures contracts, silver, platinum, palladium, and rhodium are all discussed in this section. Lastly, collectibles such as rare coins, works of art, antiques, stamps, rare books, sports memorabilia, rugs, Chinese ceramics, paintings, and other items that appeal to collectors and investors are presented.

Learning Objectives

After studying this chapter, you will be able to:

Obj. 1 Identify types of real estate investments.

Obj. 2 Evaluate the advantages of real estate investments.

Obj. 3 Assess the disadvantages of real estate investments.

Obj. 4 Analyze the risks and rewards of investing in precious metals, gems, and other collectibles.

Key Terms

collectibles
commercial property
direct investment
indirect investment
participation certificate (PC)
passive activity
passive loss
real estate investment trust (REIT)
syndicate

Pretest

True-False

T 1. (Obj. 1) In direct real estate investment, the investor holds legal title to the property.
T 2. (Obj. 1) In indirect investment, the investors appoint a trustee to hold legal title on behalf of all the investors in the group.
T 3. (Obj. 1) Passive loss is the total amount of losses from a passive activity minus the total income from the passive activity.
F 4. (Obj. 1) Investing in participation certificates is not as secure as Uncle Sam's own bonds and notes.
F 5. (Obj. 2) Generally speaking, real property equity investments are not a good hedge against inflation.
T 6. (Obj. 2) Financial leverage enables you to acquire a more expensive property than you could acquire on your own.
F 7. (Obj. 2) Limited financial liability is one of the biggest disadvantages of investing in limited partnerships.
T 8. (Obj. 3) During deflationary and recessionary periods, the value of real property may decline.
T 9. (Obj. 3) The Tax Reform Act of 1986 limits the ability of taxpayers to use losses generated by real estate investments to offset income gained from other sources.
F 10. (Obj. 4) Collectibles provide current income and they are easy to sell in a hurry.

Self-Guided Study Questions

Obj. 1

Investing in Real Estate (p. 547)

1. How are real estate investments classified?

2. What are the differences between direct and indirect real estate investments?

Direct Real Estate Investments (p. 547)

3. What has been the "real" return of owning a home during the past 150 years?

4. Why has the after-tax cost of owning a vacation home risen since 1987?

5. What is the definition of commercial property?

6. How do you determine the investment potential of commercial property?

7. What does commercial property include?

8. What type of real property investment is preferred by small investors?

9. How have many investors acquired sizable commercial properties?

10. What is an example of passive activity?

11. What is a passive loss?

12. Why have some investors been favoring undeveloped land for development?

Indirect Real Estate Investments (p. 549)

13. What is a real estate syndicate?

14. How does a limited partnership work?

15. What is a real estate investment trust (REIT)?

16. Who sells indirect real estate investments?

17. What are three types of REITs?

18. What are the differences among equity REITs, mortgage REITs, and hybrid REITs?

19. What are the risks and rewards of investing in REITs?

20. Who is most likely to invest in first and second mortgages?

21. What is a participation certificate (PC)?

22. What are Ginnie Maes and Freddie Macs?

23. Why are Maes and Macs as secure as U.S. Treasury bonds and notes?

24. How can investors buy participation certificates?

Obj. 2

Advantages of Real Estate Investments (p. 552)

A Hedge Against Inflation (p. 552)

25. How do real property equity investments provide protection against purchasing power risk?

Easy Entry (p. 552)

26. How can one gain easy entry in a shopping center investment?

Limited Financial Liability (p. 553)

27. What is your financial liability as a limited partner?

28. Who must bear all financial risks in a general partnership?

No Management Concerns (p. 553)

29. Why are there no management concerns in some real estate investments?

Financial Leverage (p. 554)

30. What is financial leverage?

31. How is financial leverage an advantage in real estate investments?

Obj. 3

Disadvantages of Real Estate Investments (p. 554)

Illiquidity (p. 555)

32. What is perhaps the largest drawback of real estate investments?

Declining Property Values (p. 555)

33. How does deflation affect real estate values?

Lack of Diversification (p. 555)

34. Why is diversification in direct real estate investments difficult?

Lack of a Tax Shelter (p. 555)

35. What is the tax shelter aspect of real estate syndicates after the enactment of the 1986 tax law?

Long Depreciation Period (p. 555)

36. What are the new depreciation guidelines for depreciating real estate investments?

Management Problems (p. 555)

37. How can buying and managing individual properties create management problems?

Obj. 4

Investing in Precious Metals, Gems, and Collectibles (p. 556)

38. What are several methods for buying precious metals?

Gold (p. 556)

39. How are gold prices affected by war, political instability, and inflation?

40. What is the basic unit of gold bullion?

41. How can you avoid storage and assaying problems?

42. How can you invest in gold stocks and gold futures contracts?

Silver, Platinum, Palladium, and Rhodium (p. 556)

43. Why do some investors prefer to invest in silver, platinum, palladium, and rhodium?

Precious Stones (p. 557)

44. What should you keep in mind when you invest in precious stones?

45. Who certifies a precious stone's characteristics?

Collectibles (p. 558)

46. What are collectibles?

47. Why have forgeries become a significant problem in the world of art?

48. What rules must you follow when investing in collectibles?

49. How is collecting for investment purposes very different from collecting as a hobby?

50. What are some caveats if you invest in rare coins?

Post Test

Completion

1. (Obj. 1) With ____________ ____________, the investor holds legal title to the property.
2. (Obj. 1) The term ____________ ____________ refers to land and buildings that produce lease or rental income.
3. (Obj. 1) The ____________ may be organized as a corporation, as a trust, or, more commonly, as a limited partnership.
4. (Obj. 1) There are three types of real estate investment trusts: equity REIT, mortgage REIT, and ____________ REIT.
5. (Obj. 2) If you are ____________ ____________, you are not liable for losses beyond your initial investment.
6. (Obj. 2) ____________ ____________ is the use of borrowed funds for investment purposes.

7. (Obj. 3) ____________ in direct real estate investments is difficult because of the large size of most real estate projects.
8. (Obj. 4) The basic unit of gold bullion is one ____________.
9. (Obj. 4) ____________ and other precious stones are not easily turned into cash.
10. (Obj. 4) An acknowledged industry leader in certifying a precious stone's characteristics is ____________ ____________ ____________ ____________.

Multiple Choice

C 1. (Obj. 1) Real estate investments are classified as
   A. pure and impure.
   B. speculative and nonspeculative.
   C. direct and indirect.
   D. liquid and illiquid.

A 2. (Obj. 1) The investment potential of commercial property, unlike that of undeveloped land or personal residence, can
   A. accurately be measured.
   B. not be determined.
   C. be guessed.
   D. not be measured.

D 3. (Obj. 1) Which one of the following statements is not correct about real estate syndicates?
   A. Syndicates provide limited financial liability.
   B. Syndicates provide professional management for their members.
   C. Syndicates provide diversification.
   D. Syndicates provide guaranteed rate of return on investment.

C 4. (Obj. 1) Which one of the following is not an example of a real estate investment trust?
   A. Mortgage REIT
   B. Hybrid REIT
   C. Preferred REIT
   D. Equity REIT

B 5. (Obj. 1) Participation certificates from the Government National Mortgage Association are called ____________ Maes.
   A. Sallie
   B. Ginnie
   C. Fannie
   D. Sonny

A 6. (Obj. 1) If you want a relatively risk-proof real estate investment, you should invest in
   A. a participation certificate.
   B. a vacation home.
   C. land.
   D. commercial property.

C 7. (Obj. 2) Real property equity investments usually provide
   A. above average returns on investment.
   B. below average returns on investment.
   C. protection against purchasing power risk.
   D. protection against deflation.

D 8. (Obj. 2) The use of borrowed funds for investment purposes is called
   A. financial average.
   B. financial yield.
   C. rate of return on investment.
   D. financial leverage.

B 9. (Obj. 3) During deflationary and recessionary periods, the value of tangible assets usually
   A. increases slightly.
   B. decreases.
   C. remains unchanged.
   D. skyrockets.

C 10. (Obj. 4) Diamond prices can be affected by the whims of
   A. the U.S. government.
   B. the South African government.
   C. De Beers Consolidated Mines of South Africa.
   D. the Gemological Institute of America.

Problems, Applications, and Cases

1. If you are a homeowner, when did you buy the house? What price did you pay for it? What improvements did you make during your ownership? How much did the improvements cost? What is the present market value of the house? Subtract the purchase price and the improvements cost from the market value. What is the appreciation value? Divide the appreciation by the number of years you have owned the home to determine average annual appreciation. Calculate annual percentage increase in value. Has the increased value kept pace with inflation? (Use the Consumer Price Index as a guideline for the years of home ownership.)

2. You have just inherited $30,000 from Uncle Harry. Since the inheritance represents excess funds, you would like to invest the $30,000. Determine how you will invest your money using the investment objectives and alternatives given below. Outline (a) your investment objectives, (b) the investment alternatives considered, and (c) why you made particular investment decisions.

   a. What are your investment objectives?

Investment objective	Possible advantages	Possible disadvantages
Safety of capital		
Liquidity		
Steady income		
Growth of capital		
Inflation hedge		
High speculative return		
Combination		

   b. What are your investment alternatives?

Investment objective	Possible advantages	Possible disadvantages
Down payment on a home		
Down payment on a rental property		
A limited partnership		
First/second mortgages		
Participation certificates		
Stocks		
Bonds		
Commodities market		
Options market		
Precious metals		

c. Investment(s) selected:

Reasons:

3. Use the following inventory sheet for your collectibles and determine percent appreciation in value since you purchased the collectible.

Item	Date purchased	Today's market value	How value was determined	Appreciation (or depreciation)	Percent appreciation	Consumer price index change
Americana 19th Cent. paintings Folk art Furniture						
Antiques						
Automobiles (antiques and classics)						
Coins: gold/silver						
Commemorative coins & medals						
Diamonds						
Fine jewelry						
Paintings						
Rare books						
Rare coins						
Rugs						
Sports memorabilia						
Stamps						
Western art						
Works of young artists						
Wine						
Other ________						
Other ________						

4. Consult "Money & Investing" section (Section C) of *The Wall Street Journal* to find the commodity futures prices for one troy ounce of
   a. gold
   b. platinum
   c. palladium
   d. silver

5. For each of the following investments, compute the current yield:

Investment	Initial cost	Value-one year later	Yield
a. rare books	$550	$625	____________ %
b. undeveloped land	$20,000	$23,500	____________ %
c. rare coins	$4,400	$3,900	____________ %

6. Read the following case from the Federal Trade Commission. What steps can an investor take to protect oneself from such scams?

   The Federal Trade Commission has charged that Professional Coin Grading Service, Inc. ("PCGS") misled consumers by falsely claiming that it provides consistent, objective grading of coins and that investment in PCGS-certified rare coins eliminates all the risk associated with the grading of coins. Under a consent decree filed August 16, 1990 in federal district court, PCGS is prohibited from making false representations about its objectivity, consistency, or the liquidity of its coins, and from making deceptive statements about the risks of investing in graded coins. (Civil Action No. 90-1982)

   Source: *FTC News Notes*, August 20, 1990.

Supplementary Case 17

Topic: Art Fraud

Text Reference: pp. 558-561

Richard Welch, a recent community-college graduate, received a letter inviting him to participate in a drawing for a free original lithograph by a famous artist. He was asked to return a postcard with his name, address, and phone number. After he returned the postcard, he was telephoned for more information, including his credit-card number.

At some point, the caller asked Richard to buy a print, using such glowing terms as "fabulous opportunity," "onetime offer," "limited edition," and "excellent investment" to describe the purchase. Richard was told that the print was the work of a famous artist who was near death and that its value would increase after the artist's death. He was assured that when the artist died, the company that the caller represented would gladly buy back the print at two to three times what he paid for it and that he could always resell the print elsewhere at a substantial profit. He was told that he would receive a certificate testifying to the "authenticity" of the print. And he was promised a trial examination period with a 30-day money-back guarantee.

Case Questions

1. Does the offer seem genuine to you? Explain your answer.
2. How can Richard protect himself against a phony offer. List at least five suggestions that you would give him.
3. If Richard bought the work of art and discovered fraud, how should he try to resolve his dispute with the company that sold it to him? Where should he complain if the dispute is not resolved?

Supplementary Reading 17-1

Thane Peterson, "Want To Buy A Piece of History? The Net has made document-collecting easier" *Business Week*, April 3, 2000, pp. 156-157.

Want To Buy A Piece of History?

The Net has made document-collecting easier

What hooked William Steiner was a Sotheby's auction 12 years ago of Albert Einstein letters. The chairman of Dryclean USA, a Miami dry-cleaning gear and franchise company, wound up buying two letters for $2,800 apiece. He has since built an eclectic collection of some 1,500 documents. "I realized I could own things signed by people I regard as the heroes and villains of history," says Steiner. "I just kept getting in deeper and deeper."

Steiner has company. Historical documents have shaken off some of their musty image with the emergence of celebrity collectors such as Bill Gates. And some segments of the market, such as early Americana and Civil War documents, are jumping (table). Steiner, for example, last year sold a July 1, 1776 letter from John Adams about the Declaration of Independence. The sales price: $635,000. Meanwhile, Web auction sites have brought a flood of new material and opened the hobby to a new audience. "Before eBay, most people just didn't know you could buy a letter by someone like Harry Truman for a few hundred dollars," says Chicago collector James Berland.

But the hobby can be fraught with peril. Mechanical pens and the practice of secretaries signing letters mean that signatures on many 20th century documents are not authentic. "We just assume that after 1965, anyone who could afford to use an auto-pen used one," says Kenneth Rendell, a dealer in Boston and author of Forging History: The Detection of Fake Letters & Documents (University of Oklahoma Press, $24.95).

Sports, rock 'n' roll, and Hollywood memorabilia are so rife with fakes that many experts recommend collecting only such documents as contracts, which are relatively easy to verify. And it's far from certain that a document will gain value. For every Jane Austen, whose surge in popularity has caused prices for her letters to spike, there's a William Makepeace Thackeray, whose prices have barely budged since 1900, says Polly Beauwin at leading London dealer Maggs Bros.

How can a novice avoid the pitfalls? The best insurance is to buy from reputable dealers or auction houses such as Sotheby's or Christie's. Top dealers tend to belong to professional groups such as the Professional Autograph Dealers Assn., which publish membership lists and codes of ethics on their Web sites (table). Good dealers also give references and guarantee refunds on items that come into question, even years after a sale.

The next step: Focus. "Pick a subject you love," says Nathan Myhrvold, who's on sabbatical from his post as Microsoft's chief technology officer. A science buff, Myhrvold is delighted with a trove of letters by British paleontologists he recently acquired. They discuss the Piltdown man, a supposed new species of human discovered in 1912 that proved to be a hoax. Collectors' magazines, such as *Pen & Quill*, can spark ideas. Collectors also peruse dealer catalogs and monitor auction sales. Ernest Hemingway buffs already are salivating over Christie's auction in New York of newly uncovered documents by the author.

In the old days, the signature was the most valuable element of many documents—so much so that signatures were regularly excised and the letters thrown away. But these days, value depends heavily on the historical importance of the contents, as shown by the nosebleed price fetched by the Adams letter. Still, you can start a collection on a budget. A less significant Adams document might sell for $4,000. And certain segments of the market, such as documents from World War II, are fairly inexpensive. Claude Harkins, a collector in suburban Kansas City, Mo., thinks World War II soldiers' letters home are a great value because they can be had for $5 to $10 each, and demand for them seems likely to grow. Similar letters from the Civil War go for $200 to $2,000, up from $1 apiece 15 years ago.

The Net is a good place to look for inexpensive documents, in part because dealers use the Web to sell items that aren't worth putting in catalogs. Jim Smith, owner of Remember When Auctions in Wells, Me., recently sold on eBay a short note signed by the late Supreme Court Chief Justice Earl Warren for just $36.

Dealers claim it's not hard to root out fakes if you scrutinize documents carefully. In *Forging History*, Rendell says crooks tend to make obvious errors. He cites a note purportedly signed by Einstein done on an IBM Selectric, a machine introduced in 1961, six years after the physicist's death. There are less obvious giveaways, too. Machine-made signatures, for example, don't leave an indentation in the paper, as real ones do. Of course, you may not be able to do these checks when buying on the Net. And tons of material of doubtful authenticity have been pouring onto Web sites. So it's best to buy only from the online arms of established dealers and auction houses. Sothebys.com and sothebys.amazon.com guarantee the authenticity of what they sell and offer refunds if a document proves to be a fake. Many prominent dealers also are now doing land-office business on eBay or via their own sites.

Most serious collectors worry far more about finding key items to fill out their collections than they do about fakes. Some search for years for, say, an ultrarare Button Gwinnett to fill out their collections of signers of the Declaration of Independence. For Steiner, the Holy Grail would be a Mozart letter or musical manuscript, now almost impossible to find. But even for those of more modest means, this is one field of collecting where you can say proudly that you're holding a bit of history in your hand.

Thane Peterson

HANDICAPPING THE MARKET

HOT	UP AND COMING	COLD
CIVIL WAR A letter by Robert E. Lee tops $5,000.	**WORLD WAR II** You can still get signed photos of some generals for $300.	**WORLD WAR I** Has never been popular with collectors.
SPORTS Soaring but prone to fakes. A signed Babe Ruth photo goes for $2,500.	**WOMEN** A Susan B. Anthony letter can still be had for $1,000.	**THE ARTS** Composers, writers, and artists are cheap: An Igor Stravinsky letter goes for $400.

DATA: REMEMBER WHEN AUCTIONS INC., BUSINESS WEEK

GETTING HELP

To find reputable dealers, check out these groups

Int'l Autograph Collectors Club & Dealers Assn. www.iacc-da.com	**Universal Autograph Collectors Club** www.uacc.org	**Professional Autograph Dealers Assn.** www.padaweb.org

Study Questions

1. How can a novice document collector avoid the pitfalls of investing in documents?

2. What was the most valuable element of many documents in the old days?

3. Is it still possible to start a collection on a budget? Explain.

4. Why is the Net a good place to look for inexpensive documents?

Supplementary Reading 17-2

Stephanie Anderson Forest, "Real Estate," *Business Week*, January 10, 2000, p. 144.

Real Estate

For much of this decade, the real estate and construction industry has been enjoying some of its best times ever. But as the new millennium kicks off, the industry will hit a plateau. "This year will be good, but it won't stack up to the boom we've seen in recent years," says Mark M. Zandi, chief economist at RFA Dismal Science, a West Chester (Pa.) consulting firm.

Blame the Fed's attempt to guide the economy to a soft landing. Following a succession of interest-rate hikes, the higher cost of financing will exert a dampening effect during 2000 on the rate-sensitive housing sector. And if the housing sector turns south, so will the construction industry, which just finished its eighth consecutive year of expansion.

After four years of record gains, the value of new single-family and multifamily residential contracts in 2000 will drop 3%, to $184.8 billion, according to The McGraw-Hill Companies' F.W. Dodge Div. At the same time, housing starts will slide 7%, to 1.58 million units. Taking its cue from housing, the total value of all U.S. construction contracts will remain virtually flat at $429 billion. That compares with an 8% jump—to $246.8 billion—in 1999.

The main culprit here is rising mortgage rates. The National Association of Home Builders estimates that the rate on 30-year fixed mortgages will climb to 7.9%, up from 7.4% in 1999. Still, measured against historical levels, mortgage rates are low, leaving room for optimism among some housing industry veterans. "As long as rates stay between 7% and 9%, we'll be O.K.," says William D. Albers, chief financial officer at Centex Homes, one of the nation's largest homebuilders. "If we go to double digits, we'll see some real slowing."

As housing loses some of its momentum, there will be fewer homeowners outfitting their new digs. That means new-store building could drop by as much as 7%. Office construction may also tumble about 3.4%, as developers add just 280 million square feet of space. But to put that in perspective, the 290 million square feet added last year marked the highest level since 1986.

Even as the market slows, however, industry executives say they are unlikely to get saddled with overcapacity, as occurred in boom-and-bust cycles past. While signs of overbuilding have appeared in some suburban office areas, like Atlanta and Dallas, inventories will remain surprisingly low in most areas. Industry execs "are more disciplined and more rational" than in the boom cycles of the 1980s, says John C. Goff, CEO of Crescent Real Estate Equities Co.

Landlords may have a different view of the market. It's unlikely that they will be able to raise office rents in 2000 as much as they have in recent years. In 1999, for example, rents were up nearly 10% over 1998. This year, real estate services firm Cushman & Wakefield Inc. estimates that the increase will be closer to the 5%-to-7% range.

In the industrial market, the picture may be the brightest. Warehouses will rock, thanks to the explosion in e-commerce. As labor shortages continue, storage space with built-in robotic retrieval and other high-tech amenities will command the highest price. "This is going to be a banner year for the Internet, and industrial [real estate] is going to be a big beneficiary," says Janice Stanton, Cushman & Wakefield's managing director of investment research.

That's what Michael K. Berry, president of Dallas-based Hillwood Properties, is banking on. Hillwood, co-owner of the 14 million-square-foot Alliance industrial complex in the Dallas-Fort Worth area, is currently adding 500,000 square feet of speculative space, largely targeted at capturing what he calls the e-commerce fulfillment business. "At the end of the day, all of these new Internet ventures still need brick-and-mortar locations," he says. And that may well be the only bit of excitement the real estate industry gets in 2000.

By Stephanie Anderson Forest
in Dallas

Study Questions

1. Why might the real estate and construction industry hit a plateau as the new millennium kicks off?

2. How do rising mortgage rates affect the housing and construction industry?

3. Why is it unlikely that landlords may have a difficulty in raising office rents?

18 Retirement Planning

Chapter Overview

As increasing numbers of Americans join the 65-and-over ranks, the United States faces a serious question—is this country prepared to meet the demands of a growing elderly population? The evidence that America is growing older is clear. In the last two decades, the 65-and-over population grew twice as fast as the rest of the population. Today, one of every nine Americans—a group of at least 25 million people—is 65 years of age or older. We begin this chapter by recognizing the importance of retirement planning. We show how individuals can analyze their current assets and liabilities to make sure they are suitable for retirement. Then, we suggest that individuals estimate their needs by considering changes in spending patterns and where and how they plan to live. Next, we describe various types of housing suitable for retirees. In estimating retirement expenses, we emphasize that expenses should be adjusted for inflation. Once expenses are estimated, we then turn to the importance of evaluating planned retirement income. Income from Social Security, other public pension plans, employer pension plans, personal retirement plans, and annuities are discussed in depth. Finally, we stress the need for living on retirement income and balancing the retirement budget.

Learning Objectives

After studying this chapter, you will be able to:

Obj. 1 Recognize the importance of retirement planning.

Obj. 2 Analyze your current assets and liabilities for retirement.

Obj. 3 Estimate your retirement spending needs.

Obj. 4 Identify your retirement housing needs.

Obj. 5 Determine your planned retirement income.

Obj. 6 Develop a balanced budget based on your retirement income.

Key Terms

annuity
defined-benefit plan
defined-contribution plan
401(k) (TSA) plan
individual retirement account (IRA)
Keogh plan
reverse annuity mortgage
vesting

Pretest

True-False

_______ 1. (Obj. 1) Most young professionals in a recent survey said they would rather save money today for their retirement.

_______ 2. (Obj. 1) Saving money comes naturally to many young people.

_______ 3. (Obj. 2) If your mortgage is largely or completely paid off, you can get a reverse annuity mortgage.

_______ 4. (Obj. 2) Your pension benefits are not considered as marital property.

_______ 5. (Obj. 3) Spending patterns of retirees do not change significantly.

_______ 6. (Obj. 3) Retirees' medical expenses tend to increase with age.

_______ 7. (Obj. 4) The housing needs of people often change as they grow older.

_______ 8. (Obj. 5) Private pension plans are the most widely used source of retirement income.

_______ 9. (Obj. 5) Social Security benefits do not increase automatically if the cost of living has increased during the preceding year.

_______ 10. (Obj. 6) Dipping into savings during your retirement years is wrong.

Self-Guided Study Questions

Obj. 1

Why Retirement Planning? (p. 569)

1. Why is it important to engage in basic retirement planning throughout your working years?

Tackling the Trade-Offs (p. 569)

2. Why is the old adage "you can't have your cake and eat it too" particularly true in planning for retirement?

3. What actions taken today can ensure a comfortable retirement later?

The Importance of Starting Early (p. 570)

4. How many years can you expect to spend in retirement?

5. Why is retirement planning both emotional and financial?

6. What three reasons make financial planning for retirement critical?

The Basics of Retirement Planning (p. 571)

7. What are the four basic steps in retirement planning?

Obj. 2

Conducting a Financial Analysis (p. 572)

8. How do you calculate your net worth now and at retirement?

Review Your Assets (p. 572)

9. What factors must you consider in reviewing your assets?

10. What is a reverse annuity mortgage (RAM)?

11. How should you handle life insurance during retirement years?

Your Assets After Divorce (p. 574)

12. How are pension benefits divided when couples divorce?

Obj. 3

Retirement Living Expenses (p. 576)

13. Why is it impossible to predict the exact amount of money you will need during retirement?

14. What expenses may be lowered or eliminated during retirement?

15. What four expenses may increase during retirement?

Adjust Your Expenses for Inflation (p. 578)

16. Why must you adjust your retirement expenses for inflation?

Obj. 4

Planning Your Retirement Housing (p. 578)

17. What factors should you consider before moving to a new housing location?

Types of Housing (p. 579)

18. Why do housing needs change when people grow older and retire?

19. What housing alternative is preferred by most people approaching retirement age?

20. What is a "universal design home"?

21. Why are contractors building universal design homes from scratch?

Avoiding Retirement Housing Traps (p. 580)

22. Why is research important before making a move to a new housing location?

23. What are some tips from retirement specialists on how to uncover hidden taxes and other costs of a retirement area before moving?

Obj. 5

Planning Your Retirement Income (p. 582)

24. What are some possible sources of income for retirees?

Social Security (p. 582)

25. Is Social Security intended to provide 100 percent of retirement income?

26. When and where should you apply for Social Security benefits?

27. What information would you need to apply for Social Security benefits?

28. What effect will it have on your Social Security benefits if you decide to retire at age 62 instead of 65?

29. Why will the full retirement age be increased in gradual steps until it reaches 67?

30. How do you estimate your retirement benefits?

31. How do you qualify for Social Security retirement benefits?

32. What are the approximate monthly Social Security benefits for workers at age 65?

33. Are Social Security benefits taxable?

34. How are your Social Security benefits affected if you decide to work after you retire?

35. Are Social Security benefits adjusted for inflation?

36. What is the future of Social Security?

Other Public Pension Plans (p. 585)

37. Besides Social Security, what are other government retirement plans?

Employer Pension Plans (p. 586)

38. What is a defined-contribution plan?

39. Why are defined-contribution plans sometimes called individual account plans?

40. What four plans may be included in defined-contribution plans?

41. What is a 401(k) plan?

42. What are tax benefits of a tax-sheltered accounts (TSAs)?

43. What is vesting?

44. What is a defined-benefit plan?

45. What is a pension plan portability?

Personal Retirement Plans (p. 588)

46. What are the two most popular personal retirement plans?

47. What are Individual Retirement Accounts (IRAs)?

48. What is the Roth IRA Plus?

49. What are some advantages of the Roth IRA?

50. What is an education IRA?

51. Should you convert your traditional IRA to a Roth IRA Plus?

52. What is the biggest benefit of an IRA?

53. How do 401(k) contributions compare with IRA contributions?

54. What are Simplified Employee Pension Plans—IRA (SEP-IRA)?

55. In what kinds of investments can you put your IRA funds?

56. What kinds of investments are prohibited for IRA accounts?

57. When can you withdraw from your IRA account?

58. How are IRA withdrawals treated for federal income tax purposes?

59. What are the income tax consequences if you withdraw before age 59½?

60. What is an IRA rollover?

61. What is a Keogh plan?

62. Why should you obtain professional tax advice before using a Keogh plan?

63. When must you start withdrawing from your retirement plans?

Annuities (p. 594)

64. What is a deferred annuity?

65. Who should consider an annuity?

66. How are annuity payments taxed?

67. What are two types of annuities?

68. What are the differences between immediate and deferred annuities?

Options in Annuities (p. 595)

69. What are major settlement options in annuities?

70. Who should select a straight life annuity option?

71. What is an annuity with installments certain?

Which Annuity Is the Best? (p. 595)

72. Which annuity option is best for you?

Will You Have Enough Money During Retirement? (p. 595)

73. What can you do if your planned retirement is less than your estimated retirement expenses?

Obj. 6

Living on Your Retirement Income (p. 597)

74. What is the first step in stretching your retirement income?

Tax Advantages (p. 598)

75. What should you do if you have any questions about your taxes during retirement?

Working During Retirement (p. 598)

76. How can your part-time earnings affect Social Security benefits?

Investing for Retirement (p. 598)

77. What are some suggested investment strategies for the "35-year-olds," "50-year-olds," and "65-year-olds"?

Dipping Into Your Nest Egg (p. 598)

78. Should you draw down your savings during retirement?

Post Test

Completion

1. (Obj. 1) You can expect to spend about ____________ years in retirement.
2. (Obj. 1) Retirement planning involves both emotional and ____________ planning.
3. (Obj. 3) The exact amount of money you will need in retirement is ____________ to predict.
4. (Obj. 3) Your daily living expenses will be ____________ when you retire than they were when you were working.
5. (Obj. 5) ____________ ____________ is the most widely used source of retirement income.
6. (Obj. 5) In employer-offered pension plans, a(n) ____________ ____________ ____________ has an individual account for each employee.
7. (Obj. 5) In employer-offered pension plans, a(n) ____________ ____________ ____________ specifies the benefit promised to the employee at the normal retirement age.
8. (Obj. 5) A(n) ____________ ____________, also known as an H.R.10 plan, is a retirement plan for self-employed individuals.
9. (Obj. 5) ____________ annuities are generally purchased by people of retirement age.
10. (Obj. 5) A(n) ____________ annuity is generally purchased by younger people.

Multiple Choice

______ 1. (Obj. 1) At age 65, what is an average life expectancy of a man?
A. 9 years
B. 14 years
C. 19 years
D. 25 years

______ 2. (Obj. 1) At age 65, what is an average life expectancy of a woman?
A. 9 years
B. 14 years
C. 19 years
D. 25 years

______ 3. (Obj. 1) What is considered the critical age to begin financial planning for retirement?
A. 24
B. 35
C. 45
D. 55

______ 4. (Obj. 1) What is the first step in planning for your retirement?
A. Analyze your current assets and liabilities.
B. Estimate your spending needs.
C. Evaluate your planned retirement income.
D. Estimate the inflation rate.

______ 5. (Obj. 3) Which of the following expenses will most likely be lower during your retirement?
A. Medical
B. Leisure activities
C. Gifts and contributions
D. Federal income tax

______ 6. (Obj. 3) Which of the following expenses will most likely be higher during your retirement years?
A. Work-related
B. Clothing
C. Medical and life insurance
D. Housing

______ 7. (Obj. 5) What is the most widely used source of retirement income?
A. Social Security
B. Employer pension plans
C. Personal retirement plans
D. Annuities

_____ 8. (Obj. 5) In which of the following employer pension plans must the employer set up an individual account for each employee?
A. Undefined-benefit
B. Undefined-contribution
C. Defined-benefit
D. Defined-contribution

_____ 9. (Obj. 5) Under what retirement plan does your employer make non-taxable contributions to the plan for your benefit and reduce your salary be the same amount?
A. Keogh
B. 401(k)
C. Gramm-Rudman
D. Defined-benefit

_____ 10. (Obj. 5) In what types of annuity is the money you pay invested in common stocks or other equities, with the income you receive depending on the investment results?
A. Installment refund equity
B. Life annuity with installments certain
C. Variable annuity
D. Fixed annuity

Problems, Applications, and Cases

1. Request a statement of your earnings record from the Social Security Administration. The postal cards are available at your local Social Security Administration office and at many U.S. Postal Service branches. There is no charge for this service of the federal government.

   Read the statement closely to understand how the information applies to you. When you receive your Summary Statement of Earnings, study the folder sent with it, entitled *Your Social Security Earnings Record.*

2. Write to the Housing and Urban Development (HUD) Office of Interstate Land Sales Registration (OILSR) to obtain free brochures on out-of-state land developers. Prepare a checklist of factors you will consider before purchasing land for retirement housing needs.

3. Check the want ads, talk with real estate brokers and with friends, and make your own survey of retirement housing costs in your community.

Apartments

furnished apartments are renting for:
$ a month for 1 ½ rooms
$ a month for 2 rooms
$ a month for 3 rooms

unfurnished apartments are renting for
$ a month for 1 ½ rooms
$ a month for 2 rooms
$ a month for 3 rooms

Houses

Four-room houses sell for:
$ to $
Five-room houses sell for:
$ to $
Six-room houses sell for:
$ to $

4. Conduct a survey of workers to determine the types of retirement plans in which they are involved. Request information about both company-sponsored plans and personal investment funds set aside for retirement.

5. Suppose you have $80,000 in savings that earn 5.5 percent interest, compounded quarterly.
   a. How much money could you withdraw each month for 15 years before reducing your savings to zero?
   b. How much money could you withdraw each month for 15 years so as to leave your savings intact?

6. Based on the following information, what annual deposit must a person make to achieve the desired retirement income needs?
   - expected retirement income needs: $22,000 a year
   - number of years to retirement: 37 years
   - expected rate of return on investment funds: 9%
   - expected annual inflation rate: 4%

   Required annual deposit $ ________________

Supplementary Case 18-1

Topic: Determining Retirement Income Needs

Text Reference: pp. 595-597

Fred Reinero is 42 and single, and has an after-tax annual income of $30,000. His annual living expenses are $28,000, and he saves the remaining $2,000. Fred believes he needs 80 percent of his annual income, or $22,400, during his retirement years to maintain his current standard of living. Of course, this amount does not allow for increases in the cost of living. Fred plans to retire at age 62 and expects to live 18 years in retirement.

Case Questions

1. How much of a nest egg, in current dollars, will Fred need to finance his retirement?
2. Assuming a 4 percent rate of inflation, how much money will Fred need during his first year of retirement? (Use the Inflation Factor Table on page 579.)

Supplementary Case 18-2

Topic: Housing Options for Retirees

Text Reference: pp. 579-582

Helen, 66, a resident of the suburban area of a large eastern city, lives alone in the house that she and her husband bought when they were first married. She has three adult children, all of whom live in other parts of the country. Helen's income is modest—she works as a salesclerk in a department store. She took this job soon after her husband's death because she could not support herself and her teenage son, the only child who was still living at home, on the insurance and Social Security benefits left by her husband.

Helen has found it increasingly difficult to maintain her large house. The costs of heating and cooling it have increased, and she must pay for minor repairs and yard work. Helen has spent most of her holidays and vacations with one of her children. However, she is quite lonely, and she misses her children and grandchildren.

Helen will retire soon. She has three financial goals: (1) to maintain enough income to support herself after she retires, (2) to have enough savings to meet emergencies, and (3) to eliminate some of the expense and responsibility of maintaining a large house.

Helen's daughter, Janet, had tried for several years to get her mother to move in with her and her family. Helen resisted until recently, afraid of losing her independence and becoming a burden. Now that Janet is divorced and could use day-to-day help with her two children, Helen has reconsidered. She realizes that once she moves in with Janet, she can sell her house and use the money for savings and living expenses. However, after careful thought, Helen has decided not to sell her house in case living with her daughter does not work out. Instead, she has arranged to have a real estate company find tenants, manage the property, collect the rent, and mail it to her (minus the company's fees) each month.

Helen knows that she should review and update her will so that her property will be handled according to her wishes if she dies or becomes unable to handle her own affairs. Because of the income that she expects from rent and Social Security and the decreased expenses that will result from sharing her daughter's household, Helen is looking forward to retirement.

Case Questions

1. What are some of the housing options that might be available to Helen after her retirement? What might be some advantages and disadvantages of each of these options?
2. Do you agree with Helen's decision to move in with her daughter? Why? What might be a few disadvantages of this choice?
3. Is it a sound financial idea for Helen not to sell her house? Why?

Supplementary Reading 18-1

Peter Coy, "To Save Or Not To Save, Uncle Sam sends the wrong message" *Business Week*, May 8, 2000, p. 34.

To Save or Not To Save

Uncle Sam sends the wrong message

Why is the personal savings rate in the U.S. so low? Conventional wisdom says it's because many people earn just enough to get by. But a new study by Steven F. Venti of Dartmouth College and David A. Wise of Harvard University calls that idea into question. They found lots of people who earn high incomes but save extremely little, as well as people with low lifetime incomes who still manage to save quite a bit.

Using data from the government's ongoing Health & Retirement Study, Venti and Wise split up the population of people nearing retirement into 10 groups, or deciles, based on their lifetime incomes. The fifth-lowest income decile, for instance, had median lifetime income of about $740,000 in 1992 dollars. Of the people in that group, savings varied from $443,000 for good savers to just $12,500 for bad savers. Here, good savers means families whose savings were higher than all but 10% of the families in the income group. Bad savers means families whose savings were lower than all but 10% of the families in the group.

Venti and Wise found little difference when they took into account chance events—both positive ones such as inheritances and negative ones such as poor health. Some families saved more because they picked higher-yielding investments. But the authors found that effect to be minor compared with the choice to save or not to save.

Peter Coy

Study Questions

1. Why is the personal savings rate in the United States so low?

2. What are the findings of a new study by Messrs. Venti and Wise?

Supplementary Reading 18-2

Peter Coy, "Longer Hours for Seniors, How big a labor force boost?" *Business Week*, May 8, 1998, p. 34.

Longer Hours for Seniors

How Big a Labor Force Boost?

Now that President Clinton has signed into law the repeal of the Social Security earnings test for workers aged 65 to 69, many people in that category will start putting in longer hours. That's the prediction of Leora R. Friedberg, an economist at the University of California at San Diego whose research helped influence Congress and the White House to back the repeal, which is retroactive to Jan 1.

Under the earnings test, this year, a Social Security beneficiary aged 65 to 69 would have lost $1 in benefits for every $3 earned above a floor of $17,000. Friedberg figures that a fairly small group of people making right around $17,000, whom she terms low earners, have held down their working hours to avoid a reduction in benefits. She predicts that they will increase their hours worked by 50%. She estimates that middle earners, who have had part of their benefits taken away by the test, will increase their hours about 18%.

Friedberg figures that since high earners made so much money that all their Social Security benefits were already being taken away, they could not lose benefits by working more. With the test removed, the benefit cut per extra hour worked will also be zero—so effectively, there's no change. She estimates that high earners will cut their hours about 4% because with their benefits restored, they'll feel richer. And because this group is big, overall hours worked by people affected by the earnings test should rise only 5%, she figures.

Actually, even when the earnings test was in place, people's lifetime Social Security benefits weren't significantly reduced. Their annual benefits were raised after they retired to make up for the pre-retirement reduction. But since most workers never understood that, they cut back on work hours as if they were being heavily taxed. That's why Friedberg is happy the test is gone.

Gene Koretz

Study Questions

1. Why will workers aged 65 to 69 start putting in longer hours at work?

2. Why is Leora R. Friedberg happy that the earnings test for workers aged 65 to 69 is gone?

Supplementary Reading 18-3

Robert Barker, "Click Back and Plan Your Retirement" *Business Week*, February 228, 2000, p. 168.

Click Back and Plan Your Retirement

With 401(k) plans holding $1.5 trillion, money that we amateurs must manage ourselves, America is making a huge bet on our ability to invest wisely. How good are the odds, do you think? I suspect they're better than many experts believe. Yet I'm also happy to see more and better advisory tools now being offered to our nation of accidental investors.

Among these are several services that give interactive financial planning advice via computer, showing how best to split retirement savings among your plan's investment options. But most (including one from Standard & Poor's which like BUSINESS WEEK is a unit of the McGraw Hill Companies) are available only on company sites.

The latest entrant, though, can be used not just through employers but by anyone on the Internet. Financial Engines took an early lead in this arena. Now Morningstar is introducing ClearFuture, with lofty ambitions. "We want to be in the behavior-modification business," Morningstar Research Director John Rekenthaler told me. "If this is going to work, it has to become more a part of people's lives."

"WHAT IF" In other words, running your 401(k) has to become, if not exactly fun, then far from the anxiety-ridden chore it is for so many of us. Curious to see how well ClearFuture meets that goal, I've been testing the service, which you can find at www.morningstar.com. (Price: $99 a year after a free, 30-day trail. Morningstar says it'll soon offer a cut rate.) An expanded version, with education, research, and tracking modules, is being sold directly to 401(k) plans, as Financial Engines is doing, too.

What did I find? Right off, ClearFuture introduced a pair of Jetsonian cartoon characters, Jake Starlight and his tail-wagging mutt, Maggie, to guide me. It also estimated how much time I might spend—20 minutes for investors with basic portfolios. Next, ClearFuture took me through questionnaires on retirement goals, plus my current portfolio and savings plan, before crunching numbers and suggesting three strategies: smooth, moderate, or bumpy investment "flights" to retirement. I picked a moderate one and took off on a "test flight" that showed me via charts and dollar figures how my balance might plunge over three, 12, and 24 months. That gave me a chance to consider how well I could stomach that much portfolio volatility and, if I wanted, to adjust it. Finally, it picked the funds for me from choices I had entered, described them in detail, and told me how much money to put in each.

It was all swift and mostly painless. It also seems aimed directly at Financial Engines, which offers forecasts for free and advice for $14.95 a quarter. Founded by economist and Nobel laureate William Sharpe, Financial Engines' excellent tool comes across as decidedly more sober, if not geeky. It is complex. It's slow to load, and its type is often maddeningly tiny. ClearFuture is sprightly, saving details for long footnotes. And when it gives advice, I found it easier to follow. I especially liked its "What If?" function. It let me test changes in such variables as my retirement date, and was admirably compact yet explicit. Instead of forecasting a percentage probability of reaching my retirement income goal given my savings plan and investments, as Financial Engines does, it gave me a range of income that I would likely have given the same assumptions. That made more sense to me.

Where both tools need sharpening is in helping the many people who hold most retirement assets outside a 401(k). Perhaps they've switched jobs and rolled fat sums into IRAs, or they're already retired. If that's you, you can get advice from either service by simulating a 401(k) portfolio. Caution: If yours is even a bit complex, you could spend hours at it. Morningstar is working on this key job, but Financial Engines now does it better. It also wins at handling the many 401(k) plans with specialized accounts. If yours offers, say, a guaranteed investment contract, you can choose a generic GIC to mimic its role in your portfolio.

Employees using ClearFuture as part of their 401(k) won't need such workarounds. But if you want to get advice by yourself via the Net, you'll find Financial Engines the better choice

For barker.online, go to www.businessweek.com/investor/ or AOL keyword: BW Daily

Robert Barker

401(k) ADVICE ON THE WEB

SITE	COMMENTS	SITE	COMMENTS
MORNINGSTAR CLEARFUTURE www.morningstar.com	Speedy, easy to understand, but adapts poorly to investors with most assets outside a 401(k) plan	**FINANCIAL ENGINES** www.financialengines.com	More flexibility for investors with many assets outside a 401(k), slower, sometimes seems opaque

Study Questions

1. What are several network services that give interactive financial planning advice via computer?

2. If you want to get retirement/financial advice by yourself via the Net, which service is your better choice? Why?

19 Estate Planning

Chapter Overview

This chapter presented us with a delicate challenge. On the one hand, estate planning should be taken very seriously. On the other hand, reading about it can be, well, deadly. We begin with the importance of estate planning. Its goal is to assure that the estate's assets go to the rightful heirs, not Uncle Sam. Next, we present personal aspects of estate planning, noting that if you are married, estate planning involves the interest of at least two people. But never having been married does not eliminate the need to organize your papers. Then, we discuss the legal aspects of estate planning. Simple will, traditional marital share will, exemption trust will, and stated dollar will are described and compared. We offer tips in writing a will, selecting an executor, and altering or rewriting a will. Next, we differentiate among living trust, testamentary trust, insurance trust, and lifetime gifts and trusts. We conclude the chapter with an explanation of federal and state taxes imposed on estates. The four types of taxes—estate taxes, estate income taxes, inheritance taxes, and gift taxes, are described.

Learning Objectives

After studying this chapter, you will be able to:

Obj. 1 Analyze the personal aspects of estate planning.

Obj. 2 Assess the legal aspects of estate planning.

Obj. 3 Distinguish among various types and formats of wills.

Obj. 4 Appraise various types of trusts and estates.

Obj. 5 Evaluate the effects of federal and state taxes on estate planning.

Key Terms

adjusted gross estate
beneficiary
charitable lead trust
charitable remainder trust
codicil
community property
credit-shelter trust
disclaimer trust
estate
estate planning
estate tax
exemption trust will
formal will
generation-skipping trust
gift tax
guardian
holographic will
inheritance tax
intestate
irrevocable trust
life insurance trust
living trust
living will
marital deduction trust
power of attorney
prenuptial agreement
qualified personal residence trust (QPRT)

revocable trust	stated dollar amount will	trust
self-declaration trust	statutory will	trustee
simple will	testamentary trust	trustor
spend thrift trust	traditional marital share will	will

Pretest

True-False

_______ 1. (Obj. 1) Most people now live long lives.

_______ 2. (Obj. 1) Never having been married eliminates the need to organize your important documents.

_______ 3. (Obj. 2) In case of death, proof of claims must be produced, or the claims will not be processed.

_______ 4. (Obj. 2) The Economic Recovery Tax Act of 1981 created estate planning opportunities and problems for many people.

_______ 5. (Obj. 3) If your spouse had separate property or if the value of your estate increased, the simple will would cause lower taxation.

_______ 6. (Obj. 3) The exemption trust will has been decreasing in popularity due to its increased exemption ($675,000 since 2000).

_______ 7. (Obj. 3) A statutory will is one type of formal will.

_______ 8. (Obj. 4) A trust is a property arrangement through which your assets are held by a trustee for your benefit or for that of your beneficiaries.

_______ 9. (Obj. 5) Whatever you give your spouse is exempt from gift and estate taxes.

_______ 10. (Obj. 5) Inheritance taxes are imposed only by the federal government.

Self-Guided Study Questions

Obj. 1

Why Estate Planning? (p. 607)

What Is Estate Planning (p. 607)

1. Why is estate planning an essential part of retirement planning?

2. What is an estate?

3. What are the two components of estate planning?

If You Are Married (p. 608)

4. What are some of the personal aspects of estate planning if you are married?

If You Are Never Married (p. 608)

5. What are some of the personal aspects of estate planning if you never married?

New Lifestyles (p. 609)

6. What are some unique estate planning problems for millions of non-traditional households?

The Opportunity Cost of Rationalizing (p. 610)

7. What are the consequences of not planning your estate?

8. Why is it essential to plan your estate while you are in good health?

Obj. 2

Legal Aspects of Estate Planning (p. 610)

9. What are the legal aspects of estate planning?

10. What are some important necessary documents, and how can they be obtained?

Wills (p. 611)

11. What is a will?

12. What is an intestate?

13. What are the effects of marriage or divorce on a will?

14. What is the cost of preparing a standard will?

Obj. 3

Types and Formats of Wills (p. 613)

15. What are the various types of wills?

16. What is a simple will?

17. What are the characteristics of a traditional marital share will?

18. What is an exemption trust will?

19. What is the main advantage of the exemption trust will?

20. What is a stated dollar amount will?

21. What is one major shortcoming of the stated dollar amount will?

22. How do you determine which type of will is best for you?

Formats of Wills (p. 614)

23. What is a holographic will?

24. Is a holographic will valid in all states?

25. What is a formal will?

26. Must two witnesses sign the formal will in your presence?

27. What is a statutory will?

28. What are serious risks in leaving a statutory will?

Writing Your Will (p. 615)

29. What precautions should you take in writing a will?

30. Who is an executor or an executrix?

31. What are some guidelines in selecting an executor?

32. Who sets the fees for executors?

33. What is a guardian?

34. What is a trustee?

35. What precautions should you take in selecting a guardian?

36. What is the difference between a guardian and a trustee?

Altering or Rewriting Your Will (p. 617)

37. How do you alter an existing will?

38. What circumstances should trigger you to review your will?

39. What is a codicil?

40. What is the purpose of a prenuptial agreement?

A Living Will (p. 618)

41. What is a living will?

42. Who should have a living will?

43. How can you ensure the effectiveness of a living will?

44. How can a living will become a problem?

Power of Attorney (p. 619)

45. What is a power of attorney?

Letter of Last Instruction (p. 619)

46. What is a letter of last instruction?

47. What should a letter of last instruction contain?

48. What is the purpose of a letter of last instruction?

Obj. 4

Types of Trusts and Estates (p. 620)

49. What is a trust?

50. What is the trustor or grantor?

51. What is a revocable trust?

52. What is an irrevocable trust?

53. Which trust offers tax advantages?

Benefits of Establishing Trusts (p. 620)

54. What are some common reasons for setting up a trust?

Types of Trusts (p. 620)

55. What is a credit-shelter trust?

56. What are the unique features of a disclaimer trust?

57. What is a marital-deduction trust?

58. What is the most popular form of marital trust?

59. What is a living or inter-vivos trust?

60. What are the advantages of a living trust?

61. What are the unique features of a self-declaration trust?

62. What is a testamentary trust?

63. What is a pourover will?

64. What is a life insurance trust?

65. What are the pros and cons of a charitable remainder trust?

66. What is a qualified personal residence trust (QPRT)?

67. What is a charitable lead trust?

68. What is a generation-skipping trust?

69. Who should consider setting up a spendthrift trust?

70. How can a generation-skipping trust be used?

Estates (p. 624)

71. What is an estate?

72. What is meant by community property?

73. Why is joint ownership of property between spouses very common?

74. What is joint tenancy with the right of survivorship (JT/WROS)?

75. What is tenancy in common?

76. What is tenancy by entirety?

77. How are life insurance and employee benefits treated for income tax and probate purposes?

78. What are the tax consequences if lifetime gifts and trusts have strings attached to them?

79. How is the estate settled?

Settling Your Estate (p. 626)

80. Who carries out your wishes if you die "intestate"?

Obj. 5

Federal and State Estate Taxes (p. 627)

81. What has happened to the maximum tax rate on estates and gifts?

Types of Taxes (p. 627)

82. What are the four major taxes you should consider in estate planning?

83. What is an estate tax?

84. Who levies an estate tax?

85. What is the difference between an estate tax and an estate federal income tax?

86. Who imposes inheritance taxes?

87. What is a gift tax?

88. Who levies a gift tax?

Tax Avoidance and Tax Evasion (p. 629)

89. What is the difference between tax avoidance and tax evasion?

90. What charitable gifts and bequests are exempted from taxes?

Calculations of Tax (p. 630)

91. How is estate tax calculated?

92. What is net taxable estate?

93. What are probate and administration costs?

94. How is your taxable estate determined?

Paying the Tax (p. 631)

95. How is the estate tax paid?

96. What are some ways of handling the estate tax?

Post Test

Completion

1. (Obj. 1) The need to take estate planning steps is especially great if you are only ____________ or ____________ years away from retirement.
2. (Obj. 2) A(n) ____________ is the legal declaration of a person's mind as to disposition of his or her property after his or her death.
3. (Obj. 2) If you die without a will, you are called a(n) ____________.
4. (Obj. 3) An "I love you" will is known as a(n) ____________ ____________.
5. (Obj. 3) A(n) ____________ ____________ is a handwritten will that you prepare yourself.
6. (Obj. 3) A(n) ____________ is a document that explains, adds, or deletes provisions in your existing will.
7. (Obj. 3) A documentary agreement between spouses before marriage is called a(n) ____________ ____________.
8. (Obj. 3) A(n) ____________ ____________ ____________ is a legal document authorizing someone to act on your behalf.
9. (Obj. 4) In a(n) ____________ trust, you retain the right to end the trust or change its terms during your lifetime.
10. (Obj. 5) Your estate administration costs run between ____________ and ____________ percent of your estate.

Multiple Choice

______ 1. (Obj. 1) A definite plan for the administration and disposition of one's property during one's lifetime and at one's death is called
   A. a trust.
   B. an intestate.
   C. a codicil.
   D. estate planning.

______ 2. (Obj. 2) A legal declaration of a person's mind as to the disposition of his or her property after his or her death is called a(n)
   A. trust.
   B. estate.
   C. codicil.
   D. will.

_____ 3. (Obj. 3) An "I love you" will is sometimes called a(n) ____________ will.
A. simple
B. compound
C. traditional
D. exemption trust

_____ 4. (Obj. 3) Which type of will has been gaining popularity due to the increased exemption ($675,000 since 2000)?
A. Simple
B. Stated dollar amount
C. Exemption trust
D. Traditional marital share

_____ 5. (Obj. 3) A handwritten will that you prepare yourself is called a(n) ____________ will.
A. formal
B. holographic
C. beneficiary
D. statutory

_____ 6. (Obj. 3) Which document explains, adds, or deletes provisions in your existing will?
A. Prenuptial agreement
B. Trust agreement
C. Power of attorney
D. Codicil

_____ 7. (Obj. 3) A person who assumes the responsibilities of providing the children with personal care and of managing an estate for them is called
A. trustor.
B. trustee.
C. guardian.
D. beneficiary.

_____ 8. (Obj. 3) Which legal document authorizes someone to act on your behalf?
A. Power of attorney
B. Letter of instruction
C. Trust agreement
D. Prenuptial agreement

_____ 9. (Obj. 4) A trust established by your will that becomes effective upon your death is called a ____________ trust.
A. living
B. testamentary
C. revocable
D. willed

_______ 10. (Obj. 5) Probate and administration costs of your estate may run between _____________ percent of your estate.

A. 2-4
B. 5-8
C. 9-12
D. 15-20

Problems, Applications, and Cases

1. Interview an employee of a bank to determine the types of trusts the financial institution has available. Use the following form to summarize your findings.

Type of trust	Features	Advantages	Disadvantages

2. Conduct a survey of lawyers to determine the costs of having a will prepared. What factors influence these fees?

3. Draft your living will based on examples shown in Exhibits 19-3 and 19-4.

4. Make a list of desirable qualities you would want in a guardian for your minor children.

5. What is a tentative unified transfer tax for a decedent who dies in 1999 and makes a gift of $1,250,000 just before dying? Use the table as shown in Exhibit 19-7.

6. Fill out this sheet and provide copies to all those individuals whom you wish to attend to these important matters.

What to do when the emergency comes

(Helpful information for others)

In case of serious illness or my death, my doctors should be called as quickly as possible. (The doctor may, in turn, suggest calling the most available ambulance or emergency service. The numbers listed here should also be listed near a telephone.)

Doctor

Telephone

Ambulance or emergency service

Telephone

Call a relative or friend who can immediately assist you in handling some of the details listed on this page.

Name

Telephone

Call a clergy member (if desired).

Name

Telephone

Call a funeral director

Name

Telephone

Newspapers in which the obituary notice should be published.

Name of newspaper

Address

Newspaper

Address

(The funeral director generally assumes this responsibility. However, check with director if out-of-town notifications of death are to be published.) After funeral arrangements and other priority matter are completed, take care of the following:

You'll need death certificates—have about 15 copies made.

Notify employer, insurance companies, associations, banks, and other institutions.

Visit or call:

The local VA office

Address

Telephone

The local Social Security office:

Address

Telephone

The information on this page conveys a sense of immediacy. Thus, it should be readily available for others.

Courtesy of Aetna Life & Casualty, 151 Farmington Ave., Hartford, CT 06156.

Supplementary Case 19-1

Topic: Retirement and Estate Planning in a High-Income Family

Text Reference: pp. 620-631

Rich, 48, and Mariann, 47, have a gross estate of $1,160,000 and a high family income. Last year, their combined gross income was about $175,000, most of which came from a medical clinic in which Rich and several other physicians are partners. The remaining income came from Mariann's part-time job and from interest and dividends on various stocks, bonds, mutual funds, tax-sheltered investments, and rental property that Rich holds.

Rich and Mariann also own, in joint tenancy with right of survivorship, a home, a summer home, and an undeveloped lot in another state; and Mariann will receive $100,000 from a trust fund next year. Their net worth is about $510,000.

Since their holdings are extensive, Rich and Mariann contacted an estate planner for help in determining the most advantageous way of organizing their estate. Naturally, they wanted to be sure that the estate was set up in such a way as to minimize tax and probate shrinkage when it was passed on, first to the surviving spouse and ultimately to their four children. They also wanted to accumulate additional assets and to minimize their income taxes.

Case Questions

1. Should Rich and Mariann retitle some of the assets they currently hold in joint tenancy, so as to take advantage of the unified estate and gift-tax credit? Why?
2. Should Rich and Mariann establish a gifting program to reduce their income taxes and build up education funds for their children? Why or why not?

Supplementary Case 19-2

Topic: Retirement and Estate Planning in a Middle-Income Family

Text Reference: pp. 610-632

Bob, 42, an account executive for a manufacturing company, makes $45,000 a year. Judy, 42, a teacher, makes $25,000 a year.

With a son and a daughter, aged 15 and 13, respectively, Bob and Judy first want to make sure that they have enough money to pay for their children's education. They also want to make sure that they can retire at about 75 percent of their current monthly income when Bob is 64. Finally, Bob and Judy want to know how these goals and the overall status of their estate would be affected if either of them became disabled or died prematurely.

Case Questions

1. Assuming a modest rate of growth in their current capital plus monthly additions by each of them, do you think that Bob and Judy will be able to finance their children's education? Would you recommend that they establish an education fund?
2. If Judy were to die prematurely, would the family face an income shortage? What if Bob died?
3. What suggestions do you have for Bob and Judy's estate planning? For example, what type of will do you recommend, and do you recommend a trust arrangement?

Supplementary Reading 19-1

Joan Oleck, "When Giving Means Getting Back, The tax advantages of donating stock," *Business Week*, April 10, 2000, p 232.

When Giving Means Getting Back

The tax advantages of donating stock

When Community Foundation Silicon valley holds a networking party to pull rich, young Internet entrepreneurs into philanthropy, a kind of gee-whiz moment often occurs, says venture capitalist Kevin Fong, managing partner of the Mayfield Fund. "One of the questions that always comes up," says Fong, "is, 'How do you contribute stock? What are the advantages?' It's amazing, when you talk to these people, that many of them are not that sophisticated when it comes to their own finances."

Yet William H. Davidow, a founding partner of Mohr, Davidow Ventures in Menlo Park, Calif., predicts a flood of giving of appreciated stock by Internet billionaires in years to come. Indeed, both Davidow and Fong are already multimillion-dollar stock donors. And they have learned that gifting stock, as the practice is called, is important both for the good it does for the world and the good it does for your taxes and estate planning. Gifting, says Martin Greif, managing director of American Express Tax & Business Services in New York, is "one of the simplest and greatest things in the tax law." So if you're sitting on capital gains you'd like to turn over to charity, here are some key points:

TAKE A DEDUCTION. The Internal Revenue Service allows you to take a tax deduction on the full fair-market value of a gift stock. IRS rules direct you to calculate its value by figuring the mean between the high and low on the day you transfer it. That means lots of charitable mileage out of shares you may have bought at rock-bottom prices. Lawrence Rapoport, manager of client accounting at Rockefeller & Co., explains it this way: Say you bought stock for $1,000 that's now worth $10,000. If you sold those shares, you would pay 20%, or $1,800, in capital gains taxes on that $9,000 profit. Instead of having $10,000 to give to charity, you'd have only $8,200. Yet if you gift the $10,000 in stock, you can claim the full amount as a deduction. Remember to hold the stock 12 months or more. Otherwise, you may deduct only original cost basis.

GIFT INSIDER STOCK. You can donate restricted stock or "locked up" shares held by initial public offering insiders. Community Foundation, for instance, is holding on to pre-IPO shares of AltaVista, the search engine and Net portal, and Snowball.com, a Web site aimed at 13- to 30-year-olds. To value restricted stock, you will need an independent appraiser, according to IRS rules. Although you are not required to engage an appraiser for stock worth $10,000 or less that is not traded on any securities market, in practical terms, you will need help to value the stock, says Greif.

KNOW THE LIMITS. The IRS allows you to donate stock worth up to 30% of your adjusted gross income and still get a current valuation. The limit for donating to a family foundation is 20% of AGI. The overall ceiling on donations is 50%, so you can augment that 30% in stock with an additional 20% of your AGI in cash. If you exceed the limit, you can carry over the excess for five years.

GIFT MUTUAL FUND SHARES. "You don't see this as much," says Morgan Stanley Dean Witter Senior Vice-President Matthew Ives, "because a mutual fund makes a distribution every year." That means fund shares tend to have smaller capital gains.

WATCH THE CALENDAR. Although you won't know your exact AGI until at least yearend, don't donate stock on Dec. 31. It might not transfer in time for current-year tax benefits. And be sure to ask your recipient charity for a donor acknowledgement letter for the IRS.

TRY A TRUST. You deposit appreciated stock in a charitable remainder annuity trust and collect annual income of, say, 6%. Upon your death, the charity receives the principal. Using a trust avoids taxes on the stock's gains and gets you a deduction, dependent on your age and the value of the annuity interest.

By Joan Oleck

GIFT STOCK RESOURCES

SITE/ADDRESS (WWW.)	COMMENTS
COMMUNITY FOUNDATION SILICON VALLEY cfsv.org	Click on "Giving," then "How to give"
FIDELITY INVESTMENTS fidelity.com	Click on "Charitable Gift Fund"
GIVEASHARE.COM giveashare.com	New site will let you donate shares over the Net
NEWTITHING newtithing.org	Help in deciding how much you can afford to give
CHARLES SCHWAB schwab.com	Go to "Charitable Giving"

Study Questions

1. Why is gifting "one of the simplest and greatest things in the tax law" in estate planning?

2. What are the IRS limits for donating appreciated stocks?

3. What if you exceed the IRS limits?

4. Why should you not donate stock on December 31?

5. How can a trust arrangement help you in donating appreciated stock?

Supplementary Reading 19-2

Toddi Gutner, "Picking Up The Pieces When A Spouse Dies" *Business Week*, March 6, 2000, p. 186.

Picking Up The Pieces When A Spouse Dies

Since retiring , my husband handled inside work and I tackled the yard. Then, on Jan. 2, he died. How to survive was the message I got very fast. What money was coming in and going out? I am alone to make decisions and learn what a lone woman must know. After 50 years of being protected in a marriage, it is a very trying and difficult time.

As this recent widow wrote me, losing a spouse is devastating. The last thing most survivors want to think about is money. But financial affairs become the most pressing matter—a trauma for women who may be at the controls for the first time. Whether or not you're new to the ways of money, collecting all the benefits you're entitled to can be exhausting. But you can make this ordeal easier.

First, obtain several certified copies of your spouse's death certificate from the funeral director. You'll need these to verify your husband's death when you apply for Social Security benefits, retirement funds, and insurance proceeds, among other things. Next, contact your husband's life insurance agent to file a claim. Or send a written request to the insurance company with a copy of the death certificate and policy number.

KEEP RECORDS. You can often download claim forms from an insurer's Web site, but you'll be required to send in the original policy. Photocopy it and request a receipt. If you don't hear from the company in 10 business days, submit a written complaint to the head of the claims department, and request a response within two weeks. If that doesn't work, ask your state's insurance commissioner to investigate. Keep records of all correspondence and phone calls. And don't forget to look for life insurance hidden in other accounts. Ginita Wall, founder of the Women's Institute for Financial Education in San Diego, advises checking with your credit union, credit-card issuers, and auto insurer to see if benefits are available.

You'll also need to contact the human resources department of your husband's employer. Ask about retirement funds, deferred salary, accrued vacation pay, unpaid bonuses, commissions, corporate life insurance, and stock options. Options typically have a 10-year life from the date they're granted. In some cases, options must be exercised within a year of the owner's death. If you're the beneficiary of your husband's retirement funds, they automatically pass to you. Notify banks, brokers, or mutual-fund companies holding your husband's other retirement plans, such as IRAs or Keoghs. Also change the beneficiary on any policies or accounts that listed your husband. Finally, call the Social Security Administration (800 772-1213). Make an appointment to go to the local office to discuss survivor's benefits. If your husband was working when he died, bring his W-2 forms for the last two years. You'll receive $255 immediately upon your husband's death. You can claim monthly benefits if you're at least 60.

You may want to have a family member or attorney help with your efforts. But even if you think you've rounded up all of your husband's assets, you may have missed some. "Try to remember every bank, brokerage house, insurance company, and employer your husband ever had dealings with," recommends Barbara Raasch, partner at Ernst & Young in New York. Once you have pieced together the financial puzzle, resist making big investment decisions in the first six months after your loss. You have to reassess your financial needs, and it's tough to do so while grieving.

Toddi Gutner

Study Questions

1. What should a new widow's financial checklist include?

2. What can you do if your insurance company does not respond within two weeks after you file a life insurance claim?

3. Why is it important to contact your deceased spouse's human resources department at work?

4. Why shouldn't you resist making big investment decisions in the first six months after the death of a spouse?

Supplementary Reading 19-3

Mike McNamee, "Keeping Trusts Out of Harm's Way, More beneficiaries say they're captives of bad managers," *Business Week*, April 10, 2000, pp. 228-230.

Keeping Trusts Out of Harm's Way

More beneficiaries say they're captives of bad managers

Trust funds: Don't those words just conjure up images of huge sums managed with loving care by tweedy bankers for the benefit of carefree heirs? Well, these days, the reality is something else. You'll still find banks running trust funds, but the average fund's size is less than $250,000, and the assets are probably part of a common pool of securities mutual funds. Individual attention? Forget about it. Today's smaller trusts are more likely to be overseen by a harried banker who's running 300 other accounts as well. And the beneficiaries? They're mad as hell—and letting their banks know about it.

Beneficiaries' complaints about trustees are on the rise. Some are massive lawsuits, such as the multimillion-dollar settlement a Texas family won for legal malpractice against the law firm that handled their grandfather's estate. Others are small-scale disputes, such as the $20,000 in fees Diane D'Arcy of Fairfax County, Va., won back from the Boston bank that produced meager returns for her grandfather's $250,000 trust. Like D'Arcy, many beneficiaries think their bank or trust company is collecting fat fees while delivering thin investment returns and stingy payouts to a captive clientele.

Are these the whinings of idle coupon-clippers or a sign of wider problems? The answer is critical, since trusts are becoming the estate-planning tool of choice for Middle America. Revocable or lifetime trusts aren't a problem, because most people who use revocable trusts in place of wills name themselves or their spouses as trustees. Battles arise over irrevocable trusts. They tend to kick in after the grantor's death to minimize estate taxes, support widows or minor children, channel funds to charities, or protect assets for a future generation. For these, careful planning and drafting are crucial to head off future trouble (table).

By their nature, trusts are ripe for conflicts. Current beneficiaries want the biggest possible payouts; their children, who usually get what's left when the trust dissolves, want to preserve assets and go for growth. "Beneficiaries say: 'It's our money,'" says Steve Fast, a Hartford lawyer. "But the trustee has to maintain that it's not—it's granddad's money, and granddad might not have known the beneficiary."

Trouble is, these days it's unlikely that granddad would know the trustee, either. Waves of mergers have swallowed up local institutions, and a trust placed with a friendly banker in Elwood, Ind., might now be managed in Detroit. Most trusts are invested in the bank's common stock-and-bond portfolio or, increasingly, in the bank's own captive mutual funds, whether those funds are world-beaters or also-rans. And fees keep climbing: Locke Glenn, a 75-year-old beneficiary in Atlanta, complains that Wachovia Bank's fees have risen eight times as fast as payouts from his grandfather's trust since 1964. Wachovia says fees have remained around 1% of trust assets.

New competition from brokers' and insurers' recently minted trust arms, as well as state-chartered trust companies, should put the heat on bank trustees. But beneficiaries complain that they're captives, because most older trusts don't allow them to remove or replace a trustee without proving major breaches of fiduciary duty. "Banks won't resign gracefully, and if you fight them, they'll use the trust's own money to fight back," says Standish H. Smith, founder of Heirs, a beneficiaries' advocacy group in Villanova, Pa. Bankers say they're responding, naming trust ombudsmen to handle complaints and resigning as trustees more often. But "sometimes you can't get around the fact that Uncle Charlie wanted the trustee to be tough," says James D. McLaughlin, director of trust affairs at the American Bankers Assn.

What can an unhappy beneficiary do? First, look at the underlying will and trust documents: They might give the trustee bank more flexibility than it thinks it has. If not, put your complaints about poor investments or lack of accountability in writing. Document the trust's shortcomings by comparing its investment returns with other balanced portfolios. Then try to negotiate with the bank to move the trust elsewhere. Litigation should be your last resort—even if you have documented performance that the bank might find embarrassing. "You have much more power over a bank when you're threatening to sue it than when you actually sue," says Bedda Emous of Fiduciary Solutions, a Boston firm that advises beneficiaries.

Replacing a trustee should get easier soon. Under a new Uniform Trust Code that states will start adopting next year, beneficiaries can ask courts to remove a trustee without proving wrongdoing as long as all the beneficiaries agree. The new rule will apply to all trusts, even old ones, that don't spell out removal procedures.

But the best defense against future trust problems is good planning. Don't rule out banks or other corporate trustees: They're stable, they will outlive your heirs, and they can bring a dispassionate view to fractious family matters. Instead consider co-trustees—pairing a bank or brokerage selected for its investment and communication skills with a family member or trusted adviser. And give the individual who is the co-trustee the upper hand in executing the trust's goals—as well as the power to switch institutions. John K. Dwight of Charlotte, Vt., has taken that course, naming his wife, Heather, co-trustee with Chittenden Trust, in trusts he has already funded for their children.

If your estate must provide both immediate income and capital for future heirs, you might consider a unitrust. This instrument will empower your trustees to invest for total return and to use capital gains, as well as dividends or interest, to pay beneficiaries' income. The result will be a better portfolio and less conflict among heirs.

Owners of closely held businesses face special challenges. "No corporate trustee wants to be stuck trying to run a business," says Providence-based planner Amy J. Leavitt of Lincoln Financial Advisors. Work out a success plan or pick an individual trustee who can set the business up for an orderly sale.

There's no way to guarantee that your heirs and trustees won't squabble. But if you let all parties know well in advance what you want done, you can curb friction. That, as much as the assets you leave, may be your best legacy.

By Mike McNamee

SMART PLANNING TO HEAD OFF TROUBLE

Lifetime or revocable trusts aren't a problem. But irrevocable trust must be drafted with care.

AVOID UNNEEDED TRUSTS
If your heirs are mature and you don't have pressing tax or generation-skipping concerns, it's easier to leave assets to them outright.

PICK THE RIGHT TRUSTEE
Avoid obvious conflicts, like giving a daughter control over her stepmother's income. And screen trustees for investment skills.

CONSIDER CO-TRUSTEES
Pair a family member or trusted adviser with a bank or broker trustee. Give the individual power to oversee the corporate trustee.

CREATE ESCAPE HATCHES
Consider letting beneficiaries vote to replace a poorly performing trustee.

MAKE YOUR WISHES KNOWN
Your trustee and beneficiaries should have a clear understanding of how you want your estate to be managed and distributed.

LET GO
Don't try to rule from the grave. Consider "sprinkle" trusts, which distribute assets to beneficiaries at set intervals or ages.

WHERE TO FIND HELP

HEIRS INC.
www.heirs.net
Advises beneficiaries and advocates trust reform

FIDUCIARY CHOICE
www.fiduciarychoice.com
Directory for banks and trust companies to post qualifications

AMERICAN COLLEGE OF TRUST & ESTATE COUNSEL
www.actec.org
Referral service for finding estate attorneys

NATIONAL ACADEMY OF ELDER LAW ATTORNEYS
www.naela.org
Directory of lawyers who handle estate, Medicare, and other concerns of the elderly

Study Questions

1. What is the average size of a typical trust fund?

2. Why are the beneficiaries of these trusts "mad as hell"? Why are they complaining?

3. Why are revocable or lifetime trusts not a problem?

4. Where are most trust funds invested?

5. What can an unhappy beneficiary do?

6. Can you ask the court to remove a trustee without proving wrongdoing as long as all the beneficiaries agree?

7. What is your best defense against future trust problems?

Supplementary Reading 19-4

Mike McNamee, "Death And Fewer Taxes" *Business Week*, April 10, 2000, p. 230.

Death And Fewer Taxes

You can't take it with you. So why do so many people hang on to their wealth until the bitter end? Especially when the Internal Revenue Service is set up to ensure that the end will be bitter—or at least expensive—indeed.

"One of the biggest mistakes wealthy people make is not giving away assets while they're alive," says Bob Carson, a tax partner and planner at Ernst & Young. "It's human nature." But defy nature. Give to your heirs while you're alive, and they'll thank you for it. They'll net more after taxes than if you leave the same assets in your estate. Give wisely, and you can wipe out the 55% IRS levy on estates of $5 million or more.

Gifts enjoy two tax advantages. Up to $10,000 that you give to each recipient in a year is excluded from gift and estate taxes. Give more, and the second tax break kicks in: The gift tax is levied only on the amount you give, while the estate tax is levied on your whole estate—including the tax. Say you give your children $1 million. In the 55% bracket, you'll pay $550,000 in tax. Leave $1.55 million in your estate, and the IRS will take 55% of it. It will get $852,500, and your kids will net $697,500—30% less.

Astute planners say you shouldn't just give—you should give early. On top of the $10,000 annual exclusion, the tax code gives you a lifetime credit that lets you transfer $675,000 without paying gift or estate taxes. (The excluded amount will rise to $1 million in 2006.) "That's your coupon, and you should spend it wisely," says Thomas R. Livergood, a financial planner with Balasa & Hoffman Inc. in Schaumburg, Ill., Give $500,000 in stock to your kids today, directly or in trust, and you'll pay no tax. Wait 10 years—when the stock has risen, say, to $1.3 million—and the same gift will net the IRS $165,000 in taxes.

The best way to keep wealth in the family is to combine the gift-tax advantage, your lifetime credit, and IRS-approved discounts for gifts that are structured in certain ways. Say you put $1 million worth of stock and real estate into a family limited partnership (FLP). Name yourself the general partner, with the power to decide how assets are managed, but give 99% of the partnership to your children as limited partners. Since your kids can't manage or sell the property, their shares are deemed impaired and can be reported on a gift-tax return at less than full face value. A discount of 35% would wipe out the tax. But proceed with care: The government is cracking down on deep-discount FLPs, especially those funded with marketable stocks or bonds. A skilled planner, lawyer, or accountant can structure an FLP that will withstand an audit.

The biggest hurdle to lifetime gifts, planners say, is persuading clients to let go. "These aren't people who need to worry about their next meal," says Livergood. "But they still have to be persuaded to give up some wealth and control." If this sounds like you, get a financial analysis to see how much of your wealth will outlive you. Then, remember the estate planner's rule: "Tis better to give than to bequeath."

Mike McNamee

Study Questions

1. Why do so many people hang on to their wealth until the bitter end?

2. What tax advantages do gifts provide?

3. What is the best way to keep wealth in the family?

4. Comment on the statement: "Tis better to give than to bequeath."

Chapter 1 Answers

Pretest *True-False*

1. T (p. 3)
2. F (p. 6)
3. F (p. 12)
4. T (p. 17)
5. T (p. 12)
6. F (p. 14)
7. F (p. 4)
8. T (p. 8)
9. T (p. 21)
10. F (p. 23)

Post Test *Completion*

1. personal finance planning (p.3)
2. adult life cycle (p.12)
3. goals (p.4)
4. opportunity cost (p.6)
5. Economics (p.13)
6. time value of money (p.17)
7. inflation (p.14)
8. Liquidity (p.21)
9. Values (p.12)
10. plan (p. 23)

Multiple Choice

1. C (p. 3)
2. B (p. 4)
3. A (p. 18)
4. B (p.12)
5. B (p. 13)
6. A (p.16)
7. D (p. 8)
8. C (p. 21)
9. D (p. 23)
10. C (p. 23)

Problems, Applications, and Cases

1. a. $501.38
   b. $1,395
   c. $310.80
   d. $1,724.10
2. Answers will vary.
3. Answers will vary.
4. a. estate planning
   b. planning
   c. managing risk
   d. borrowing (or spending)
   e. obtaining (or planning)
   f. savings (or planning)
   g. borrowing (or planning)
   h. investing (or planning)
5. Answers will vary.
6. Answers will vary.

Chapter 2 Answers

Pretest *True-False*

1. T (p. 38)
2. T (p. 37)
3. F (p. 39)
4. T (p. 42)
5. T (p. 47)
6. T (p. 62)
7. T (p. 63)
8. F (p. 67)
9. T (pp. 49-52)
10. T (p. 54)

Post Test *Completion*

1. screening (p. 67)
2. targeted (p. 63)
3. job (p. 37)
4. mentor (p. 55)
5. cover letter (p. 65)
6. chronological (p. 62)
7. informational (p. 47)
8. career (p. 37)
9. selection (p. 67)
10. functional (p. 63)

Multiple Choice

1. B (p. 39)
2. A (p. 47)
3. D (p. 62)
4. B (p. 63)
5. C (p. 65)
6. B (p. 65)
7. C (p. 67)
8. A (p. 67)
9. C (p. 51)
10. C (p. 50)

Problems, Applications, and Cases

1. Answers will vary.
2. Answers will vary.
3. Answers will vary.
4. Answers will vary.
5. Answers will vary.
6. Answers will vary.

Chapter 3 Answers

Pretest *True-False*
1. F (p. 73)
2. T (p. 74)
3. F (p. 75)
4. F (p. 77)
5. F (p. 77)
6. T (p. 78)
7. T (p. 81)
8. F (p. 85)
9. T (p. 86)
10. T (p. 90)

Post Test *Completion*
1. Liquid (p. 75)
2. variance (p. 86)
3. balance sheet (p. 74)
4. take-home pay (p. 79)
5. liabilities (p. 75)
6. cash flow statement (p. 77)
7. Insolvency (p. 77)
8. allocations (p. 85)
9. net worth (p. 77)
10. safe-deposit box (p. 73)

Multiple Choice
1. B (p. 73)
2. A (p. 74)
3. A (p. 75)
4. D (p.77)
5. B (p. 77)
6. C (p. 80)
7. B (p. 77)
8. B (p. 81)
9. B (p. 86)
10. A (p. 91)

Problems, Applications, and Cases

1. Student activity.
2. Balance sheet:
   Assets: $29,234
   Liabilities: $2,193
   Net Worth: $27,041

   Cash flow statement:
   Income: $2,112
   Payments: $2,102
   Surplus: $100
3. Student activity.
4. Answers will vary.
5. Answers will vary.
6. a. variable
   b. variable
   c. fixed
   d. variable
   e. variable
   f. fixed
   g. variable
   h. variable

Chapter 4 Answers

Pretest *True-False*	Post Test *Completion*	*Multiple Choice*
1. T (p. 98)	1. credit (p. 104)	1. B (p. 98)
2. F (p. 98)	2. excise (p. 98)	2. D (p. 98)
3. T (p. 98)	3. capital gain (p. 121)	3. A (p. 99)
4. F (p. 99)	4. tax audit (p. 117)	4. C (p. 101)
5. T (p. 101)	5. Earned (p. 99)	5. A (p. 102)
6. F (p. 104)	6. inheritance (p. 98)	6. D (p. 106)
7. F (p. 106)	7. itemized deductions (p. 101)	7. B (p. 107)
8. F (p. 109)	8. exemption (p. 102)	8. A (p. 117)
9. F (p. 117)	9. exempt (p. 120)	9. D (p. 118)
10. F (p. 122)	10. exclusion (p. 99)	10. C (p. 119)

Problems, Applications, and Cases

1. Taxable income $28,550
2. Student activity.
3. Answers will vary.

Chapter 5 Answers

Pretest *True-False*

1. T (p. 132)
2. T (p. 132)
3. F (p. 134)
4. T (p. 132)
5. F(p. 138)
6. F (p. 146)
7. F (p. 144)
8. T (p. 150)
9. F (p. 150)
10. F (p. 159)

Post Test *Completion*

1. savings and loan association (p. 138)
2. rate of return (p. 146)
3. Demand (p. 132)
4. share and draft account (p. 150)
5. automatic teller machines (p. 134)
6. certificate of deposit (p. 144)
7. asset management account (p. 133)
8. credit union (p. 139)
9. compounding (p. 146)
10. time (p. 132)

Multiple Choice

1. B (p. 140)
2. C (p. 132)
3. D (p. 138)
4. C (p. 133)
5. A (p. 146)
6. A (p. 148)
7. D (p. 149)
8. B (p. 150)
9. C (p. 159)
10. D (p. 161)

Problems, Applications, and Cases

1. Answers will vary.
2. Answers will vary.
3. Answers will vary.
4. a. $599.20
   b. $887.60
   c. $259.21
   d. $1,453.83
5. Answers will vary.
6. Answers will vary.
7. Corrected (adjusted) checkbook balance: $230

Chapter 6 Answers

Pretest *True-False*

1. T (p. 165)
2. F (p. 166)
3. F (p. 169)
4. T (p. 170)
5. T (p. 176)
6. T (p. 177)
7. F (p. 183)
8. T (p. 187)
9. F (p. 187)
10. T (p. 192)

Post Test *Completion*

1. Credit (p. 165)
2. closed-end credit (p. 169)
3. open-end credit (p. 169)
4. Line of credit (p. 169)
5. character (p. 183)
6. capacity (p. 183)
7. Collateral (p. 184)
8. 20 percent (p. 176)
9. seven years (p. 180)
10. The Fair Credit Billing Act (p. 187)

Multiple Choice

1. C (p. 166)
2. A (p. 168)
3. D (p. 169)
4. A (p. 169)
5. B (p. 183)
6. D (p. 183)
7. C (p. 176)
8. A (p. 180)
9. B (p. 187)
10. D (p. 190)

Problems, Applications, and Cases

1. Students will find various and varying information in their credit files.

2. a. open-end
   b. incidental
   c. incidental
   d. closed-end
   e. closed-end
   f. incidental
   g. open-end
   h. open-end
   i. closed-end
   j. open-end

3. The student responses will vary. Here are possible answers:
   a. yes
   b. yes
   c. no
   d. maybe
   e. yes
   f. no
   g. maybe
   h. no
   i. no
   j. maybe

4. Answers will vary.

5. Yes. Alyssa meets all the tests of the Fair Credit Billing Act. The purchase is over $50, within her home town and home state, and she has made a good faith effort to resolve the matter.

6. No. Mark has not made a good faith effort to resolve that matter. The TV repair problem may be unrelated to the earlier service call he made to Ace TV Repair Shoppe.

7. No. Amy can't withhold the payment because the purchase was not over $50.

Chapter 7 Answers

Pretest *True-False*
1. T (p. 199)
2. F (p. 200)
3. T (p. 204)
4. T (p. 204)
5. F (p. 213)
6. T (p. 216)
7. T (p. 216)
8. F (p. 216)
9. T (p. 220)
10. F (p. 220)

Post Test *Completion*
1. cheaper (p. 199)
2. growing (p. 200)
3. consumer finance companies (p. 202)
4. commercial banks (p. 202)
5. finance charge (p. 204)
6. annual percentage rate (p. 204
7. Fair Debt Collections Practices Act (p. 213)
8. Consumer Credit Counseling Service (p. 216)
9. Chapter 7 bankruptcy (p. 220)
10. Chapter 13 bankruptcy (p. 220)

Multiple Choice
1. B (p. 203)
2. A (p. 202)
3. A (p. 209)
4. C (p. 204)
5. D (p. 211)
6. A (p. 213)
7. C (p. 213)
8. B (p. 216)
9. B (p. 220)
10. C (p. 220)

Problems, Applications, and Cases

1. To find the interest rate on a loan, use the simple interest formula:
   I = P x R x T (PRT)
   = $2,000 x 0.10 x 1 = $200
   Total owed at the end of one year = P + I = $2,000 + $200 = $2,200

2. Over the first year, you have the full use of the $2,000 principal and, therefore, incur an interest obligation of $200 ($2,000 x 0.10 x 1). This first year's interest expense, however, is payable at the *end* of the second year.

   Over the second and last year of the loan, you again have full use of $2,000, for which another $200 interest obligation is incurred and due at the end of the second year. At the end of two full years, you must repay the two years interest ($200 + $200 = $400), in addition to the original amount borrowed ($2,000). In other words, you have to pay interest *only* on the amount borrowed and *not* on any accumulated interest charges.

   Total loan repayment = principal + interest charges on the principal only.
   = P + I or
   = P + (P x R x T)
   = $2,000 + ($2,000 x 0.10 x 2)
   = $2,000 + $400
   = $2,400

3. P = $1,500; R = 0.132 or 13.2/100; and T = 6 months or ½ year. The amount due on the loan consists of principal plus the half-year's interest on the principal:

   Total loan repayment = $1,500 (1 + 0.132 x ½)
   = $1,500 (1 + 0.066) = $1,500 (1.066)
   = $1,599

Note: While the simple annual interest rate is 13.2%, the amount of interest charged for half the year is 6.6% or ½ of 13.2% of the principal.

Since the total amount due is $1,599 and the amount borrowed is $1,500, the difference of $99 ($1,599 - $1,500) is the total amount of interest on the six-month loan.

4. a. Creditor
   b. Consumer
   c. Consumer
   d. Consumer
   e. Debt collector (The debt collector loses business. The creditor, too, may still be incurring high collection costs as a result of the Act.)
   f. Consumer
   g. Debt collector
   h. Consumer (The creditor has shifted the higher costs of debt collection to consumers. However, the creditor may still incur costs if reducing the availability of credit also causes business to decrease.)

5. a. Illegal. A debt collector cannot use a post card to communicate with a customer.

   b. Legal. As long as the creditor does not go by a different name when collecting debts, he/she is not covered by the Fair Debt Collection Act.

   c. Legal. A bank collecting its own debts is not covered by the Act.

   d. Illegal. A debt collector cannot call at an unusual or inconvenient time (before 8 a.m. or after 9 p.m.)

   e. Illegal. ABC Stores is covered by the Act because it goes by ABC Collections, Inc., when collecting debts. (6 a.m. is generally considered an unusual time.)

   f. Legal. A department store collecting its own debts is not covered by the Act.

   g. Legal. A credit union collecting its own debts is not covered by the Act.

   h. Illegal. A debt collector cannot call a consumer at work if such contact is prohibited by the employer.

   i. Illegal. Because a debt collector legally cannot "throw a consumer in jail," he/she cannot threaten to do so.

   j. Legal. The creditor may repossess the furniture so it can be stated as possible consequence of nonpayment.

6.

Cost of credit	APR
a. $232	10.77%
b. $114	22.62%
c. $500	10.91%

7. The nominal rate of interest on the loan is 0 percent.

8. The real rate of interest is minus seven percent.

Chapter 8 Answers

Pretest *True-False*

1. F (p. 240)
2. F (p. 240)
3. T (p. 247)
4. F (p. 247)
5. T (p. 250)
6. T (p. 251)
7. F (p. 253)
8. T (p. 254)
9. T (p. 255)
10. F (p. 256)

Post Test *Completion*

1. nit pricing (p. 248)
2. Small claims court (p. 255)
3. mediation (p. 254)
4. Impulse buying (p. 247)
5. legal aid societies (p. 256)
6. Arbitration (p. 254)
7. service contract (p. 251)
8. class action suit (p. 256)
9. cooperative (p. 247)
10. warranty (p. 250)

Multiple Choice

1. C (p. 238)
2. B (p. 240)
3. C (p. 248)
4. D (p. 247)
5. C (p. 250)
6. B (p. 245)
7. A (p. 253)
8. B (p. 254)
9. C (p. 256)
10. B (p. 256)

Problems, Applications, and Cases

1. Answers will vary.
2. Scoring results: Brand A 5.3; Brand B 6.2; Brand C 5.9.

   Based on this analysis, John would buy Brand B, but he should also consider other factors in his purchasing decision, such as comments from friends, ratings by consumer organizations, and brand reputation.
3. Answers will vary.
4. a. Highway Traffic Safety Administration
   b. U.S. Postal Service or Federal Trade Commission
   c. Food and Drug Administration
   d. State Consumer Protection Office and Securities and Exchange Commission

Chapter 9 Answers

Pretest *True-False*
1. T (p. 281)
2. T (p. 285)
3. F (p. 286)
4. T (p. 288)
5. T (p. 290)
6. T (p. 293)
7. T (p. 293)
8. F (p. 295)
9. T (p. 299)
10. T (p. 301)

Post Test *Completion*
1. Amortization (p. 296)
2. condominium (p. 288)
3. balloon (p. 298)
4. deed (p. 301)
5. lease (p. 285)
6. Points (p. 295)
7. buy-down (p. 300)
8. escrow account (p. 302)
9. Earnest money (p. 292)
10. closing costs (p. 301)

Multiple Choice
1. C (p. 284)
2. B (p. 285)
3. A (p. 288)
4. D (p. 287)
5. C (p. 290)
6. D (p. 290)
7. B (p. 295)
8. B (p. 296)
9. C (p. 300)
10. B (p. 302)

Problems, Applications, and Cases

1. (1) Total annual home purchase expenses ($790 x 12 x $420) — $9,900
   (2) Deductible portion of expenses ($8,900 + $1,575) — $10,475
   (3) Multiply deductible items by tax rate ($10,475 x 0.28) — $2,933
   (4) Subtract (3) from (1) to obtain after-tax cost of buying — $6,967
   (5) Multiply rent by 12 to obtain annual renting costs — $7,800

   In addition to these financial aspects, George and Alicia should also consider the money needed for a down payment, chances of having to move in the near future, freedom from being responsible for repairs, as well as other personal and financial factors.
2. Answers will vary.
3. Answers will vary.
4. Answers will vary.
5. a. an FHA mortgage or buy down
   b. a balloon mortgage or variable rate mortgage
   c. a second mortgage or variable rate mortgage
   d. a conventional mortgage
   e. a graduated payment mortgage

Chapter 10 Answers

Pretest *True-False*

1. F (p. 318)
2. T (p. 319)
3. T (p. 321)
4. F (p. 321)
5. F (p. 325)
6. T (p. 325)
7. F (p. 326)
8. T (p. 328)
9. T (p. 330)
10. F (p. 332)

Post Test *Completion*

1. Comprehensive physical damage (p. 330)
2. actual cash value (p. 325)
3. Property damage liability (p. 329)
4. Vicarious (p. 318)
5. Driver classification (p. 332)
6. Financial responsibility law (p. 326)
7. negligence (p. 318)
8. Collision (p. 329)
9. umbrella (p. 321)
10. Medical payments (p. 328)

Multiple Choice

1. C (p. 318)
2. C (p. 319)
3. B (p. 321)
4. A (p. 322)
5. C (p. 325)
6. B (p. 327)
7. D (Pp. 328, 329)
8. C (p. 329)
9. C (p. 332)
10. A (p. 332)

Problems, Applications, and Cases

1. Student activity.
2. Student activity.
3. a. medical payments
   b. property damage liability
   c. bodily injury liability
   d. comprehensive physical damage
   e. uninsured motorists protection
   f. collision

Chapter 11 Answers

Pretest *True-False*
1. T (p. 339)
2. T (p. 343)
3. F (p. 343)
4. T (p. 345)
5. F (p. 346)
6. T (p. 346)
7. T (p. 351)
8. F (p. 352)
9. T (p. 359)
10. F (p. 367)

Post Test *Completion*
1. stay well (p. 343)
2. health insurance (p. 343)
3. Disability income insurance (p. 345)
4. Hospital expense insurance (p. 350)
5. Surgical expense insurance (p. 351)
6. Physical expense insurance (p. 351)
7. Blue Cross (p. 359)
8. Blue Shield (p. 359)
9. Medicare (p. 363)
10. Medicaid (p. 367)

Multiple Choice
1. C (p. 339)
2. A (p. 345)
3. D (p. 344)
4. C (p. 346)
5. C (p. 351)
6. A (p. 351)
7. B (p. 351)
8. A (p. 359)
9. B (p. 359)
10. C (p. 363)

Problems, Applications, and Cases

1. Answers will vary.
2. Answers will vary.
3. Answers will vary.
4. a. major medical
   b. basic protection
   c. basic protection; major medical; disability income
   d. basic protection
   e. supplemental policy (dental insurance)
   f. basic protection
5. Larry probably does not need health insurance because he is covered through Liz's employer-sponsored health insurance plan. However, Larry should obtain disability income insurance and possibly a decreasing term insurance.
6. Since Pam's ex-husband is responsible for the children's health care bills, she does not need additional health insurance coverage, but she should purchase disability insurance.

Chapter 12 Answers

Pretest *True-False*	Post Test *Completion*	*Multiple Choice*
1. F (p. 375)	1. life insurance (p. 376)	1. B (p. 375)
2. T (p. 376)	2. easy method (p. 378)	2. B (p. 378)
3. F (p. 377)	3. participating policy (p. 380)	3. A (p. 380)
4. F (p. 378)	4. Term insurance (p. 380)	4. D (p. 383)
5. T (p. 380)	5. whole life (p. 383)	5. C (p. 390)
6. F (p. 383)	6. group insurance (p. 386)	6. A (p. 386)
7. T (p. 389)	7. beneficiary (p. 389)	7. B (p. 391)
8. T (p. 391)	8. Interest-adjusted (p. 395)	8. C (p. 391)
9. F (p. 394)	9. annuity (p. 399)	9. D (p. 395)
10. T (p. 399)	10. annuity (p. 399)	10. A (p. 400)

Problems, Applications, and Cases

1. Student responses will vary depending on where they live.
2. Student responses will vary from state to state.
3. The answers given here are recommended. With more information, it would be possible to give logical reasons for other answers:
   a. straight life or term
   b. term
   c. straight life
   d. term
4. Answers will vary.
5. Single persons living alone or with their parents usually have little or no need for life insurance.
6. Households with small children most often have the greatest need for life insurance.

   Based on the insurance agent's rule of thumb that a "typical family" will need approximately 70 percent of the breadwinner's salary for seven years, Barry will need about $147,000 worth of life insurance on his life.

   Since Mary does not work, we can use a "non-working spouse" method of determining life insurance needs. The youngest child reaches age 18 in 16 years. Simply multiply 16 by $9,000; therefore, Barry needs $144,000 of life insurance.

Chapter 13 Answers

Pretest *True-False*	Post Test *Completion*	*Multiple Choice*
1. T (p. 410)	1. three (p. 411)	1. B (p. 411)
2. F (p. 410)	2. Safety, risk (p. 414)	2. B (p. 419)
3. T (p. 411)	3. interest rate (p. 417)	3. B (p. 419)
4. F (p. 414)	4. Liquidity (p. 420)	4. D (p. 420)
5. F (p. 420)	5. common stock (p. 421)	5. D (p. 420)
6. F (p. 420)	6. preferred stock (p. 421)	6. C (p. 422)
7. T (p. 421)	7. one, thirty (p. 421)	7. B (p. 423)
8. T (p. 421)	8. mutual fund (p. 421)	8. B (p. 423)
9. T (p. 427)	9. financial planner (p. 427)	9. C (p. 428)
10. F (p. 432)	10. ordinary (p. 429)	10. A (p. 431)

Problems, Applications, and Cases

1. Answers will vary.
2. Answers will vary
3. Answers will vary.

Chapter 14 Answers

Pretest *True-False*	Post Test *Completion*	*Multiple Choice*
1. T (p. 442)	1. proxy (p. 443)	1. D (p. 442)
2. T (p. 444)	2. stock split (p. 445)	2. B (p. 448)
3. F (p. 447)	3. Callable (p. 447)	3. D (p. 448)
4. F (p. 448)	4. defensive (p. 450)	4. C (p. 449)
5. F (p. 449)	5. price-earnings (p. 459)	5. C (p. 460)
6. T (p. 449)	6. fundamental (p. 460)	6. B (p. 462)
7. F (p. 466)	7. securities exchange (p. 463)	7. B (p. 464)
8. T (p. 468)	8. account executive (p. 465)	8. A (p. 466)
9. F (p. 471)	9. direct investment (p. 472)	9. D (p. 470)
10. T (p. 474)	10. option (p. 474)	10. C (p. 474)

Problems, Applications, and Cases

1. Answers will vary.
2. a. Book value = $8.80 per share
   b. Earnings per share = $3.20
   c. Price-earnings ratio = 14
3. a. Current yield = 3.1 percent
   b. Total return = $1,400
   c. Annualized holding period yield = 8 percent
4. The price-earnings ratio is a key factor that serious investors use to evaluate stock investments. Generally, a low price-earnings ratio indicates that a stock may be a good investment and a high price-earnings ratio indicates that it may be a poor investment. Since the price-earnings ratio for Watson Plastics, Inc. is above average for firms in the same industry, Watson Plastics may be a poor investment at this time. Before making your investment decision, you may also want to consider some of the other factors that are described on pages 449-462 in Chapter 14.

Chapter 15 Answers

Pretest *True-False*

1. F (p. 483)
2. T (p. 484)
3. F (p. 486)
4. T (p. 486)
5. T (p. 489)
6. F (p. 490)
7. F (p. 494)
8. T (p. 494)
9. F (p. 501)
10. F (p. 502)

Post Test *Completion*

1. corporate bond (p. 483)
2. maturity date (p. 484)
3. subordinated debenture (p. 486)
4. sinking (p. 487)
5. interest, value, repayment (p. 489)
6. registered (p. 489)
7. $1,000 (p. 494)
8. general obligation (p. 495)
9. bid (p. 498)
10. market (p. 502)

Multiple Choice

1. B (p. 484)
2. A (p. 486)
3. D (p. 487)
4. B (p. 489)
5. A (p. 490)
6. B (p. 494)
7. B (p. 496)
8. D (p. 498)
9. A (p. 502)
10. C (p. 502)

Problems, Applications, and Cases

1. Answers will vary, but you may want to compare your answers with the material in Exhibit 15-6.
2. a. 6.94 percent
   b. 8.33 percent
   c. 9.03 percent
   d. 10.42 percent
   e. 11.11 percent
3. Answers will vary.
4. Answers will vary.
5. a. 8.42 percent
   b. 4.76 percent
   c. 11.67 percent
   d. 10.79 percent
   e. 15.29 percent

Chapter 16 Answers

Pretest *True-False*
1. T (p. 514)
2. F (p. 514)
3. F (p. 516)
4. T (p. 517)
5. F (p. 520)
6. T (p. 522)
7. F (p. 528)
8. F (p. 525)
9. T (p. 532)
10. T (p. 537)

Post Test *Completion*
1. professional, diversification (p. 514)
2. closed-end (p. 514)
3. net asset value (p. 514)
4. contingent deferred sales load (p. 517)
5. balanced (p. 521)
6. small cap (p. 521)
7. professional-advisory (p. 528)
8. prospectus (p. 525)
9. Capital gain (p. 532)
10. capital (p. 534)

Multiple Choice
1. D (p. 514)
2. C (p. 516)
3. B (p. 517)
4. D (p. 517)
5. C (p. 520)
6. D (p. 520)
7. B (p. 523)
8. D (p. 532)
9. A (p. 537)
10. A (p. 537)

Problems, Applications, and Cases

1. Matching questions
   1. c (p. 514)
   2. i (p. 517)
   3. b (p. 514)
   4. g (p. 517)
   5. d (p. 516)
   6. a (p. 514)
   7. e (p. 517)
   8. h (p. 517)
   9. f (p. 516)
2. Answers will vary, but you may want to review the material on pages 519-522 while completing this exercise.
3. Answers will vary.
4. a. The net asset value per share is $14.67.
   $588,600,000 ÷ 40,124,200 = $14.67 per share.
   b. The commission on a $2,000 investment would be $120.
   $2,000 x 0.60 = $120.
5. a. The current yield for this investment is 5.6 percent.
   $0.60 ÷ $10.75 = 5.6 percent.
   b. The total return for this investment would be $180 loss at the end of 12 months.
   200 shares x $0.60 = $120 current return.
   200 shares x $1.50 = $300 dollar loss ($12.25 purchase price - $10.75 selling price = $1.50 per share loss.)
   $120 current return - $300 future loss = $180 total loss on the transaction.

Chapter 17 Answers

Pretest *True-False*
1. T (p. 547)
2. T (p. 547)
3. T (p. 548)
4. F (p. 552)
5. F (p. 552)
6. T (p. 554)
7. F (p. 553)
8. T (p. 555)
9. T (p. 555)
10. F (p. 558)

Post Test *Completion*
1. direct investments (p. 547)
2. commercial property (p. 548)
3. syndicate (p. 549)
4. hybrid (p. 550)
5. limited partner (p. 553)
6. Financial leverage (p. 554)
7. Diversification (p. 555)
8. kilogram (p. 556)
9. Diamonds (p. 558)
10. Gemological Institute of America (p. 558)

Multiple Choice
1. C (p. 547)
2. A (p. 548)
3. D (p. 549)
4. C (p. 550)
5. B (p. 552)
6. A (p. 552)
7. C (p. 552)
8. D (p. 554)
9. B (p. 555)
10. C (p. 558)

Problems, Applications, and Cases

1. Responses will vary.
2. Responses will vary.
3. Responses will vary.
4. Responses will vary.
5. a. 13.6%
   b. 17.5%
   c. –11.4%

4. Students will most likely list the rules provided by the Federal Trade Commission and the American Numismatic Association.

Chapter 18 Answers

Pretest *True-False*	Post Test *Completion*	*Multiple Choice*
1. F (p. 570)	1. 16 to 20 (p. 570)	1. B (p. 571)
2. F (p. 570)	2. financial (p. 570)	2. C (p. 571)
3. T (p. 573)	3. impossible (p. 576)	3. C (p. 570)
4. F (p. 574)	4. less (p. 576)	4. A (p. 571)
5. F (p. 576)	5. Social Security (p. 582)	5. D (p. 576)
6. T (p. 577)	6. defined-contribution plan (p. 586)	6. C (p. 577)
7. T (p. 579)	7. defined-benefit plan (p. 587)	7. A (p. 582)
8. F (p. 582)	8. Keogh plan (p. 594)	8. D (p. 586)
9. F (p. 582)	9. Immediate (p. 595)	9. B (p. 586)
10. F (p. 598)	10. deferred (p. 595)	10. C (p. 594)

Problems, Applications, and Cases

1. Student activity.
2. Student activity.
3. Answers will vary.
4. Answers will vary.
5. a. $647
   b. $368
6. Male: $2,249.95
   Female: $2,746.98

Chapter 19 Answers

Pretest *True-False*

1. T (p. 607)
2. F (p. 608)
3. T (p. 608)
4. T (p. 611)
5. F (p. 613)
6. F (p. 613)
7. T (p. 614)
8. T (p. 620)
9. T (p. 627)
10. F (p. 629)

Post Test *Completion*

1. five or ten (p. 608)
2. will (p. 611)
3. intestate (p. 611)
4. simple will (p. 613)
5. holographic will (p. 614)
6. codicil (p. 617)
7. prenuptial agreement (p. 617)
8. power of attorney (p. 619)
9. revocable (p. 620)
10. 5 to 8 (p. 630)

Multiple Choice

1. D (p. 607)
2. D (p. 611)
3. A (p. 613)
4. C (p. 613)
5. B (p. 614)
6. D (p. 617)
7. C (p. 616)
8. A (p. 619)
9. B (p. 622)
10. B (p. 630)

Problems, Applications, and Cases

1. Student activity.
2. Answers will vary.
3. Answers will vary.
4. Student activity.
5. Tax on $1,000,000 is $345,800
   Tax on additional $250,000 at 41 percent is $102,500
   Total tax is $448,300 ($345,800 plus $102,500)
6. Student activity.